Staying Afloat

LIFE ABOARD HOUSEBOATS, BARGES AND LIVEABOARDS

JERI CALLAHAN

Seattle, Washington
Portland, Oregon
Denver, Colorado
Vancouver, B.C.
Scottsdale, Arizona
Minneapolis, Minnesota

ISBN: 1-59404-001-X
Library of Congress Control Number: 2004110919

Printed in the United States of America

For additional copies call 1-800-201-7892, extension 52

For more information contact:
Jeri Callahan
PMO Box 258, Lake Union Mall
117 East Louisa Street
Seattle, Washington 98102
www.discoverhouseboating.com

Design: David Marty Design
Illustrations: Anita Lehmann

Peanut Butter Publishing
An Imprint of
Classic Day Publishing, LLC
2100 Westlake Ave. North, Suite 106
Seattle, WA 98109
www.classicdaypublishing.com
Email: info@classicdaypublishing.com

PREFACE

In 1994, Seattle's once derelict houseboats attracted both national and international attention with the release of the hit movie *Sleepless In Seattle*. The film featured Tom Hanks as a recent widower living with his young son in one of Lake Union's houseboats. Subsequent publicity about our floating neighborhood has typically featured the *Sunset Magazine* or *Architectural Digest* genre of houseboats.

Yet, what meets the public eye is only half, if that much, the story. Among my neighbors, a professional horticulturist with a multitude of container plants blanketing his deck, had to disinvite me to a three-person meeting; there was only room for two to sit in his large, yet overflowing, home. When I reconfigured my plumbing, I showered across the dock at my neighbor's for several weeks. A Boeing engineer, he used a wooden crab trap as his coffee table, pumped music from an old upright player piano and ate the identical bologna and cheese sandwich every night until his new wife varied the menu. A couple who each have doctorate degrees, (in education and nutrition, respectively,) were living in a garage-size houseboat when they submitted the lowest bid to replace the roof on neighbors Tom and Peggy Stockley's houseboat.

A creative couple several docks south bathe in a giant copper feed tub next to a wall entirely covered with wine bottle corks. With space at a premium, bikes, exercise equipment, or a coat tree sometimes occupy houseboat living rooms. Access to living rooms is often by way of the kitchen or beyond bed and bath to reach the views of the lake from the back channel side of most houseboats.

In my own first floating home, a gray shingled shoebox about the size of a freight train caboose, the front door opened to a narrow passage between a bunk bed built over a dresser and the tiny bathroom. I've since moved kitty-corner across the dock to a 600-square-foot quasi-Victorian with more than twice the space. My old fir floor reveals the site of former walls along with a long gone cat that left paw prints of white paint. Young cedar trees, stripped of bark, support my sleeping loft, rust inevitably forms at the drain of my claw-foot bathtub, and I've yet to repair the horizontal cracks in my living room walls that appeared when new stringers leveled my floor.

My accessories include two framed hand-embroidered Chinese Mandarin cuffs acquired by a missionary great-aunt of my father and a photo of my year-old grandson in a small brightly painted porcelain frame from Mexico. The antique tiger maple drop-leaf breakfast table of my childhood is opposite my computer on an L-shaped desk I improvised from a second-hand contemporary credenza.

While I cherish my light, comfortably furnished home with views of both open water and wooded shore land, I'd hardly consider it a candidate for the Sunday paper's magazine section.

This book aims to offer a balanced picture of the community by profiling a variety of people who live on the lake. While I've indicated approximate locations of various individuals' homes, they are deliberately vague to ensure the owners' privacy. I trust my readers will honor my neighbors' willingness to share their life afloat by respecting that privacy. The Floating Homes

Association welcomes visitors at a tour of houseboats every two years. For information about the next tour call the FHA office at (206) 325-1132.

From the Mid-Twenties

Floating Home Dutch Door

ACKNOWLEDGMENTS

When Howard Droker handled the legal details involved in the purchase of my first houseboat in 1988, he gave me an autographed copy of his definitive work on Seattle houseboat history, *Seattle's Unsinkable Houseboats*. Most of my understanding of our community's past comes from his thoroughly researched dissertation, originally written for a PhD in History. Another scholar, Donald Wysocki, wrote *The Gentrification of Bohemia; Change in Seattle's Houseboat Community* for his Master's thesis in Geography. Donald asked me to collaborate with him on a book about houseboats until a job offer from Microsoft took precedence. Although Duse McLean had been urging me to write about houseboats as Droker's book approached being out-of-print, Donald served as the catalyst for what you now hold in your hands.

A variety of friends and acquaintances reviewed the pending book and offered many constructive comments. They include Claudia Nelson, my favorite person with whom to be "on deadline;" John Miller, who has never been to Seattle but always trusted me to ghost write for him; and Catie Burns, my Indiana cousin and free lance writer.

Houseboaters Tom and Peggy Stockley, Art Holder, George Johnston and Jann McFarland, along with Eastlake neighborhood activist Jules James, also reviewed the manuscript.

In terms of patience Jeff Garbacz of RE.PC Recycled Computers and Peripherals takes the prize for leading me through the time-devouring learning curve of a new computer and printer. Followed up by the invaluable help of the men in my family, Charlie, Keith, and John Callahan; friends Pete and Lee Mullen; and neighbors Doug Hunt and Derek Stanley.

For help with the more recent generation of computer technology, necessitated when the screen of my previous laptop displayed nothing but beautifully colored wavy vertical lines, I'm indebted to Scott Leopold for guiding me in the selection and ordering of my brand new Dell computer. Neighbor Michael Shelton helped with software and I never would have made it through another learning curve without the tutorials of Padre Cesar Hernandez, a guest from my time in El Salvador and a man of exceptional grace, good humor, tact, and patience.

I owe connecting with my publisher, Elliott Wolf, to my neighbor Cynthia Moffett. One summer afternoon she excitedly told me about a woman taking photos on our dock for a future coffee table book on houseboats. Cynthia told the photographer about my long envisioned book, obtained Elliott's name and phone number and urged me to call him. Elliott has been exactly the combination of task master, mentor, and professional I needed; he even offered me the use of his home computer one day when I was on deadline and my printer was misbehaving.

As for my anonymous editor, what more could anyone want? He never complained about my inconsistencies in following style rules, abrupt changes in font sizes, or frantic last minute changes. He tactfully led me thorough my first experience writing a book, which I've learned differs significantly from whipping out a feature article or another "Over the Teacups" social column. And yes, that was a long, long time ago.

My designer, David Marty, not only amazes me with the wonders he works using the latest technology, but obviously rates as a first class artist. He also graciously drove from his studio in Edmonds to Seattle and back during the week before Christmas without any complaints that such a trip was necessitated by my confusing the dates of an earlier meeting scheduled in Edmonds.

Long before I met Elliott, Hanna Jay, who operated "Jay Walking tours," raved about the drawings of architect Anita Lehmann. Once I met Anita and saw her work, I knew she was the ideal illustrator. Her elegantly crafted sketches contribute immeasurably to portraying the ambiance of life afloat.

Houseboater Art Holder, who replaced my stringers, also made the time to shoot my photo as he indulged in one of his favorite hobbies. Jann McFarland, current Office Manager for the Floating Homes Association, deserves much credit for always cheerfully providing me with yet another name and or phone number.

I'm particularly grateful to all the current and one time denizens of Lake Union who've shared their experiences with me; what a privilege to meet and know such interesting folks. I've also realized there could probably be at least a dozen more books about those who choose to live on the water; the stories just go on and on.

I'll also forever treasure Tom Stokley's consoling comment when I bemoaned the reality that my writing always could be improved, "Jeri, a book is never finished; it's abandoned."

Finally—I speak not only for myself, but for most of us floating folk, we treasure the commitment, savvy, and dedicated efforts of all those who gave so much of themselves so that we can all continue to stay afloat.

DEDICATION

TOM AND PEGGY STOCKLEY

Tom and Peggy Stockley personified for many the essence of life afloat. Peggy always preferred a dip in the lake to shopping, even if it was her fourth or fifth swim of the day. The two shared one closet and Tom often proclaimed, "If you buy a new pair of shoes, you have to throw an old one away." Rather than sleep in the bedroom, they chose to convert the futon in the open and sunny corner "den" to a bed every night so they could awaken to the morning sky. Tom could be found writing his weekly wine column on his laptop computer almost anywhere, including on the dock. His overflowing office at the back of their house was smaller than many contemporary bathrooms.

Immediate neighbors always knew when Tom hosted a wine tasting; partially consumed wine bottles appeared at their front doors. About every six weeks the weight of all the wine delivered to the famous wine columnist caused the oil in his skillet to flow to the northeast side. Tom, thoughtfully sorting according to taste, shared his abundance with everyone on the dock. In his weekly wine column Tom addressed the general public; one never found a hint of elitism in his approach to his favorite beverage. "I never participate in a wine judging where I have to wear a tux," he'd say. He happily provided a free wine-tasting event for the owner of a struggling new local Italian restaurant where he liked the food.

The Stockley's hospitality was a given. Fellow houseboaters paddling or sailing by often accepted the offer of a glass of wine. Tom and Peggy were usually the first to invite newcomers on the dock to sample something from one of Tom's many cook books. Both always spread the word of a skinny dip off their back deck on summer nights with a full moon. More visibly the Stockleys and their neighbors the Donnettes could be seen weeding new plantings on neighborhood public property. Nothing formally organized; they simply saw a need and did it.

Lost in Alaska Flight 261, January 31, 2000.

Tom and Peggy were not only generous with their time; they also contributed to a multitude of their favorite causes. No need to have their names published as donors, or to be seen at elegant, pricy fund raisers or social events. They simply wrote and mailed checks to everything from the Youth Symphony Orchestra to the Pike Place Market.

A quote from Emerson hung on a plaque next to their front door, "The ornaments of our home are our friends who frequent it." Many were blessed to have been among those ornaments.

CONTENTS

Preface iii

Acknowledgments vii

Dedication xi

The Lay of the Lake 1

In the Beginning..3

The Last Duwamish Houseboater 7

Childhood Memories of Portage Bay.......................11

Lake Union in the Late Forties 15

Student Days on Portage Bay 17

Sturdy Stock 21

Houseboat Patriarch..27

"Just a Guy"..33

Baby on Board 39

A Child's Eye View..45

The Hathaway Home 49

Huck Finn Revisited 57

Wheeling Around 61

The Old Boathouse 69

Phoenix Dock 75

Decidedly Different 79

Roanoke Reef..85

Trend Setters 91

Too Handy? 99

Home at Last...105

Hooked on Boats 113

The Sally S. 121

Fluke's Folly 127
Whose Lake is This? 131
Art Lover in Residence 135
Shooguy 141
Clowning Around 147
A Benevolent Bachelor 153
Tui Tui 159
An Airplane in a Houseboat? 169
The Accidental Owners 175
Downsizing, and Then Some 187
Romance Afloat 195
Creative Housing Solutions 199
Houseboat Treasures 203
A Kind Place 211
Hine Sight 217
A Touch of Europe 223
Caroline's Home 233
Journalist to Professor 237
Why Would I Go Anywhere Else? 245
It's Magic 253
She's Come a Long Way 259
Ann of Lake Union 267
Creature Comforts 277
A Cast of Characters 283
"I Couldn't Believe It" 289
Stringers Art 295
Vintage George 299
The Moving Man 305
Through the Year 311
Glossary 317

THE LAY OF THE LAKE

The pioneers called the site of Seattle's remaining house-boats *Tenas Chuck*, the Chinook Indian trading jargon for Little Water. Salmon fought their way from the salt water of Salmon Bay up a narrow stream to deposit their eggs along Lake Union's fresh water shoreline or the streams that flowed into it.

Bear, deer, cougar and elk roamed the surrounding forest. Both Queen Anne Hill on the west and Capitol Hill to the east plunged into the small lake carved by glaciers centuries ago. To the east Portage Bay led to a narrow strip of land the native coastal tribes used to cross from the waters of *Tenas Chuck* to *Hyas Chuck*, the Big Water of Lake Washington. A few small streams fed the little lake in addition to the snow melt flowing down from the Cascade mountains.

By the 1900s the gritty industrial Lake Union was clearly the "basement" of Seattle while Lake Washington began to emerge as more of an elegant parlor.

Lumber mills and their floating log booms, the brick yards that rebuilt the city after it burned, a gas plant to fuel the city's street lamps, ship yards that built and repaired both war ships and pleasure boats lined the shoreline. When the canals linking Lake Union to Puget Sound on the west and Lake Washington to the east were completed and the Chittenden Locks opened in 1917, pioneer Thomas Mercer's dream that

1

the small lake would some day unite the two bodies of water became reality.

Today Seattle's houseboats nestle amid a grab-bag of industrial, commercial, residential, educational and recreational uses lining the shore of Lake Union and its eastern arm, Portage Bay. The gasification plant which converted coal into gas is now a city park; the old steam plant has been renovated and occupied by a Scandinavian bio-tech company. But some of the old water-dependent users remain: dry docks, marinas, boat repair shops and houseboats. On the east side of the lake, fourteen 150- to 300-feet-long houseboat docks jut from the shore immediately north of the white National Oceanographic and Atmospheric Administration (NOAA) ships. Further north in Roanoke Bay, two modern and one older houseboat docks run parallel to the shoreline. Of the many houseboats that once lined the west side of the lake, only three long adjacent docks, tucked in between marinas, and a cluster of about thirty floating homes on either side of the south end of the Aurora Bridge remain. At the north end one solitary long dock anchors thirteen houseboats east of the Aurora bridge in Fremont. A small dock with only six houseboats nestles just west of Jensen's Motor Boat Works and the University of Washington on the north side of Portage Bay. On the opposite shoreline, various configurations of homes and docks, ranging from vintage cottages moored directly on the shoreline near the I-5 freeway bridge to the eleven sleek architect-designed homes of Portage-at-Bay, hug the shoreline.

Please refer to map on page 320.

IN THE BEGINNING

Seattle's earliest live-aboards and houseboaters included mostly fishermen, dock workers and sailors living cheaply on Elliott Bay.

A fisherman's wife might prefer a do-it-yourself cabin on an old oyster barge to accompanying her husband to the Alaska fishing waters. Sailors sometimes shared living quarters, often alternating their time in port. Locals simply enjoyed the proximity to work and cheap housing available to anyone capable of building a simple shelter against the winter storms. By 1902, houseboats were prominent enough to warrant newspaper coverage. The *Seattle Post-Intelligencer* ran a full-page spread including several photographs on "Seattle's Unique Floating Population." All of the featured houseboats squatted among the fishing boats and freighters wintering in Elliott Bay.

"No rent or taxes to pay, no lawns to mow, no book agents to dodge, and with but a few of the so-considered necessary evils ordinarily attending life in a civilized community, such a condition might appeal to one as an ideal existence. Yet such is the life of nearly a thousand of Seattle's population, a floating population not in name alone, but in fact.

"Down along the waterfront at this time of year, tied up to the pilings out of the way of the shipping, are to be seen scores of shanty-boats and hundreds almost of small fishing boats floating

on the lazy tide. Curls of blue smoke from tiny chimneys denote
that they are used as habitations, and such is the case, for here
is where the old-time fishermen and many of the dock employees
make their homes."

Donald Wysocki summarized the character of this free-floating community in his thesis, *The Gentrification of Bohemia; the Fall and Rise of Seattle's Houseboats*:

"Unlike earlier homesteads or later housing developments, the houseboaters' domain was not claimed, founded, subdivided, platted, taxed, bought and sold, planned or developed."

As for Lake Union and its eastern arm, Portage Bay, Howard Droker quotes a reference in the 1904 Polk City Directory to "Rodney Allabach, Hominy Salesman, Boat House, Lake Union." Droker wrote the definitive book on houseboat history, "Seattle's Unsinkable Houseboats" as his dissertation for a Doctorate in history.

An entirely different floating community, built by contractors hired by the well-to-do, sprang up in the early 1900s on the then distant western shore of Lake Washington. These houseboats and their owners, including H. A. Chadwick, the editor of an independent political journal; T. Daniel Frawley, the well known actor; and B. L. Muir, developer of the Leschi neighborhood, frequently made the local press.

Lake Washington homes included tiny bungalows, large homes built on barges, self propelled houseboats, and large structures with salons and staterooms that doubled as residential clubs for young people.

An article in the Aug. 2, 1908 Seattle Post-Intelligencer magazine section describes the home of the Terrell brothers moored at 34th Street in Madison Park.

"While my escort admired the launch, rowboats and canoe I
listened to the auto piano and cautiously glanced around the

premises. The living room nearly covered the main deck, and the hardwood floor was strewn with fur rugs. The mission sofa was well supplied with cushions covered with leather and linen, hand decorated to suit the masculine taste. The book cases were filled with stores of knowledge ranging in interest and amusement from histories and classic epics to ragtime jingles.

"As we listened to selections from operas and classic melodies I further noticed that besides the auto piano there was an old pianoforte which had staged it through dance hall scenes, and there were stringed instruments around on the floors, which indicated that the natures of their owners were attuned to the harmony of sound. "

While the music played on for those on Lake Washington, the City ordered all the houseboats out of Elliott Bay in 1908, ostensibly for polluting the water with their sewage, an issue that continued to sully their image for over fifty years. Owners who felt their homes were worth saving moved south to the Duwamish River where they either pulled their homes onto dry land at high tide or tied up along the shoreline.

Seattle native Jerry Kostakis describes a group of about twenty houseboats on the west side of the Duwamish in the 1920s. "They all had hoses for water, wires for electricity, sometimes phones, and usually little outhouses at the back. They also all had gang-planks that went up and down with the tide. I remember as a twelve year-old delivering the Sunday paper to Mr. Kourkoumelis' houseboat in the middle of a cold, rainy, pitch dark night. I slipped on his gang plank and fell into the freezing cold river. Fortunately Mr. Kourkoumelis heard my yowling and came to my rescue. He pulled me out of the water, took me inside his house, cleaned and warmed me up, gave me some dry clothes and then helped me finish delivering those heavy Sunday papers."

Jerry also recalls another houseboater on the Duwamish, the wrestler John Pencote whose fame sprang from his exceptional strength. Pencote was banned from his trade after killing an opponent during a wrestling match. He was so strong numerous contemporaries insist he actually bent the bars on his jail cell window.

In the later 1930s Fred Fischer, who currently owns a moorage in Portage Bay, towed a small powered house scow from Tacoma to moorage on the Duwamish, when Todd Shipyards transferred him to Seattle. The $5.00 per month moorage fee and proximity to work made an ideal combination.

During the Great Depression of the 1930s houseboats offered cheap housing throughout Seattle. A local dentist who grew up on Queen Anne Hill recalls delivering a weekly advertising paper to the Westlake houseboats. "Sometimes the occupants would literally be standing at the door waiting for me, the newspaper was their weekly supply of toilet paper," he explains.

When Seattle eliminated the last sewer outfall into Lake Washington in 1938 with the completion of the Henderson Street sewer, the Health Department ordered the eviction of all houseboats without chemical toilets. The remaining houseboats were eventually evicted during WWII. Some marginal houseboats went out in flames in the middle of Lake Washington, but many migrated to Lake Union and Portage Bay, much to the consternation of their upland neighbors.

When WWII quickly pulled Seattle out of the Depression, the City declared both the floating Hooverville houseboats on the Duwamish, as well as the landed shanties, unsafe and illegal. The Coast Guard removed all of the Duwamish houseboats except those few whose occupants moored on property they owned. All remaining houseboats on Lake Washington were also evicted, leaving almost all Seattle's remaining houseboats on Lake Union.

THE LAST DUWAMISH HOUSEBOATER

West Seattle resident Frank Sardarov's family once shared the same address with Fred Strom, the last of the Duwamish houseboaters. The Sardarov family lived at 4838 W. 12 Avenue S.W., one of several streets on a small parcel of level land between West Marginal Way and the Duwamish River opposite Kellogg Island. The island, just south of the West Seattle Bridge, emerged when the Army Corps of Engineers straightened and dredged the river to create a shipping channel. About forty families lived along the original route of the Duwamish north of where Puget Creek flowed down from the steep hillside and into the river.

The Yakima Indians used to paddle down the Duwamish to the creek and trade their produce and fruit for salmon and halibut to bring back to their families east of the Cascades. Strom bought his riverside property, at the end of a dead-end road, for $500 in the mid-1930s. Once Strom owned property, the hardworking and resourceful Swedish immigrant bought two very substantial cedar logs to support the house he built himself.

Strom had worked in lumber mills throughout Seattle and built his houseboat so he could row to and from work in the various mills that lined the Duwamish.

Frank Sardarov recalls, "We used to go swimming in a swimming hole right where the water was coming down from Puget creek; it was right beside Strom's house. We even had a picnic table rigged up down there because the water was so nice and clear. I delivered the daily newspaper to Fred Strom. He was one of the finest men in the whole community. He was very meticulous and clean."

Strom treasured the surrounding greenery, fishing from his deck for a salmon for dinner, and the great blue herons that nested in the trees above. There was plenty of room for his cats to roam on the shore. Frank remembers Strom's kitchen had a nice linoleum floor and a very old wood burning stove.

"Fred had his place all fixed up. He was a real gentleman. The houseboater who lived next door to Fred was the biggest bootlegger on the Duwamish River. He used to come down in his boat from British Columbia and would bring in whiskey. Once we found a fellow about thirty yards from Fred's house lying on the floor with a woman and a keg rigged up above them. The beer was almost pouring into them from a hose attached to the keg. The girl was drunk out of this world. She used to jump into the river naked and go swimming. We called her Russian Mary. She'd stay two months or so with one guy and then move over to another one. She was working her trade in all the houseboats from Edmonds Street to Alaska Street."

When Frank married and began his own family, he and his wife Helen hired Fred Strom to build a fence so their children could safely play in the yard. Frank knew the work would be first class. Fred Strom was in his eighties when the Port of Seattle entered his life. It was 1975 and the Port needed some additional land for a barge terminal. The level parcel of property where Frank had once lived and where Fred still moored his houseboat proved ideal for the Port.

"Once the Port bought the site," says Frank, "everyone had to move out. There were still about 120 people living there. Then vandals started taking everything from bathtubs to doors to stoves, anything they could get there hands on, so the Port put a cyclone fence around the area."

But Fred Strom didn't want to sell his property; he wanted to continue living in his houseboat. It was probably the only home he'd ever known, built from scratch and lived in for forty years. He hired an attorney to represent him, and the Port gave him a key to the cyclone fence so he could have access to and from his house. Strom eventually lost his case and died several years later.

Frank reports that when the Port actually began leveling the property a large number of Indian artifacts turned up. Construction was abruptly halted and anthropologists began researching the area. "When the Port condemned the property," says Frank, "they put the family names on the roof of each house. I was invited to go up in a plane with a fellow from the Port when there were only three houses left. I pointed out my old house to him. The Port fellow commented that my house was built on the original site of the Indian Long House where the Duwamish held all their pot latches. It was sacred ground."

The envisioned barge terminal site has since evolved into a park with informational signage about its history which includes the name of the Sardarov family. The Duwamish tribe has bought the property across the street and plans to build a new Long House. Kellogg Island, designated in the late1970s as a bird sanctuary, offers a green patch along the waterway's industrial area. Salmon have begun to return to the now cleaner Duwamish waters and great blue herons soar above the tide flats.

Would that somewhere, somehow, Fred Strom knows his former neighborhood is once again a green oasis in the midst of an industrial area.

CHILDHOOD MEMORIES OF PORTAGE BAY

Vivian Cushman, now living in Bennet, Nebraska, vividly recalls her early years on Portage Bay where her family lived at the foot of Shelby Street.

"First of all I remember when my two older twin brothers, Phil and Ruben, wanted to take me for a boat ride. I loved attention from my older brothers so of course I wanted to go. We headed toward the southeast end of the lake where there were a lot of cat tails. I didn't want to go through them because I was afraid there might be spiders. But they pushed on while I held my breath because there were lots of spiders and their sticky webs. We finally came to a much worn path on the eastern corner of the marsh land. It was the portage that the Indians used to go back and forth between Lake Washington and Lake Union. The place was all overgrown except for this pathway. Early settlers had built a wooden "railroad track" along the portage so they could move coal and logs from Lake Washington to Portage Bay."

When the family first moved to their new home on Shelby around 1910, they'd sometimes see a beautiful Indian princess from a group that camped down by Roanoke Street near the west side of today's Montlake Cut. She would groom herself as elegantly as possible and then parade by in a canoe paddled by some very good looking young Indians. The princess would always wave and shout "Kla-hoy-ya," as she went by. Vivian and her family didn't know what the words meant, but her sister would call "Kla-hoy-ya" back to the princess. The family assumed the phrase was a common greeting, and according to *The Chinook Jargon and How to Use It,* published in 1909 by George C. Shaw, their assumption was right on target.

One of Vivian's neighbors, Jake Hoover, lived with his sister Hattie in a little house on stilts. He rented out canoes and rowboats. An avid sportsman, Jake tended to make fun of Vivian's industrious, religious and well educated family. Jake had lived near the source of the Missouri River in northern Montana before he moved to Seattle. He was always talking about his friend Charlie Russell, the famous Western painter. He claimed that one day in Montana when he was fixing dinner near his camp fire he looked up to see a young man approaching his camp.

"Have you eaten" Jake asked.

"No." he replied.

"Do you have a grub stake?"

"No."

"The poor guy didn't even have a horse. So I took him in for the winter and really saved his life," claimed Jake.

The Cushman family never really believed their funny old neighbor, Jake Hoover, knew the famous Charlie Russell.

But then one day Charlie Russell actually did come to see Jake.

"His stories were true!" says Vivian. "When we heard Charlie Russell was right next door to us, my brother Reuben rushed out to try to meet him, but by that time he was walking back down the street to catch the streetcar."

"I learned to row when I was four years old. I don't remember it, but I've been told my parents looked out one day and saw me in the middle of the lake. Eventually I rowed back home. I do remember when I was very little I managed to get out of the house and onto the dock. Peering over the edge of it I lost my balance and fell into the lake. Fortunately my dress caught on a nail which kept me from going clear under. Joe Hall, a close family friend, was visiting us. He heard my mother scream when she looked out the window and saw me fall in. Immediately he rushed out, grabbed me, and turned me upside down. He spanked me all the way back to the house to get the water out of me. I couldn't forget that."

Vivian describes the day the lake dropped an eventual total of ten feet. They were building the locks and she reports that someone put a stick of dynamite in the wrong place.

"I was coming home from Seward Elementary after school and the minute I came over the hill I could see that the lake was much lower. Twelve to fifteen houseboats between the University Bridge and Shelby Street were left high, dry and tipping down toward the center of the lake. The furniture inside was rolling around. Some of our neighbors helped by rushing inside the slanted houseboats and moving the furniture to the downhill side of the rooms. These were well-to-do people who had very nice furniture, some of them even had pianos, but they were willing to help the poor folks in the beached houseboats."

Even as a child, Vivian remembers it took three attempts before the successful completion of the Montlake Cut. The first two times the contractors failed to pour the cement high enough to keep the surrounding land from collapsing.

"Once they finally got it right," says Vivian, "everyone wanted to see the grand opening. Phillip, Ruben and I were watching all the activity from a dirt bank. As the time for the opening drew near my brothers said, 'Come on; let's be the first ones to go through the cut.' I refused to go; the steep banks scared me. Phillip and Ruben used my rowboat and were actually the first to go through the new canal. The next day their picture was in the newspaper."

"One day the Polar explorer Roald Amundsen anchored his ship, The Maude, at the foot of our street. About ten Eskimo men were standing around on our lawn watching a huge ten-foot high pile of polar bear skins. It didn't take long for all of us neighborhood kids to gather around. Soon someone discovered you could climb up the pile of polar bear skins and slide down.

"I was twelve years old at the time and feeling too mature to slide down with all the children. But I finally decided even though I was a twelve-year old, I would probably never have another chance to slide down a pile of polar bear skins. Phillip and Ruben were working on our car, and the Eskimos, who had never seen such a thing, had gathered around them to watch. Just as I started toward the pile of skins one of my brothers said something to the other one. Suddenly the horn honked loudly. All the Eskimos jumped a mile. Then everyone had a big laugh. About that time the Eskimos sensed that Mr. Amundsen was coming, and they shooed all of us kids away from the polar bear skins.

"So I missed my chance," says Vivian.

Happily, Vivian has had many other chances: an idyllic marriage, travel abroad, forty years as an adored teacher, two affectionate children and probably the chance to be the only living person who remembers seeing polar bear skins at the foot of Shelby Street.

LAKE UNION IN THE LATE FORTIES

Lucy and Blair Kirk offer a sample of Lake Union in the late 1940s, when they bought a houseboat moored at Lake Union Dry Docks. The fifty by sixteen foot-long house had been rented primarily by students, who furnished their small rooms to replicate everything from a giant spider web to a New Orleans bordello. The Kirks paid a tug boat operator twenty-five dollars to move the long and skinny houseboat to a shore-side moorage about eight blocks north.

Compared to the house boat community's rather Bohemian reputation at the time, Lucy and Blair were relative straight arrows. She worked for the telephone company and he sold drapery hardware, which made them something of an anomaly among their neighbors.

One of their neighbors, a handsome bachelor named John, lived in the end houseboat. His Irish charm was not lost on women. Often in the late evening the Kirks would hear his woman come down the dock, knock on his door, and yell, "Open up, John. I know you're in there." Soon the Kirks would hear the staccato clicks of high-heeled shoes retreating down the dock.

When Blair told his neighbors he planned to put in large picture windows, they cautioned him against doing so. At that time, the Lone Star cement plant anchored industrial activity at the south end of the lake. Big ships, giant cranes and pile drivers, and tug boats pulling log booms and barges often created substantial wakes. These wakes sometimes rocked the houseboats so forcefully they broke their windows. But the innovative Blair mounted each window in a thick layer of packing material which cushioned the glass placed inside the frame. He insists you could actually see the window move in its frame when the house rocked.

Blair recalls a blustery fall evening when he looked up from reading the evening paper and gasped, "Lucy, they've moved Queen Anne Hill!" Their home was drifting north with only its phone line holding it to the dock. Lucy called the telephone company with an SOS to notify the Coast Guard. The operator insisted Lucy supply the Coast Guard phone number.

"Don't you understand," exclaimed Lucy, herself a telephone company employee, "the phone line is our only connection to the dock, and we're likely to lose that any minute!" Lucy finally located the Coast Guard number just before the phone line broke. A Coast Guard cutter found their floundering houseboat within the hour, but it was four hours before the Coast Guard crew managed to return Blair, Lucy, and their still intact house to the dock.

"Then we moved to the south side of the dock," says Blair, "where we weren't so likely to get blown away by those strong so'westers."

STUDENT DAYS ON PORTAGE BAY

A later view of Portage Bay comes from long-time Seattle resident Maid Adams. She recalls her houseboat days among graduate students when she and her husband David lived on a dock in Portage Bay directly opposite the Seattle Yacht Club. In deference to the docks view of Seattle's premiere yacht club and its proximity to Broadmoor, one of Seattle's few gated communities, residents jokingly referred to their moorage as "Broadmoor by the Sea." Since the site was also adjacent to an extensive marshland, they'd often hear the slap of beaver tails at night as their furry neighbors ventured out from the nearby dam. Daylight afforded frequent glimpses of various water foul, including a great blue heron perched on a pole.

"I've always felt those days were a magical period in my life," says Maid. "Waterfront has always been prime real estate in Seattle, and here we were actually living ON the water for a mere $35 per month. The marsh teemed with wildlife in a completely natural setting. With no other dock near us we were completely removed form the world and yet we were in the midst of a thriving big city."

She and David were at the end of the relatively small dock with only nine to ten houseboats, but they housed a variety of people: some involved in their careers and working full time, older retired folks on a small income, a few students typically supported by their working wives, and a couple with a new-born baby.

"We had a warm sense of always being able to call on one another if we needed help. Even better, there was an almost contradictory mix of privacy in our individual homes yet intimacy with our neighbors. For instance, we had a very small water pipe, and if the winter temperature dipped below freezing some of us lost our water. You don't ordinarily shower or bathe in someone else's home, but on the dock it was a given that those nearer the shore who still had running water expected their waterless friends to drop in for a shower."

Maid always waited for people to get to know her before she revealed her exact address. In those days Seattle viewed house-boats as marginal housing inhabited primarily by disreputable outcasts. "I wanted people to know me before they passed judgment on something they didn't know anything about. It was a burdensome feeling, because I felt very good about where I lived and the people who lived there; to have this sense of shame was very uncomfortable and totally the opposite of what it is now.

Maid reminisces, "We'd often row over to other docks and get together for wonderful parties. We'd gather for informal potlucks with mostly hamburger and cheap table wine. Sometimes we'd glance over to watch the folks at the Yacht Club with their cocktails and *hors d'oeuvres.* Often we'd raise our glasses in salute, certain that we enjoyed our shared cama-raderie just as I'm sure they enjoyed theirs."

The parking lot for their dock was located strategically close to the University of Washington stadium. During one Husky football season the dock denizens came up with the idea of rent-ing out space in their parking lot to the hordes of football fans

Portage Bay

heading for the stadium. The parking money was a welcome bonus for the struggling students and retirees until the dock owners got wind of their enterprise. On the day of the next home football game the docklords sent several of their own people to collect the parking money.

"Every two or three months the owners sent their agent down to collect the moorage fees," says Maid. "He always wore a suit and tie that made him look like an undertaker, and his facial expression clearly indicated he felt he was among the dregs of society."

When Maid knew a baby was on the way, she couldn't imagine dealing with diapers in a houseboat, so they moved to the land shortly before their son arrived. After graduate school, raising their son and numerous volunteer activities Maid ended up creating and directing a Women's Center at Green River Community College. Still active and teaching part time, Maid feels like she has come full circle. She recently sold her home in Madrona and moved to a condo in a co-housing community near downtown Seattle. In her self-operating community everyone pitches in with various tasks such as mowing the lawn, cleaning the common bathroom or cooking for fifty people once a month in the common kitchen. Although Maid can't hear beavers playing under her landed condo, she once again enjoys a sense of community in an urban setting.

STURDY STOCK

Once voters funded a sewer around Lake Union, Alfa McClung, along with more than two hundred other house-boaters, lost her moorage. Born on a North Dakota farm in 1898, the originally land-locked Alfa bought her floating home at the age of 55.

After high school graduation she had worked in a variety of jobs in North Dakota where she honed her secretarial and book-keeping skills. Still single at thirty-eight, she decided to book passage on a cruise to Alaska. The only single man on board ship, Maurice, singled out Alfa from the crowd. The classic ship-board romance culminated when they returned to Seattle and Maurice declared they had two choices. Either Alfa returned to North Dakota and they would never see each other again, or they get married right then and there. Alfa chose the latter, and the two bought their relatively large houseboat in 1954. A receipt lists the cost at $10.

She began working in the stationery department at the Bon Marche, one of Seattle's two major department stores. Maurice roamed the country in search of his fortune while Alfa paid the bills. She wrote to Maurice, "Don't you really think we should do something about the heat? The only way I can stay warm is to turn on the oven and sit right in front of it." To her last days on the dock a variety of mostly small Oriental rugs layered

Alfa's floor to mitigate the cold drafts. Maurice died only two years after they bought the houseboat.

In that era Alfa probably moored her home in various available locations. Many houseboaters took advantage of vacant street ends. Alfa's house was moored at the current site of the National Oceanographic and Atmospheric Association (NOAA) when the city leased the property to the federal government. Alfa, along with over seventy other houseboat owners, was summarily ordered to vacate within six weeks. Fortunately, in the early '60s, several dock owners worked with the State for permission to extend their docks to accommodate some of the evicted homes. Alfa was able to move to one of the extended moorages on Fairview about three blocks north of the NOAA site.

She easily adapted to her new neighborhood where the afternoon sun filtered through the bamboo curtains of her large side windows and she could wave from her back porch to anyone swimming by in the channel. After Alfa retired from the Bon Marche in 1971, she enjoyed having the time to test her skills at sketching and oil painting, play her cherished piano, listen to operas and to branch out from container gardening into working the narrow strip of land above the breakwater. With a little help from her next door neighbor, noted horticulturist Bob Lilly, Alfa tended flowers in the land above the breakwater between two cork screw willows.

Alfa also became a local version of the Humane Society, beginning with inheriting a cat named Rover when his owner moved away. It soon became common knowledge that any cat needing a home could find it at Alfa's.

Alfa eventually developed Parkinson's disease. At some point she had become a Christian Scientist, no doubt much to the chagrin of her strongly Lutheran family. As the years went by, her gardening efforts dwindled. Unlike most houseboats, hers actually had a fence all the way around it which enabled her to safely putter with the container plants on her deck. Her neighbors, especially Bob Lilly, began gradually taking on more and more of the plant maintenance.

"We were both strong independent people," says Bob, "and Alfa had a strong sense of propriety and responsibility. I don't know of anyone who ever saw her without her wig. She knew I was doing some of her gardening, so we had an informal non-agreement that I would do as much gardening for her as I wanted and she in turn would bake as many chocolate cakes for me as she wanted." Bob chuckles as he comments, "Alfa's eagerly devoured chocolate cakes were always delivered whole as her contribution to dock potlucks, but my cakes always had one piece missing. Maybe she felt she had to sample them to make sure they were up to her standards."

Bob adds, "I noticed at some point that she no longer would eat in public. I suspect as her co-ordination diminished, she preferred the privacy of her home. But she always continued to want to show me her Christmas cactus when it bloomed, and I always wanted Alfa to see my night blooming Ceres. Tom and Peggy Stockley, her across the dock neighbors, came into her house every Sunday morning when someone always took Alfa to the local Christian Science church. They cleaned out the cat litter boxes, vacuumed, and tided up her house. I'll never know whether she knew they did that for her."

As Alfa's eyesight began to fade and she grew increasingly hard of hearing, dock neighbors checked every morning to make sure her kitchen curtains were open, an assurance she was up and about. In spite of her failing vision, Alfa's favorite pastime was knitting sturdy wool socks for almost everyone she knew. She kept a small black notebook with the names, foot size in inches, and color preferences of lucky recipients.

Almost every day Alfa, with the help of her cane, walked the hundred yards of so to Pete's Supermarket Market, where she'd buy groceries for herself and cat food for Misty and Tela, her constant companions. Alfa had a preference for spam and lima beans, alternating with some sort of "Hamburger Surprise." One day after a light snow, a clerk at Pete's who often waited on Alfa carried her groceries down the steps to her dock and walked her safely home. "George (the owner of Pete's) has always told me to look after her," Bob explained. "She's all right; I just wanted to make sure she didn't slip on the way home." A week later, Bob was proudly showing everyone in the neighborhood his new treasure, a pair of blue and gray "Alfa socks."

Alfa was one of the last customers of the two tiny oil tankers, *Blondie* and *Dagwood*, which plied the lake selling heating oil. When one of the tankers sank, the last owners, the Timmermans, went out of business, but not before presenting Alfa with an electric heater to replace her old oil one. Alfa had become something of a foster grandmother to the Timmerman's various off-spring, and several years later received an invitation to a family wedding. Neighbor Peggy Stockley took her shopping at the Bon Marche, where she always remained a loyal customer, to find an appropriate dress. Fortunately, the dress was a warm one; snow covered the ground the day of the wedding. Tom and Peggy Stockley helped Alfa avoid a fall on the slippery dock and Bob Lilly drove through the snowy streets to the nuptials. As Bob says, "It was probably the only formal occasion where we all were appropriately dressed."

One evening, as neighbors were chatting, they suddenly realized that although Alfa had opened her kitchen curtains in the morning, no one had seen her during the day.

They went to check on her and found Alfa unconscious on her bed. She'd had a stroke and spent several months in physical therapy. Dock neighbors organized to make sure that someone came at least once a day to visit and feed her. Alfa spent her last several years at the Jacobsen House nursing home on Capitol Hill where neighbors often brought one of her cats for a much enjoyed visit.

Dock neighbors who knew Alfa remember her every spring when the clump of Shasta daisies she planted at the side of one of the corkscrew willows burst into bloom. Bob Lilly continues to maintain her potted forsythia as it migrates from one houseboat to another. Those fortunate to have them still treasure their "Alfa socks" on a cold winter night.

HOUSEBOAT PATRIARCH

Howard Droker lived on Terry's dock when he wrote *Seattle's Unsinkable Houseboats* and penned one of the best descriptions of Terry Pettus.

"One of the biggest mistakes the opponents of floating homes ever made was to raise the ire of the tall, white-bearded patriarch of houseboats, Terry Pettus. Terry brought political savvy, a genius for organization and publicity, eloquence, a biting wit, and an overwhelming sense of human dignity that had evolved from a lifetime of experience as a newspaper reporter, union organizer, and radical editor."

Nurtured in an Indiana clergyman's family, appalled by injustices toward the working man both before and during the Depression, and jailed during the McCarthy era for refusing to identify (squeal would be a more appropriate term during that frightening time) any fellow members of the Communist party, Terry had had his fill of political battles when over 200 houseboats lost their moorages in the early 1960s. It wasn't until he and his wife Berta were evicted from their Westlake dock that he realized he had to become involved in the fledging Lake Union Vessels Association.

Fortunately for Terry and Berta, threatened houseboaters had already formed the Association when the City, eager to eliminate the still slightly disreputable and shabby houseboats now that the new sewer justified doing so, refused to grant moving permits to evicted houseboats. Without such permits, houseboat owners had little choice but to let the City destroy their homes. Houseboaters researched the issue and learned they could circumvent the City policy by working with the United States Customs Agency. Evicted owners mounted outboard motors on the deck of their floating homes, chose a name for their "vessel," decided on a Captain and First Mate, and requested an inspection by the Customs Office. The Customs official inspected the boat, estimated the tonnage, assigned a registration number and issued an official license to the owner of the now "Registered Vessel."

When Terry and Berta were stopped by the Seattle Harbor Patrol Police while the good ship "Tenas Chuck" was being towed to temporary moorage on the east side of the lake, one can only imagine with what glee Terry showed the police officer his official license and status as a Registered Vessel.

Once Terry began working with the Lake Union Vessels Association, he inevitably emerged as its leader. Acutely aware of the importance of nomenclature when dealing with political issues, he adopted the term "Floating Homes Association," to convey a more appropriate image of permanent single family residences. Houseboaters who joined the FHA could obtain discounts at paint, hardware, and lumber yards to help them spruce up their homes. Dock meetings featured speakers or discussions on container gardening, connecting to the new sewer, exterior painting, and health and safety concerns.

His persuasive powers actually convinced houseboat owners (notorious for their "I'll march to my own drummer, thank you," attitude), to request the City to assess the value of their houseboats and tax them as personal property. Some of the older houseboats still proudly display their official small metal plate with the King County Assessor's number.

Frequently quoted as saying, "You can't fight City Hall because your can't find it," Pettus adroitly side-stepped City Hall by working with individuals on the City Council, including Wing Luke, Paul Kraabel, and A. Ludlow Kramer. He also sought common ground with the uplanders, who'd always disdained the once tawdry dwellings, by urging the community to work not only to save their homes, but to save Lake Union for water dependent use and public access including views.

Pettus tackled the issue of connecting floating homes to the sewer, by stating, "If we can get a man to the moon, (Neil Armstrong had only recently been the first man to walk on it) "we can surely find a way to move S H I T from individual houseboats to the new sewer." Ken Kennedy, master plumber and owner of a Portage Bay houseboat, proved Terry right by designing a simple gravity flow system from individual houseboats to a sump pump under each dock that pumped the effluent to the city sewer.

Once the City finally zoned all moorages where houseboats hooked up to the newly completed Lake Union sewer as residential, with accompanying height restrictions to fend off developers, the major struggle to save floating homes ended. Without Terry's leadership, coupled with the houseboat owners willingness to be the first known floating community to properly dispose of their sewage, Lake Union's houseboats would have been lost forever from the lake scape.

Terry and Berta eventually found permanent moorage on Wandesford dock, where he continued to pursue his passion for history. Although Terry never had the opportunity for a college education, he would often read up to six hours a day. Berta tended her container garden and hosted the many friends that enjoyed their company until she died in 1973. He pursued his passion for history, made a series of oral history tapes for the University of Washington, and was featured in a public television documentary about his experiences during the McCarthy era. He managed to travel to England where he took a history course at Oxford University.

Terry died of a massive heart attack at the age of eighty, just hours before he was scheduled to leave the hospital after a bout with emphysema. He had just called fellow floating home friend Dixie Pintler to report how eager he was to return to his beloved houseboat. As Pintler says, "He gave his whole life to this community, totally. He was the most civic-minded person I've even known in my life."

Five years after the death of Washington's Senator Warren Magnuson, noted *Settle Times* columnist Emmett Watson described a late night gab fest with Pettus around his wood-burning stove.

Watson points out that Terry joined the Communist party in the 1930s from his despair over the plight of the common laborers, the blacks, and the poor. As Watson put it, "Terry was a gifted, sensitive writer and news reporter. Like so many intellectual idealists of the 1930s, he saw Communism as the only systematic way of dissolving economic injustice. What did it matter that he was wrong, as so many were? He cared. Terry was a Communist in those bleak days when America became paranoid about communists, radicals, socialists, and even ordinary liberals. When called before Congressional investigators Terry declared, 'I'll tell you anything you want to know about me or my activities, but I will not tell you about others.'"

As a consequence Terry spent nine months in prison. When released he was shunned as if he were a Biblical leper. No one would hire him or publish his work, former friends avoided him, and his world shrank to Berta, their houseboat and a few loyal neighbors.

Watson continues with Terry's story. "One day a man phoned Terry; he wanted to meet him in a local park. The mysterious caller explained that he couldn't risk being seen near Terry's house. When Terry met the man he gave him an envelope as he said, "This comes from an old friend of yours. He wants you to have it because he knows how tough things are for you now. He can't come out in the open because it would damage him politically. But he wants you to know he remembers how you helped him get elected."

Watson said, "It was Warren Grant Magnuson, wasn't it?"

Terry answered "Yes, it was Maggie."

Like Terry, Maggie cared.

"Just a Guy"

"When Caryl and I married as students at the University of Washington, houseboats were cheap and romantic," says Bill Keasler, president of the Floating Homes Association. The house they bought was indeed cheap; it cost all of $150, a bargain price even in 1969. However, there was a catch.

Since the seller intended to build a more lucrative high-rise apartment building on his lake property, his rental houseboats could be bought for close to their salvage value. Bill and Caryl bought the last of the original half a dozen homes moored on the Fairview Avenue dock only because they found moorage for it just east of Gas Works Park

"That dock was gloriously Lake Union," says Bill, "full of old ships, barges, eclectic houseboats, and various live-aboards. Once we had our "new" old houseboat towed over to its new dock I did a fair amount of remodeling during the year or so we were there."

Next, Bill virtually created a short dock just beyond a small yellow house on stilts on the south shoreline between the I-5 Freeway and University Bridge. "Once we moved there we realized how noisy it was; you couldn't even hear yourself think. We wanted out."

Finally the Keaslers found what they thought would be a permanent moorage site on the east side of the lake, far from

the noisy bridge traffic. Bill began work as an electrical engineer at Boeing. Caryl started her teaching career at a Bellevue
school on the east side of Lake Washington. With the added
income the couple invested in a second houseboat on the near-
by Wandesforde dock.

Life was good until their dock owner exercised his right to
move his home to the Keasler's moorage site. He offered them
space on the same dock where their houseboat had been
moored when they first bought it. That dock had reverted to a
houseboat moorage when the Shoreline Management Act as
implemented on Lake Union not only limited the height of new
buildings on the shoreline but also prohibited any new construction without water-dependent usage.

"I didn't want to move back to the old dock," says Bill. "It was
in the shadow of the new five-story Union Harbor
Condominium. "We ended up with our house tied up to the
apple tree at the end of Boston Street without any utilities. A
city inspector came by the next day and gave me two weeks to
vacate the street end. I put an ad in the paper 'Houseboat for
Sale, Best Offer.'"

"The next day somebody came by; I don't even remember his
name, and bought it. He towed our houseboat up to Friday
Harbor in the San Juan Islands and turned it into a marina
office. Fortunately we could move into our rental houseboat, but
we couldn't avoid the financial loss.

"At the time of the eviction Terry Pettus, president of the
FHA, had collapsed from emphysema in London. There was a
leadership vacuum in the FHA so I was persuaded to step into
the leadership position."

Bill had barely gotten acquainted with the partially floating
FHA office when a lobbyist called with alarming news. A bill
designed to make any form of rent control in Washington State

A Partially Floating Office

illegal had just passed the State House. Since the City had zoned only a limited area of Lake Union for residential use, specifically where houseboats had connected to the new sewer, the zoning created a captive tenancy for moorage owners. The FHA had worked for years crafting a legally acceptable Equity Ordinance that gave dock owners the right to a fair return on their investment and also linked rent increases to the Consumer Price Index. If the bill passed the Senate, it would overturn years of work and once again tip the balance toward dock owners.

"Fortunately," says Bill, "we caught the bill before it got to the Senate. I was green as grass, but we flooded Olympia with houseboaters, called everybody we knew that supported our cause, asked them to write their legislator and call everyone they knew and ask them to do the same. We held special meetings to keep members informed of our efforts. It was my baptism by fire in Olympia. Very scary and time-consuming, but also very exciting. The vote in the Senate was overwhelmingly in our favor and we had learned what buttons to push."

Bill and Caryl's daughter Karen was born shortly after he became president of the FHA and currently attends the University of Washington. "We taught Karen how to swim before she learned to walk," says Bill.

Bill has somehow managed to keep not only his family afloat, but also lead the FHA through such items as:

1979 — Governor Dixie Lee Ray vetoes a measure tacked onto a mobile home bill in an attempt to wipe out the Houseboat Equity Ordinance.

1981 — First public tour of selected houseboats declared a smashing success with 500 tickets sold at $10 each.

1983 — Both floating home and moorage owners once again work together successfully to combat proposed four hundred percent increase in state lease fees.

1984 — After six years of struggle, revised Equity Ordinance finally becomes law. Terry Pettus joins in celebration shortly before his death.

1986 — Seattle Shorelines Master Program revision begun. To include "Safe Harbor" provision for evicted houseboats, which will allow them to moor in a non-conforming location until new moorage can be found.

1989 — University of Washington announces plans for South Campus expansion which includes eviction of six houseboats from University-owned land on north side of Portage Bay. FHA and Portage Bay communities convince the University to modify its plans.

1992 — State drafts new lease for all aquatic lands that requires lessees to accept responsibility for clean up of any contamination. Houseboaters, aware of industrial history of Lake Union, balk at assuming liability for previous polluters.

1993 — Annual spring meeting features a speaker on possible effects of an earthquake on floating homes. Answer: we'd be tossed as if in a shaking teacup.

1996 — The massive weight of snow on two successive days after Christmas tilts numerous houses and almost sinks several of them. Neighbors pitch in with shovels and Seattle fire boats pressure spray snow off the roofs of threatened homes.

On the lighter side, the Association publishes a quarterly newsletter that includes a community column titled Waterlog. Some snatches from the column written by Shari Lockwood:

"Neighbors hanging out one summer day on Tenas Chuck heard the strains of Beethoven's *Ode to Joy* announcing the beginning of a roof-top wedding across the channel. Surprised neighbors cheered as Chris Blumfield-Brown and Geraldine Dibden tied the knot that day. Chris works for Microsoft and French-born Gerri is into boat-finishing and sailing and currently works for Lake Union Mail. Their cat, Matalo, wore a bow-tie for the event but didn't make it up the ladder to the roof."

In the "Flora and Fauna" section the columnist writes, "Many people have reported bald eagle sightings over Lake Union this summer. I almost wrecked my car when one flew up over me from the lake as I was trying to merge onto I-5 from the Boylston on ramp. We have a resident bullfrog who croaks at all hours in the 2200 block of Fairview."

The Association maintains a partially floating office staffed by a part-time office manager. Every month the twelve Board members crowd into the tiny office to deal with everything from state lease issues to a second printing of their playful and practical cook-book, "Floating Kitchens."

Bill doubts houseboat owners will ever again have the combination of crisis and personality, exemplified by the evictions of the early sixties and the leadership of Terry Pettus, that energized the community at that particular time.

He's proud of the successes of the Association compared to most community groups. An increasing number of Seattle's 487 floating homes now own their moorage sites, one of the major goals of the FHA, but Bill cautions that the need to protect and represent the community's interest will continue indefinitely. He also points out that although no major crisis has popped up recently, it's often during the quiet times that potential threats to the community are being drawn up. "I've built up a trust relationship with the decision makers; in a sense I've become a credible lobbyist for the houseboat community, and that takes time.

"Even though the price has become somewhat outrageous, houseboats remain the cheapest waterfront in the city, and for those lucky enough to be here, we'll continue to live in God's pocket, as Terry Pettus would often say."

Bill is beginning to feel that after twenty-five years it may be time for new leadership. He modestly insists "about the only thing I bring to the party is a sense of continuity and context, but otherwise I'm just a guy."

Perhaps true, but this "just a guy" has led the houseboat community from the first public tour of selected houseboats to coping with the effects on Lake Union of a distant Alaska earthquake.

Thanks, Bill.

Baby on Board

A couch pillow with the saying, "Heaven seems a little closer in a house beside the water," clearly reflects the sentiments of houseboaters Jon and Arminda Phillips. The couple met when Arminda was working at the Bellevue branch of REI (Recreational Equipment Company) and John, a Corvallis, Oregon native, spent a summer working at the same store.

After dating for six years, the two became engaged and married just four months later. "We didn't want to live together until we were married so it seemed like the perfect time to purge all of our assorted individual stuff. We decided to downsize into a couple and began looking for a houseboat. We'd been on several of the bi-annual houseboat tours, and even though we knew we wanted to have children, we also love swimming, rowing, water-skiing, kayaking, scuba-diving and all those water sports. We figured we'd live on a houseboat until we had a toddler."

Jon and Arminda found an ideal situation. An older houseboat couple needed to move to a landed condo. The condo was not quite yet available but the couple wanted the equity out of their floating home. So Jon and Arminda bought their houseboat in the fall of 1999 and let the previous owners continue living there while they spent a month-long honeymoon in Italy.

"We moved in on Halloween Eve of 1999," says Arminda. "It was crazy. I was so upset we were moving on one of my favorite holidays, I went out and bought about twenty pumpkins. So here we were out in the dark and cold madly carving away at these pumpkins."

After their first week on the lake Jon and Arminda realized they never wanted to leave, not even when they had a toddler. "We just decided that somehow, we'd make it work," declares Arminda.

After fifteen years at REI with major management responsibilities, Arminda wanted a break before taking on motherhood. She decided to resign from REI and enroll in the University of Washington's two year photography program.

Meanwhile, Jon happily continued his work at Microsoft, especially since he's six foot two inches and their ceiling was only six feet high. He only could stand up straight in the small peak area of the roof.

"It wasn't very comfortable," admits Jon, "but we lived in it for a year while designing our remodeled houseboat. We discovered the walls weren't structurally sound enough to add any more weight to them, so we ended up having to knock down the original house and start from the logs up."

Since both wanted to live in an intimate community of small, low profile houseboats, they opted for only an additional two hundred square feet for a second bedroom and a rooftop deck for expanded outdoor space. With only one parking space per houseboat and very limited on-street parking, their dock will probably continue as one with cottage-like smaller homes.

"I like the quaintness of our small, intimate little village. Besides, if I can't clean the kitchen, Swifter the floor and tidy up the house in half an hour, I'm not a happy camper," admits Arminda.

Their compact remodeled home attests to their love affair with Italy, where they've spent every September since their honeymoon. The exposed structural beams, soft wood floors with square nails, (the nails took six weeks to obtain and nearly drove their contractor crazy!) Carrara marble for the kitchen counters, and a big deep rectangular porcelain sink all have roots in Italy. The hand carved walnut refectory dining room table with both matching benches and chairs had a previous life in an Italian convent.

Fortunately, both the remodel and Arminda's studies at the University were completed shortly before Scout arrived on Dec. 10, 2002.

Scout came home to the antique rocking cradle that her father had slept in, a changing table above a dresser and below a light with dangling reflecting crystals, large letters of the alphabet lining the top of the walls, a rocking chair for mom, and a very welcoming community.

"I can't imagine a more loving place to be with a new baby." declares Arminda. "Within a week we were walking the three mile loop around Portage Bay with Scout in her little pack, and we'd often come home to find dinner waiting for us at our front door or little gifts or tokens for Scout from various pretend aunts and uncles. Whenever I went out with Scout any neighbors who saw us had to see her, ask how she's doing and dote on her. While they probably won't admit it, we found it was the men, especially the bachelors, who seemed most adoring."

Arminda recalls that Scout was still tiny when two neighbors across their channel, Alan and Mac, were using a very loud planer to refinish their floor. Scout found the noise very disturbing, and a day or so later when they ran into Alan he noticed she was crying. "Is it the planer, Arminda?" he asked. She explained that Scout was too little to understand and the noise did upset her. The next day the noisy planer was gone.

"It was just a matter of his being aware that the noise was bothering a new little person on the dock whom he adores. For me, it's a remarkable example of what neighbors do for each other without making anyone feel guilty or like they owe you anything. I don't know where the planer went, and I still see new wood coming in to their house, so they must be doing the planing somewhere else."

Arminda and Jon both respect the challenges of raising children on the lake and have intentionally taken appropriate precautions. Before Scout arrived, they designed their windows and doors to accommodate child-proof gates. They added an old fashioned claw tub knowing how much kids like to play in them and included lots of storage space in their peaked roof accessible from an inside rolling library ladder.

As soon as Scout was six months old, Arminda began taking her for swim lessons at their local sports club. "I think at this point the lessons are more about teaching Mom safety practices with a child in the water than teaching baby to swim, but I've learned a lot already.

"We've talked to various couples who've had children here on the docks, and they've all said essentially the same thing at some time in the conversation.

"It's not your child who's going to fall in the water, it's their friend. You will have rules. Your child will know when you walk outside, you put on your life jacket. You'll have a little nail where you keep the life jacket and your child can reach it. It's someone else's kid who starts running around and suddenly just zips out the door and then falls in. Never have a birthday party or a play day down here until everyone can swim."

Arminda continues, "This is such a unique situation. Our houses are so physically close to each other, yet we never feel intruded upon. There seems to be an unwritten rule that when you're passing by on the dock if neighbors are out on their deck you stop by and chat. If you have company or if Jon and I are eating on our upper deck, that's respected. We were a little concerned about our next door neighbor, Peter, whose bedroom window is only about fifteen feet from Scout's. We feel very blessed because so far she has been a very easy baby. We tell him "You're the really lucky one she's so good, because you can probably hear her as soon as we do!"

"Every day when I walk down the dock I feel like I'm on vacation; people here are comfortable with themselves and happy. No matter where you live on the lake, we all have that connection.

"Not long ago one of our neighbors, an incredible woman who's been a pilot, a sheriff's deputy, and co-author of ten books on hiking trails and such, had a stroke. She temporarily couldn't read, write, or always find the right words. Instantly without a word everybody rallied together to help her. One neighbor brought groceries, others helped with cleaning and cooking and I drove her to doctor appointments. It was just so natural, and now she's almost fully recovered. It was such a beautiful thing to see the fluidity of it, like the water that surrounds us, everybody gathered around and swept her up. It was such a joy to do my small part.

"Afterwards, I'd go home feeling so safe and secure, because I realized that if something like that happened to me, I'd experience the same support."

In addition to pitching in to help their neighbor and welcoming Scout into their family, the past year also included the time consuming process of buying their dock. The owner had passed away and her heirs wanted to sell it. "We did it in just a year," says Arminda, "but it felt like forever. We just closed three weeks ago. Since most of us are on owned real estate we're now brand new condo owners. The house at the end is mostly on land owned by the state, but the owner negotiated a thirty year lease with the Department of Natural Resources. The two houseboats closest to the land are on a street that runs along the shore and can never be used as such. With minimal help from an outsider, we decided as a group on the value of each separate moorage. We still haven't done any by-laws as the last two summers had been torpedoed by the process, so the consensus was just to let the dust settle and then come October we'll try to finish up."

Jon and Arminda realize their now eight month-old daughter's world is rapidly expanding beyond the universe of the blanket on which she currently kicks and coos. Scout has outgrown the cradle, Arminda will soon have to move her computer from the nursery, and Scout will soon be a toddler. "Then she'll be able to ride the rocking lamb I just had to get for her," says the ever positive Arminda. "I'm not sure what we'll do about the pink pedal car I bought. You know how it is; we want our children to enjoy the same things we fondly remember."

A Child's Eye View

One morning, Joey's teacher asked her class how their day began. Joey raised his hand and reported, "Well, I was watching some ducks swimming in the channel when I saw this great big bird take off. It had a white head and brown body, so it must have been an eagle. After the eagle took off, I saw a beaver swimming by the house across the channel."

"My, where do you live?" asked the teacher.

All in a typical day for nine year old Joey LaMarche, who at dusk rarely sees eagles, but can always spy a few bats flying near the shoreline not far from his houseboat home. As one might expect, Joey's favorite sport is swimming.

The tall blond youngster attends St. Benedict's school where his class mates practically vie for invitations to his Lake Union houseboat. How he gets from Eastlake to the Wallingford area school is simple, "My Dad usually drives me there, and then Mom picks me up."

Mom, Mary Callahan LaMarche, commutes by bus to her job at a downtown hotel where she's the Chef Concierge. The job gives her the flexibility to head home when most of the hotel guests have made their plans for the day with the help of Mary and her staff.

Dad Paul, an avid sailor, owns a business offering sail boat rides or rentals of his boat, Neptune's Car, which he moors on

Elliott Bay. Unlike Mary's clients, Paul seldom has customers until he's safely deposited Joey at school.

On almost any summer day the agile nine-year old confidently takes off in his own sailboat. "I named it Jaws," says Joey, "sort of after the movie. I started taking lessons two years ago with my friend Chris at the Seattle Yacht Club. At first, there were six of us on a boat, then last year it was only four. I still take lessons, but now I can go out on my own. I guess you could say it's my version of a bicycle."

Vacation time for the LaMarche family usually involves a sailing trip. Not long ago they traveled as far south as Mexico. "We left from somewhere other than Seattle," he says, "and what I noticed most in Mexico was that they speak a different language. I couldn't understand them."

Consequently, Joey appreciated a more recent trip by plane to New Zealand. His dad Paul wanted to be a part of sailing's premier event, the 2003 American's cup race, held off the coast of Auckland, New Zealand. "I liked Australia even better than New Zealand," says Joey, and I liked that they spoke English in both countries."

His mom adds, "He seems to instantly pick up the various accents, and after only a few days in Australia we had a hard time convincing folks that we were in fact from the United States. Joey sounded so like an Aussie they couldn't believe it."

As for his birthday, a major event in any child's life, the family usually celebrates the January 19 date at their cabin near Crystal Mountain. Skiing is Joey's favorite winter sport. Thanks to their cabin near Crystal, Joey isn't really complaining when he comments, "The only snow I've seen down here is when we had like an inch of snow on the dock."

One of his earliest memories is of the Fourth of July Fireworks annually launched close to the eastern shore of the lake and not far from the LaMarche home. "It felt like they were going to come right in my face," he remembers. "I've gotten used to it now, and it's really neat we're so close." More than one adult has experienced that same feeling if they're as close to the fireworks barge as Joey is.

Joey also enjoys a grand stand seat at his home for the practice sessions of the Blue Angles prior to their annual appearance at Seattle's annual Sea Fair Festival in early August. "Those look like F-18's" he'll announce, as several of them fly almost directly overhead. Like father, like son, Joey also can identify various other planes as well as a large variety of boats. On Halloween Joey does a little Trick or Treating on the dock, but since he's the only child on the dock his parents then take him over to Wallingford. There he joins his fellow classmates from St. Benedict Elementary for some Trick or Treating in their neighborhood.

As for pets, Joey says, "I have a hamster named Hermy. My dad won't let me have a dog until I'm in high school." Probably a wise decision, considering dogs need several daily walks off the dock in search of dirt. For right now Joey takes good care of Hermy, and no doubt he'll soon be ready for the responsibilities of a dog.

THE HATHAWAY HOME

One look at the lean, long-legged Nick Hathaway and it's no surprise the high school freshman's passion is long distance running. His older sister, Katie, attends the University of Utah on a swimming scholarship. Mom, JoEllen, teaches Physical Education at local Roosevelt High School, leaving dad, Andy, as the only desk-bound member of the clan.

An ordinary family, except that the only home Katie and Nick have ever known floats on the north shore of Lake Union. The Hathaway's live aboard a sixty-five foot classic yacht, the Twin Isles, moored east of Gas Works Park.

Nick's long legs come in very handy when his home has drifted away from the dock. Boarding or leaving the Twin Isles requires a set of five stair steps to bridge the different levels of the boat and the dock. A four to five foot gap between the boat and the stair steps can be very intimidating, but Nick leaps easily from one to the other. He competently pulls the boat up closer to the dock for less agile folks. Nick began competitive swimming when he was only seven, but it's the blue ribbons he's won as a member of the Rain City Flyers running club that are thumb-tacked to the wall in a corner of the living room.

In mid-May of 2002 the Hathaways suddenly had to move their home to a different moorage site. As the family was eating a late dinner in the galley down below, Nick commented he thought he smelled smoke. News not to be taken lightly when you live within "spitting distance" of neighbors on a wooden dock. The family headed upstairs where they instantly realized a major fire had erupted on one of the three related docks. The growing conflagration, fueled by exploding gasoline tanks on the already burning boats, triggered a quick escape.

Nick explains "We just got off the dock as fast as we could. We didn't have enough time to start our engines. They're the original ones made in 1940 that start on compressed air so it's about a forty-five minute process. We called on the marine VHF (very high frequency) radio where my dad announced the name and size of our boat and that we were shoving off the dock without power."

"We see you, push off, and we'll pick you up as soon as you get off the dock," they radioed back. A lot of boaters were already out there, and the Match-Maker, a big boat about our size, came and passed us a tow line. With the wind coming from the north we had to push ourselves away from the dock to help the Match-Maker overcome the inertia of our size before we got underway. They towed us across to Wards Cove dock on the east side of the lake. Since it was fishing season most of their big fishing boats usually moored there were up in Alaska. Along with several other big boats we were able to temporarily moor in those vacant spaces."

JoEllen adds, "We felt lucky that we all happened to be at home. It was a Friday night and we were having a late dinner, but the moment we saw the smoke we realized WOW! This is trouble. Its amazing that most boat fires are caused by electrical failures, but it's almost impossible to determine whether the wiring in the boat is responsible or sudden surges in the power lines leading into the boats."

The fire they escaped continued leaping from one boat to

another. Water pumped by a small fireboat operated by the Seattle Police Harbor Control, headquartered at the north end of the lake, was of little use against the chemicals unleashed by the intense heat. Flaming boats cut adrift ignited a second dock before a properly equipped Seattle fireboat, the Alki, arrived over an hour later to dose the conflagration. The fireboat had to travel from its station on Elliott Bay around Magnolia Bluff, through the Ballard locks, down the ship canal, and finally into Lake Union.

While no lives were lost, hearts were broken at the loss of some irreplaceable classic boats, many being lovingly restored. The extent of the financial losses motivated the city to finally move one of its two big fire boats from Elliott Bay into the ship canal on the fresh water side of the Ballard locks.

JoEllen adds, "We only had to spend a few nights moored at Wards Cove. We had water and electricity and our holding tanks handled the black water. We used our cell phone until we could connect to a regular one. We were really lucky we found our new moorage."

"But I wasn't able to log onto the Internet for almost a month," remembers Nick.

"Nothing came out of place when we were towed to our new dock; we were in the same house, just in a different place. Our other dock was good. We were at the end. A few girls about my age lived there at various times but there were never any boys. I like this dock because it's smaller. We don't have to walk so far from the car," says the teen who runs every day.

As for raising a family on a boat, JoEllen feels even as toddlers the kids had a sense of the boat and the fifteen feet between the edge of the deck and the lake. "If we were going to be out on the back deck with friends and people roaming all around, we'd put life jackets on the kids. And then after they'd had swimming lessons, around age three, once either Andy or I were in the lake, we'd drop them into the water using a line tied to the back of their life jackets."

"I never liked swimming in a life jacket," says Nick. "and I remember it was kind of hard to get out of the water. My parents would take a ladder we kept on the deck and tie it up to the boat railing so we could climb up onto the deck."

Nick began swimming competitively only four years later, but it's his sister Katie who is the fish of the family. Before she left for college Katie did ten practices a week. This past summer she coached at the Wedgwood swim club. She also swam with the Salmon Bay Aquatics Club at various pools in the winter. That team has had national swimmers and Olympic qualifiers.

While Nick can't remember losing any toys in the lake, he does admit to falling in several times, but it wasn't from the Twin Isles. The family had motored over to visit some fellow live-aboards at the south end of the lake. The then eight year-old eagerly stepped from their small boat onto the rub boards of their friend's boat. Dad Andy had already decided to make another pass at docking next to the large boat, and Nick suddenly found the space between his one leg on their friend's boat and the other on the family dingy stretching wider and wider. "It was a little scary. I knew how to swim and all, but I still had all my clothes on, including my shoes.

"Then there was the time I was feeding some geese. I was leaning down with a cracker trying to get the geese to eat out of my hand. One of the geese was real grabby and always seemed to get most of the food. It was the boldest, but I was determined to give the cracker to a different goose. This guy kept trying to get my cracker and kept pulling at it until I lost my balance and fell off the dock."

When Nick was a land-less pre-schooler a thoughtful family

friend built a little red sandbox to replace the missing dirt of a typical house. The family put the imported "dirt" on the back deck where Nick played with his collection of cars, trucks, back hoes and cranes. His dirt toys are now stashed away in a wooden toy box that doubles as a table surface in the living room.

When it was time for a bicycle, JoEllen recalls, "We kept the bike covered on the bow deck. It was a little tricky getting it off the boat, but we'd take Nick and his bike to our big parking lot when there wasn't much traffic so he could bike around in circles. One day when he was getting kind of antsy for a new bike, we accidentally knocked his small bike overboard while using the hose. Nike said, 'Oh well, now I gotta get a new bike.' He was just hoping; we were able to retrieve the small one."

"Summer's really nice here," says Nick, "because with the breeze off the lake it's rarely hot, and we can jump in the water if we want to cool off. We go out in the Boston Whaler, mounted with a winch for lowering it into the lake, and we can cruise around. On the Fourth of July we go up on the bridge and have this perfect view. It's like the fireworks are getting closer and closer to you every time. There are so many people down here at Gas Works Park; it's really crowded."

Although Nick feels their location at the north shore of Lake Union somewhat isolates him from his classmates, he enjoys the family's summer travels in their very own home. "We usually head for the San Juan Islands and the inside passage east of Vancouver Island, with stops at Nanaimo, Desolation Sound, and various other small towns. I like Nanaimo best because it's a good sized city; they're lots of places to see. We often meet up with other members of the Classic Yacht Association for various events, like races, barbecues, and just hanging out together. And we all take turns handling the boat when we go out."

JoEllen adds "We had a stool for the kids to stand on when

they first started steering the boat so they could see through the window."

"In winter it gets windy and cold," says Nick. The storms can knock us around so much that books slide off the tables, sometimes dishes fall and break, and we've lost several lamps. It's noisy and keeps me awake at night sometimes. We've had a lot of stuff fall in the water. One of our deck tables blew right off.

"Christmas is just the same here as anywhere else; we have a tree and open presents and such. I usually get drafted to help put lights up outside and sometimes a tree on top of the boat.

"The first Sunday of December we go to the near-by public boat launch and take pictures of the jet-skiers that dress as Santa and his reindeer. Rudolf has his little red nose and all. Every year they lead the parade for special people like handicapped kids. It's pretty fun."

Nick likes being able to see where he lives from the I-5 ship canal bridge. JoEllen has realized that while she and Andy savor the ever changing vistas and activity on the lake, both Katie and Nick have never known anything else. "Our kids don't notice, because they've always lived here, but there's always something different to look at. We know the difference between looking out at the same thing every day and living here on the lake, but our kids don't."

Nick thinks he was about ten when he began to realize he lived in a rather unusual home.

"You don't really think about it, it's just what I do. My friends think it's cool; they like to jump off the boat and into the water. But they go like "Whoa, I've never seen anyone who lives in a boat before."

Nick says, "I definitely have a smaller space than most of my friends, but I don't think we have as much stuff as other people do, so it sort of evens out. But I think we have too much stuff for the space. We just have one TV; I don't know where we'd put another one.

"I think a boat is a lot more work than a house. I'd like to live in Seattle where I grew up, but I'd like to have a little more space."

Wherever Nick and his sister Katie eventually choose to live, what do you bet there will be a boat somewhere in their lives?

HUCK FINN REVISITED

In the mid-1990s five kids lived on one of the Fairview Avenue docks. Biko Tabor was the only one born in his floating home, three days after Christmas in 1985. As an infant Biko slept in a manger-like crib built into the wall above his parents' bed, but he long ago graduated to a dinghy suspended from the ceiling in his own bedroom. Biko's dad, Langston, entered fatherhood at forty-two. Langston always enjoyed telling the story of driving about one day when the water-locked Biko, about three, pointed to a construction project exclaiming, "Look, Mom, look Dad! Dirt! Look at all that dirt!"

Langston suddenly found himself the single parent of a seven-year old when a fatal aneurysm struck Biko's mother and the child she was about to deliver. It was 1993, the year when President Clinton named Langston Minority Contractor of the Year. Biko remembers the trip back to the other Washington for the ceremony in the White House Rose Garden. "It was really boring, lots of speeches that went on and on. I fell asleep."

As one of the old-timers on the houseboats, Langston occasionally would skinny dive into the water on a hot day, although he wore a suit when swimming home from his office, Tabor Electric, half a mile to the south.

The long narrow entry hall of the Tabor home had a strip of green carpet with a hop scotch game outlined on it and an appropriately equipped child's workbench built into the far corner. Marine life thrived in an aquarium, supplied with water pumped from the lake, that sat in the kitchen window above the sink. Langston hung a punching bag from Biko's bed, the dinghy with a ladder up it that was suspended from the ceiling. A vintage Thunderbird sailboat floated off the back deck and a ladder reached through an opening in the porch roof to a summertime outdoor sleeping area. The roof also stored a collection of inner tubes and various other float toys.

Langston and Biko's lives improved dramatically when the Handron kids, Matthew, twelve; Jonny, ten; and Caitlin, seven, all moved into the house right across the dock. The three Handron youngsters bedded down at night on foam cushions in the 10-by-12 foot loft under a pitched roof and above their parents' bedroom/office. The loft overlooks a knotty-pine living room where the Handrons and anyone else who happened to be around gathered at the large coffee table for vegetarian meals. A wood-burning stove tucked in the corner heats the small home.

Matthew, Jonny and Caitlin shared the same bathroom with their parents along with the only television set in the household. There's no swing set in their yard, in fact there's no yard. Since their dad, Mike, home schooled the boys, they had to wait until mid-afternoon for the other kids to come home. Mike saw that the youngsters vacuumed, cooked, and cleaned, as well as monitored the dumpster and recycling bins that serve the thirty-one neighboring houseboats. Mike often sent Matt or Jonny to buy the family groceries at near-by Pete's Market.

Mike had retired from a career in the insurance industry, so he taught the kids sailing in their Catalina Twenty-five sailboat, led the threesome on expeditions to Seattle's court house, museums, Science Center and parks, and monitored their academic progress.

Mom, DeAnne, works as Director of Management Consulting with Ernest & Young, one of the major accounting firms. Deanne also worked effectively with Caitlin when she would snuggle up with Mom for help sounding out words.

Jonny rowed on the lake with Carter Warmington, who lives at the end of the dock, and Matt loved the everyday swims during the summer months. The kids floated back and forth between the Handron house and Langston's place, with occasional stops at other neighbor's homes, including a professional writer who works at home. In summer, the swimming hole off Langston's back deck often resembled a miniature United Nations when Biko's play group from preschool days converged on the dock.

Both Mike and Langston recognized and utilized the myriad teachable moments on the lake. Summer sailing lessons incorporated physics, reading, group problem solving, vocabulary, social studies, math and astronomy along with the thrills.

When the Handrons first bought their floating home in the summer of 1995 for just under $100,000, they intended to use it as a week-day Seattle base so they could avoid the commute into Seattle from their suburban Issaquah home fifteen miles east.

Once they spent a few weekends in the dark stained turn-of-the-century cedar shingle bungalow, with the kids swimming, spying turtles, paddling on the lake, and roller-blading with Biko and Carter in the parking lot, they decided to rent out their home in Issaquah and move permanently to the dock.

As Mike says, "The first week-end here, the kids had a ball. They marveled at the turtles, geese and ducks, played around in the water, and Matt even caught a fish; he was ecstatic. It was all straight out of Huck Finn."

As the children grew, their needs changed. The Handrons now spend the school year in a larger home on the land, but they usually manage to return to the lake during the summers. Looking forward to the time when they can permanently return to the lake, Mike and DeAnne recently purchased another houseboat at the end of their dock.

When Biko was twelve years old Langston suffered a fatal stroke. Their next-door neighbor, Levi Moten, whose son Shinzo was Biko's age, along with the entire dock, literally wrapped Biko in love. Biko's extended dock family, especially Levi and the Handron family, took Biko under their wing and made it possible for him to remain in the only home he had ever known until Biko himself was ready to move on.

The good news is that another family with two children recently bought the Tabor house and during the past year two dock families had babies and a third is expecting their first child.

Wheeling Around

"I'm so lucky," says Bam. "I think my houseboat is the only one here where I can get to and from the dock in my wheel chair." Bam (her younger sister couldn't manage Betty-Ann, and her last name is Morse) had a stroke about five years ago, but the plucky lady from Woods Hole, Massachusetts manages quite nicely, thank you, in her vintage home.

In the summer pots of red geraniums on her south deck brighten the brown cedar shakes covering her long narrow home at the end of Roanoke Bay's Hamlin Pier. The old house-boat on cedar logs contrasts sharply with the larger two story contemporary homes of Roanoke Reef opposite her on the south side of underwater Edgar Street.

The house itself might be called Bam's scrapbook. "I like to pick up a variety of furniture," she acknowledged. "I have all these different kinds of chairs. When my family back East died I had some of the furniture shipped here. I've always liked to sleep in the front room with the view of the lake. After my stroke I had to get a lower bed; that's why I have two of them in here now."

Now that she only has the use of her left hand Bam no longer uses the wood burning stove at the front of her spacious living room. Her two beds, one of antique maple with spooled foot and headboards; and her current one, a captain's bunk with drawers underneath, occupy opposite corners. Along with the various chairs a large desk, an even larger table, a fully stocked book shelf and a glass door cabinet add to the comfortable clutter of the room.

As Bam steers her wheel chair toward the kitchen she indicates several irregularities in the living room floor, "You can see my current living room once included two smaller separate rooms," she explains.

Once in the kitchen she points to the bathroom off the back wall.

"I know it's a strange place for a bathroom, but the entrance was originally accessible from a different direction. After my stroke I had to remodel it and Sid (McFarland) discovered the rotten floor was on the verge of collapse. Since it all had to be rebuilt, I changed the entrance to off the kitchen so it would be closer." An antique roll top desk and large old wood ice box are behind the living room wall, while the kitchen sink, stove, dishwasher and refrigerator line the wall on the dock channel. A long work table/counter parallels the appliances with space for Bam's wheel chair in-between the two.

The site of the former kitchen, which Bam moved so she could be closer to her guests when entertaining, now holds a hodgepodge of everything: a stunning antique bird's eye maple chest, now partially visible under boxes of dishes and gardening equipment, seven yellow Kodak boxes with slide carousels, various extension cords, a box of mouse killer, another box filled with balls of various colored string, two large accordion type kites she bought in Taiwan and not even Bam knows what else.

"I finally got rid of all the yarn and quilting materials I had. I began knitting in sixth grade when we knitted socks for the soldiers fighting overseas. I enjoyed knitting when there was

Roanoke Bay

nothing else going on, but the quilting took more planning and concentration. It was so disappointing discarding some of the patterns I had chosen; I had to keep some of them.

"I have a friend who comes down here every Monday evening and helps me sort through it all. Margie used to work for me and she's interested in seeing what we'll discover. Until we had a convenient recycling container, where I knew what I threw out would be reused, I tended to just pile stuff back here. I'll admit I have a hard time throwing anything away."

The plucky Bam arrived in Seattle after graduating from Maine's Bates College with a degree in Physics, not exactly typical for a girl in those days. Her senior thesis was in Oceanography and Bam hoped to go to sea just as her Coast Guard father had done.

"After graduation I worked at Wood's Hole during the summer and a cohort who had been in Seattle suggested I apply for a position in the Oceanography Department at the University of Washington. I took the advice, was offered a job, accepted it, and drove out to Seattle. After only two weeks on the job, I was out in

Puget Sound on board the University's research vessel, the Brown Bear, measuring the water to determine its characteristics.

"I loved it"

During Bam's time at the UW, she spent a good chunk of several years in Taiwan assisting in measuring the quality of the ocean waters. Her contribution was a salinometer, a specific instrument for quantifying the amount of salt in the water, brought from the University of Washington.

"We could only go out to sea when weather permitted, so there was a lot of down time. Fortunately, we lived at an international house and there was always someone who spoke English. I was the only female, and they didn't quite know what to do with me. I'd learned how to handle that at the University, since I was usually the only woman on board when we went to sea."

Bam's first houseboat was a rental she found on Portage Bay, an ideal location for University students or employees. Without a yard to mow, the maintenance was minimal, and it was refreshing to have her own four walls when she returned from the close quarters aboard the Brown Bear. Not long after moving in, shortly after she'd returned from a month at sea, Bam heard a knock on her door. A woman wanted to look at the houseboat. Somewhat puzzled, Bam gave her a brief tour and then the woman asked, "Does the furniture go with it?"

"I soon learned that whenever you rented a houseboat it was usually for sale. My first houseboat was actually moored on one of the three moorages that were condemned to make way for the viaduct to the new Evergreen floating bridge to the East Side. I liked living on the water and decided I wanted to buy a houseboat, but I couldn't afford those on Portage Bay."

Bam managed to find a houseboat in her price range on the north side of Queen Ann Hill moored on the ship canal below

Seattle Pacific University. She eagerly settled into her own home even though larger house boats in front of her blocked any view of activity in the ship canal. After several tranquil years, she realized that her moorage owner was never going to connect to the city sewer system. She also knew only those houseboats on docks where they could properly dispose of sewage would be allowed to remain on the lake. It was time to move once again.

This time Bam ended up on her current moorage at the foot of Hamlin Street. "I came here before we hooked up to the new sewer, when all our waste water went out onto the logs and into the lake. I remember looking down and seeing pink toilet paper floating by. The dock owner paid for installing the sewer system under the dock, but we were responsible for the plumbing underneath our houses and connecting to system. Thirty-five years later we still have the same pump at the head of the dock."

However, Bam's moving days were not over. Her houseboat was nowhere near the end of the dock, so one day when a neighbor mentioned the owner of the end houseboat planned to sell it, Bam jumped at the opportunity.

"The previous day a colleague at work had asked me if I knew of any available houseboats," says Bam. "At that time realtors seldom handled houseboats, so without mentioning it to my work colleague, the very next day I specifically asked the owner if she wanted to sell. When she said yes, I immediately told her I wanted to buy it.

"As a leased moorage, I only had to buy my home. I pay a monthly rental fee to the dock owner for my moorage. I started out with a twenty year lease but now I'm on a month-to-month basis. I'm not worried, our dock owner, Dave Rosenquist, is very fair."

Over her thirty-some years in the end houseboat Bam has witnessed a cluster of houseboats and moorages at the end of

Edgar Street evicted and the structure where Bill Boeing built his first airplane torn down. All to make way for the projected six story over-the-water condominium, Roanoke Reef. Bam recalls the ear-shattering noise of construction when it began in 1971 right outside her front door. Pile drivers drove in over 250 concrete pilings, and a major portion of the first floor parking garage was constructed on the pilings. The project served as a magnet for land use issues, specifically shoreline use, from its beginnings in the late sixties.

As the legal jousting dragged on for years, catamaran live-aboards set up housekeeping on the giant platform, fishing boats moored there during the off season, and a marine engine repair shop sprouted up. Finally, in July of 1980, the local community celebrated the demise of the giant over-the-water Roanoke Reef. Jubilant neighbors, who had spent time, money and energy to save the lake for water dependent use, contributed a dollar to rent a pick-ax and whack away at the huge concrete platform.

In the mid-eighties Bam's new dock owner added a short dock next to the land for new two-story houseboats. He also installed a floating sailboat dock on property leased from the state on the outer side of Bam's dock. "I like the outer dock," says Bam. "It's limited to sailboats and provides some protection from rough water, wakes from boats going too fast, and all the looky-loos. I'm glad we can't go any higher than the peak of the current roof. I prefer the openness of this dock rather than the dock behind me with large two-story houseboats."

Bam might add she has an intriguing additional cost once a year on her floating home. She discovered after she'd bought it that a tiny edge of her roof hangs out over Edgar Street, so she pays the city a token amount once a year for using that space.

Bam loved her work at the University, but when money

became scarce in 1976 she lost her position as Lead Oceanographer. "I could have been a secretary; they offered me another position, but I said 'no thanks; that's not quite what I had in mind.' But I still keep in touch with several of my former colleagues."

Next Bam enrolled in various computer courses and then began working with physically handicapped children, first in Edmonds and then in the Federal Way area. "I went to all the different schools and helped handicapped kids with adaptations to computers so they could use them. It was thrilling to help the kids be able to use and enjoy the new technology. I did that until I had my stroke when I was 64. I retired a year ahead of schedule."

In addition to the woman who comes down weekly to help Bam sort through all her accumulated "stuff" in the former kitchen, Bam has a friend who comes in from Poulsbo every other week. She calls ahead for Bam's grocery list, buys all the items on the list along with a lunch, and then brings everything down to Bam's where they enjoy lunch and conversation. Another friend now living up north in Marysville cuts Bam's nails every other week and buys the items on Bam's "Costco list" for her. Often on Fridays someone picks her up for a fairly regular weekly luncheon of fellow employees in the Oceanography Department at the University. "The restaurant where we've met for years is right next to a QFC grocery store, so I can buy things on sale there," says Bam. "I eat less than I used to and have lost considerably weight, and that's good. I'm lucky that I can't taste or smell as well as I once did. When neighbors at Roanoke Reef barbecue out on the deck I'm sure it smells and tastes very good, but it no longer tempts me."

Bam has another friend who annually plants her container garden for her, especially the red geraniums that line her front porch. Another friend put a two by four board around the edge of her deck to make sure her wheel chair never would accidentally go overboard. He also built a railing along her side deck so she could hold on to it while practicing walking.

"Even though here on our dock people tend to be more private and individual than on other moorages, I know my neighbors are always close at hand. My friends that come down usually bring my mail to me, or neighbors will deliver it if they notice there's mail in the box. I'm very lucky."

Bam may be in a wheel chair, lack the eyesight she once did, as well as some of her hair, but she still holds an annual Christmas party where guests have a chance to view all the brightly decorated boats as they cruise by on the lake during the Christmas season.

"It's usually about fifty to sixty people, but everyone brings really wonderful appetizers, not just chips and a dip. They sort of float in and then float out so the house is never too crowded."

One can only hope this determined lady whose face triggers memories of Renaissance paintings of radiant saints with halos above, can enjoy many more years hosting Christmas parties in her beloved houseboat.

The Old Boathouse

Dick Wagner, Founding Director of the world famous Center for Wooden Boats, a hands on maritime museum, owes his presence in Seattle to an impulse. He'd grown up in New Jersey, completed his graduate degree in architecture at Yale, and was headed toward a job in San Francisco. He drove west with a fellow Yalie who had just completed a graduate degree in forestry and landed a job in Aberdeen, Washington. The two agreed to cut expenses by driving west together.

"Seattle fascinated me," says Dick. "I couldn't resist exploring it before going on to San Francisco." Dick's impulse to explore Seattle stretched into realizing he wanted to stay. His career as an architect began at the Boeing Airplane Company. However, during his first year Dick and his motor scooter had a major confrontation with a car that left him hospitalized.

"Being laid up in the hospital for three months gave me time to think. What is it about Seattle that intrigues me? In 1957 it was a blah city, with rather ugly buildings, situated in the midst of snow-capped mountains, funny little islands with Spanish names, and an abundance of both salt and fresh water. What is it that's so special about this place?

"As I puzzled this out in the hospital it dawned on me; it's the people. At first I thought they were boring; they seemed to have so little passion; then I realized people here are really laid-back.

"I've always felt Lake Union was fascinating; it has a mystique for me. Here it is smack in the middle of a vital city—it should have been inaccessible, surrounded by either the corporate headquarters of the major companies or their owners, fenced off and guarded by snarling dogs. Yet you could walk anywhere around the lake. I wandered down on the houseboat docks, poked around the marinas, and even picked blackberries when I ran across them."

Dick continues, "The lake was clearly under-utilized economically, and the houseboat people were far more diversified than they are now. The common denominator was poverty, which meant students, artists, blue-collar workers, and folks on pensions. Only a few had cars, so the neighbors were much closer. There were shared dinners, shared home-brew, and shared resources. It was close to an ideal urban environment: a terrific diversity of culture, ethnic groups, and educational levels sharing this unique life style in rickety old shacks packed along docks less than five feet from each other in places."

Shortly after his three months in the hospital, Dick quit his job at Boeing and began working for individual architects. Although he only made about half the salary he'd had at Boeing, he enjoyed the work more.

Then, Dick bought a houseboat under the Aurora Bridge. It was a lucky move; the house next door was shared by three women and Dick married one of them.

"Before we married, Colleen's house mates had moved out. Once we became man and wife we bought the houseboat for $500. It's a good-sized home that had originally been over on Lake Washington at the end of the Madison Street trolley line. This was in the days before we were discovered by the county assessor so there were no personal property taxes on our home."

Their large white houseboat with a red gabled roof with a five

–foot beige brick chimney has since become a National Historic Site. "That was another episode in the long period of angst we went through to save our houses," says Dick. "It was a period of desperation and creativity. Our dock lord announced he planned to kick us all out, so we figured applying for the historic designation might save our house. First Washington State certified its historic value, then it was recommended for and listed n the National Register of Historic Sites.

"The dock had some interesting characters," Dick recalls. "We had Grover Stackhouse, a happy alcoholic, who had put up a little pilot house on his roof. He would sit up there with a bottle of Muscatel in his hand as he chatted with the world in general and made comments on the passing scene.

"Then there was Harvey Layman. I'll never forget one Sunday morning when a slight wake from a passing boat proved to Harvey that he had not maintained his houseboat very well. All of Harvey's stringers, the big wooden beams that rest on the cedar logs and support the sub-floor, suddenly started falling apart. Harvey was nonchalant about it all as the houseboat finally reached the point of stabilization. His entire home had disappeared except for the stack of his oil stove sticking out above the water.

"That same morning a stranger in a suit, tie and white shirt came down on the dock and asked me if I knew Harvey. I assured him I did and asked why he wanted to know. The stranger explained that Harvey was behind in payments on a loan he'd taken out on his house. I nodded and pointed to the stove stack just above the waterline. The guy studied it, grasped the situation, turned slightly pale, and left without a word."

The slightly less colorful Dick and Colleen settled into houseboat living. When their first child arrived, Colleen resigned from her job as an art teacher so she could be home with the baby. She noticed that during the summer Dick seemed more interested in restoring one or two of the old boats tied up at their dock than his chosen profession. So she suggested they invest their savings in a few more boats and open a Mom and Pop living museum of wooden boats. In the spring of 1968 the couple launched The Old Boathouse. They ran ads along the line of "Row a boat like the one your grandfather used." Business was slow at first, but eventually they connected with a whole network of folks interested in the old wooden boats.

"I was reluctant at first to start renting our boats," Dick admits, "it's sort of like renting out your children. But Colleen knew me better than I did; she knew my soul cried out for it."

That summer they'd take the baby and head for breakfast at the Pike Place Market; then they'd come back home and work together on their boats. They never expected to make a profit, but as summer wound down it looked like they were on to a good thing.

Dick went back to work in the fall, but fortunately the job ended by spring. The Old Boathouse thrived. It generated lots of free publicity, a steady stream of customers knocking on their door, and within a few years a successful and predictable income. A second child arrived and Dick delighted in being able to see the kids grow up.

About that time, Colleen realized the family was being over-run by visitors; curious, interesting people who were nonetheless robbing them of the fun of it all. She suggested that with so many people involved in The Old Boathouse they should try to organize them.

Dick says, "We talked about maybe having people come over once a month, getting a fuller menu of maritime skills and instructions. I kept stalling, but finally in 1976 I could feel myself getting tired and irritable. I decided Colleen might be right. So we invited twenty of the most notorious free loaders we knew to come over. About forty people showed up.

"Right at that meeting I asked everybody, `What do you think about this being the first planning meeting for a hands-on living museum of wooden boats?' I remember seeing Colleen's eyes; she looked a little panicked. This meant we would no longer be the only ones in charge; we would be one of many. As it turned out it's really been as much fun as the Old Boat House. It just never seems like work.

"It seems to me we used to have a lot more time to just hang out on the dock. To live here now requires a certain amount of income—whether you steal it, smuggle it, inherit it, or work for it. Still, the people attracted to houseboats are unique and creative. I'd never trade it for anything else."

Phoenix Dock

The story of Phoenix dock begins on Westlake Avenue North near the eight-story Associated General Contractors building at the south end of the lake. In 1961 the property owner notified the twenty-three houseboat owners moored on his dock that they would soon be evicted. The dock managers, Joe and Cora Adamec, didn't want to lose their houseboat, so they bought some lake property on the east side of Lake Union south of Roanoke Street. Next the Adamecs had their underwater land dredged to accommodate houseboats, including their own. They towed the surplus dock from Westlake over to their new site where some of the evictees found moorage space. They christened the recycled dock Phoenix to celebrate its rising from the ashes of eviction to a new life on the east side of the lake.

Joe Adamec operated a steam plant at Boeing, and Cora, his wife, ran the dock like a modern Tug Boat Annie. If anyone who didn't live on the dock dared to park in the street immediately above their property, Cora would instantly appear, sometimes wielding a boat hook, to chase away the startled intruder as she shouted salty expletives.

Joe and Cora never attempted to gouge their tenants with exorbitant moorage fees nor issue arbitrary eviction notices. Both Adamecs participated fully in their local Masonic Lodge. Since they were without heirs, Joe and Cora willed their estates to the Shriners' Hospital for the treatment of burned and hand-icapped children.

Cora had elephantiasis, which along with her heavy drink-ing and advancing years, led to chronic brain syndrome, or in laymen's language, poor judgment.

Several years after Joe's death Cora was hospitalized for complications of elephantiasis. The seventy-five year-old woman, who nurses described as "confused and disoriented," was unable to sign her admission form. That same day Cora's attorney, H. Joel Watkins and his law partner, David D. Webber, called on her at the hospital. They arrived with a seven-page, single-spaced real-estate contract and option-to-purchase agreement for Adamec's houseboat moorage. Before they left, Cora had penned her shaky signature on the document, Webber notarized it, and Watkins and Webber had bought the moorage. Hospital records show that two days after signing the bill of sale Cora was confined in a strait jacket because of her mental state.

Jean Elmer, who has lived in one of the two end houseboats on Phoenix since 1979, led the fight to protest the sale, certain that Cora never intended to sell the dock, especially at the value assigned by the tax assessor, typically considerably below mar-ket price.

An attorney for the Shriners filed an unsuccessful lawsuit in Superior Court on their behalf. He did not introduce medical evidence of Cora's condition because he felt the whole transac-tion was so irregular that such evidence wasn't necessary.

"We took it as far as we could," sighs Jean, "but we finally had to give up. The Bar Association, a respected local judge, even our Congressman; all declined to get involved even though they knew the facts. I can't believe anyone would ever take money from burned and crippled children, but those attorneys did."

Four and a half years after Cora's attorney bought her dock for $77,200, he sold it to Jeff Wright of the well-known Howard S. Wright Construction Company for $307,500.

Wright, a home-owner on Phoenix, upgraded the dock to sell the individual moorage sites. He replaced the original wooden dock with a concrete one six feet north of the original site, moved electrical wires from overhead poles and ran them under the dock, and dredged a new houseboat site next to the shore.

Once Wright brought the dock up to city code, he sold the moorage sites as individual condominium lots. The condo conversion was possible since all eleven homes on Phoenix are at least partially on real estate rather than state leased land, which can not be sold. Beginning in 1985, homeowners who could afford it paid from $46,100 to $54,500 for their property. The security of ownership and by-laws that allow expansion have led to extensive remodeling. Residents landscaped a grassy area on the shoreline where they can picnic while children play in the shallow water.

Jean Nelson savored a near perfect week-end summer day from her end houseboat as a neighbor rowed by in his inflatable boat. His daughter swam nearby and occasionally grabbed a tow. Kayaks, sailboats, and windsurfers scooted past. Her paddling neighbor aimed a giant water cannon on anyone in range while another neighbor practiced fly-casting off the end of the dock.

"We have summer camp down here," she mused. "I never went to summer camp, but this is what it must be like. Boats, sunshine, kids and grown kids playing in, on and around the water. I think we'll always have summer camp down here. I hope my house will stay in the family, and my son's grandchildren can enjoy summer camp on the lake."

The battle waged over Cora's attorney buying the dock, the

emotional roller-coaster involved in buying one's moorage site, and the disruptive impact of many subsequent changes have all subsided. Phoenix homeowners, which include an architect who has designed numerous floating homes, a single mom who owns and operates an expresso stand at Sea-Tac airport, and a former City Council member who treasures the privacy he can enjoy on the dock, have themselves risen from the ashes.

DECIDEDLY DIFFERENT

The Westlake dock Marty Greer calls home, unlike most, angles slightly from the above shoreline. It's also unusual in that you reach it by way of twelve stair steps right next to a small commercial building housing a yacht rigger, cookie distributor, hair salon and other small businesses. There's also a distinct break between the first four and last four houses on the south side of the dock A finger pier with three sail boats tied up to it floats in the otherwise vacant space.

Another not so obvious difference results from City parcel divisions and the vaguery of underwater real estate combined with Department of Natural Resources leases. The twenty-four houseboats on two docks are divided into two co-ops along plat lines rather than dock locations. Consequently, the dock where Marty lives, includes the dock south of her and the houses moored there, but not the dock where she anchors her houseboat. The other co-op includes her dock and the floating homes moored on the north side of it. The two co-ops share maintenance and utility costs of the two docks.

And then there's Marty's spacious two-story house which she and her former husband moved into on New Year's Eve of 1986. The previous owner had replaced an ancient little shack using stock from his business, Seattle Building Salvage, located in Fremont at that time.

"Everything in this home came from somewhere else," declares Marty.

"He used the flooring from the original little shack for the kitchen wall, wood from a Montana barn panels the dining room and upstairs, and the stained glass window in the stairwell to the second story came from a Capitol Hill Church."

The cedar paneled bathroom includes somewhat Victorian brass faucets and soap dish while the old ceramic sink rests in a large wooden barrel, perhaps used at one time as a rain barrel.

Big black hinges hold the barn wood guest closet door to its frame. One plank on the door has been severely clawed at some time; perhaps by a cat using it as a scratching post. "It's the ultimate in recycling," declares Marty.

Marty has made few changes to the recycled home. "I took out various shelves and cupboards from the living room wall facing the view so that I could have space for my art. We took one look at the wiring and decided to have that redone. The year that the Chimney Sweep refused to clean our old wood burning Franklin stove, which was illegally too close to the wood wall, we put in a properly installed Vermont Castings model.

"A good friend, Karen Berry, designed and painted the make-believe fish pond on the kitchen floor. When Sage, my step-grand-daughter, was younger she would jump into the pond for some imaginative play; now she jumps right into Lake Union for a swim.

"I made our coffee table using patterns from Afghan kalim rugs. Underneath you can see a smaller coffee table patiently waiting for me to find another place for it. Other than that; it's pretty much as we bought it."

When Marty and her husband moved back to Seattle after three years in San Francisco, Bob's son had just graduated form high school, so they became empty-nesters. Bob thought a houseboat would fit right in with his love of sailing, and after looking at almost ten different floating homes, they found the right one.

"We happily settled into Tuesday night Duck Dodge races and thanks to a wonderful neighbor, I found myself involved in all sorts of floating homes activities. I've organized many of our bi-annual houseboat tours over the past fifteen years.

"Years ago my little neighborhood of houseboats had the most wonderful parties. We used to have egg toss contests across the channel, even Leonard and Marie, always a little tipsy by about two in the afternoon, participated. We had little rubber raft races up and down the channel, but the best, the very best, was our lip-sync contest. We built a stage complete with curtains over on Cathi and Richard's house, and every single person in every house did a lip sync. We had this fabulous woman who was a former Vaudeville star as our Mistress of Ceremonies. We had built a bridge of log rafts in the channel so we could freely come and go between the two docks, and we had the old paint float out there with benches for our judges. It was absolutely hilarious; we even had an applause-ometer.

"At Christmas time we decorated to the hilt. We'd always have the Kayak Carolers come to two or three houses, and for several years one of our neighbors rented a float and put a piano on it. She even invited a professional piano player to accompany the carolers. We also had contests for door decorating. Every year we'd have a rummage sale to fund the next year's parties."

Several years after Marty and Bob returned to Seattle their friends from sailing days in San Francisco, Jonelle Johnson and her husband, moved to Seattle and ended up on a houseboat in Portage Bay. Jonelle needed help with her growing business of taking watercolor painters on tours in Europe.

"I'd been working in a law firm," says Marty, "but I was ready

for a change, so in 1991 we organized as a company and started doing four or five tours a year. We've been doing these tours
for the past twelve years or so. Jonelle teaches the painting and
I organize everything, handle all the reservations, keep track of
the money, and serve as concierge for all the clients, so to
speak. It is a wonderful experience, and I've had some great
travels, but it's WORK! Definitely not all glamorous.

"I also started working as a print-maker at Beta Press, a fine
arts press that does Intagio (etching) prints for some very well-
known artists. But about two summers ago the owner's husband got transferred to New Jersey. Now I go back once a year
to print with her. If I had my druthers I'd be print making, but
since I can't pursue that career, I've taken up landscaping."

Marty recently married Gerry Greer, an architect.

"I own this house free and clear; it's my little heaven with all
my art work. But Gerry has a collection of eight or nine old
1950s and 1960s muscle cars and all his tools and he's not
going to leave those things. I mean, where could he park all
those cars? We have enough trouble parking the cars we already
have. We married over a year ago, but we live in two houses. So
we're here sometimes, at his place in Lake City sometimes. He
thinks my house is kind of a vacation home sort of thing, like
this isn't real. I say, 'well, you live in your workshop!'"

Gerry has a house in Twisp, built in 1897, in the Methow
Valley east of the Cascade mountains. Originally from Australia
and England, Gerry had met a woman while traveling in Greece
who invited him to come to Twisp. He took her up on the offer
and worked there as a log peeler, a bartender, and a wrangler.
He also bought the oldest house in Twisp. Gerry's a pilot so the
couple usually flies to Twisp on weekends where they're working at restoring the house.

"To this day my favorite thing to do in the summer is wait

until about 5 o'clock, when everybody begins to get home from work, and just walk up and down the dock with a wine glass or cocktail. We visit with everyone, hear what's going on, and a lot of us jump in for a swim. I so enjoy playing with the neighbors, making my garden grow, and the Tuesday night Duck Dodge. I would never leave here in the summer. Even with my art tours everyone says, 'why don't you do these in the summer.' And I say, well, because I live in Seattle. If you leave Seattle in the summer you might as well not live here."

ROANOKE REEF

"We get lots of queries about the almost triangular shape of our home, "says Bob Koenig, "and there **is** a logical explanation. Here at the end of the dock we're right at the intersection of Fairview Avenue and Edgar Street, which cuts across the north end of our condo site at an angle"

"What? A houseboat at the intersection of two streets?" you ask.

Bob's wife MJ explains, "I understand that when city planners originally platted Seattle, many of the streets were already built on what used to be tidal marshes or fill. I guess they thought someday Lake Union might be filled in, so they platted the streets across it." The old timers were partly right; extensive fill has shrunk Lake Union to two thirds its original size.

Bob and MJ's youthful figures and appearance belie their ten years of retirement. Born and wed in Salem, Oregon, they've returned to the Northwest after Bob's career in corporate telecommunications took them from Portland to Seattle to Iran, with stints in Seattle, Denver, Phoenix, and finally on to London.

They especially enjoyed their time in Tehran where they actually lived among the locals. "Our kids were too young to learn the language," says Bob, "but they learned some of it. We loved the people; they were so very gracious. The food was wonderful, especially some of the lamb dishes.

"The climate and mountains felt like we were back in Denver. The Shaw loved to ski, so there were marvelous skiing facilities in the mountains. Our kids learned to ski there along with all the Iranian families who were on the slopes."

Gary worked for the Iranians and reports they didn't have a big problem with the cultural differences. "Except maybe the fact that most of the marriages were still being arranged," he adds. "It was assumed that once you married you would simply live in an additional floor of the groom's parents' home. I'm not sure they still had dowries, but the distribution of assets after any future divorce was actually negotiated before the wedding. Family ties are very strong there."

Bob, MJ and the children had to leave rather abruptly when the Shaw was overthrown. "It was a rather scary experience, but we were quickly evacuated," recalls MJ.

MJ had trained as a nurse, but soon realized that decision came from her father's work as a hospital administrator. Once their two children were in school she returned to the classroom for a degree in design.

"I found I loved it," she says, "and I went on to develop my own career working primarily in office or commercial design." When they first bought their triangular houseboat in 1996 MJ did some basic remodeling, but after several years her talents led them to practically redo the entire home.

"The house was outdated," she points out, "and I learned that our site was larger than our home. By pushing out several walls and filling our entire site, we were able to increase the square footage by about a hundred and fifty feet. It doesn't sound like much, but when you live in a small space another room means a lot. We also re-did the basement to include what I call a 'guest womb.' It's the best place to sleep in the whole house. It's totally dark, you don't hear any noise at all, and you

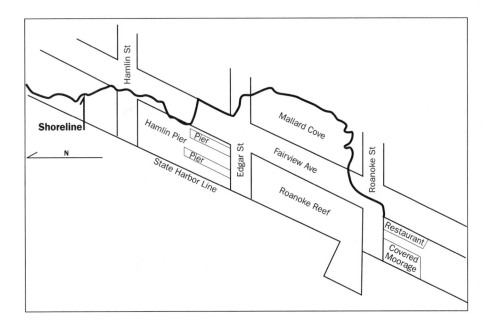

can feel the gentle rocking of the lake; it's truly like a return to the womb."

And yes, you read correctly; the Koenig's have a basement, and here's why.

Roanoke Reef is one of only three docks, beginning with Portage-at-Bay, built specifically for houseboats after the completion of the Lake Union sewer in the mid-1960s. By that time cedar logs were no longer readily available nor cheap, so houseboat floats began to be made of Ferro-cement and Styrofoam. Because contractors built forms for the float, just as they do for basements, they could design the form to include a basement.

Increasing the size of their home meant having it towed to the Foss ship yard on the Canal where demolition of the previous walls was a far less complex matter than if their home had remained in Roanoke Bay. Also, the house has practically no deck space from which to work on it. At Foss the contractors could rotate the house as they worked on its various sides. The distant location also eliminated the impact of a major construction project on their neighbors.

The basement of their sleek new home now includes the usual washer, dryer, and hot water heater along with a heat pump that draws heat from the lake to keep them warm and cozy. As is typical of many end or view houseboats, the first floor tends to include mostly the bath and bedrooms. Bob's office on the first floor is tucked into the narrow end of the triangle that borders the dock. He admits the view of all the activity on the lake is somewhat distracting.

"Just the other day I say a small wooden barge with an attached outboard motor cruising by. Two couples were seated at what looked like a card table enjoying dinner on the water. All the traffic on the lake amazes me. I've seen everything from the early morning rowers to the newest stern-wheeler cruise ship, the Empress of the North, on its way to the Lake Union Dry Docks. We feel like we're literally in the middle of all the action."

On the second floor, a large space, broken only by a kitchen island, functions as their living room, dining area and kitchen, all with a spectacular view of sunsets over the Aurora Bridge, the Christmas ships at Gasworks Park and the summer Tuesday night Duck Dodge sail boat races.

Both MJ and Bob love to cook, so the kitchen is the latest in high tech design, including a gas six burner stove and two ovens. The original kitchen cupboards no longer hang from the ceiling, but are lined up against a wall where the petite MJ is better able to access their contents. In the living room area a fifty inch plasma TV screen opposite the couch offers entertainment during the dark days of winter.

In the summer they enjoy use of their fourth level, the roof top deck. "I'm an avid gardener," declares MJ, "and I'm eager to get some plants and trees up there to soften the current barrenness of it." Knowing she and Bob think nothing of biking twenty-five miles or more on the Burke-Gilman trail, there's no doubt it won't be long until her decorative touch is added to the upper deck.

Bob and MJ not only live in a distinctive home; the dock itself isn't exactly what one would call run of the mill. The almost suburban modern two story homes, including some with basements, the unobstructed view of the ten houses on the west side and the peek-a-view of those opposite them, and their proximity and easy access to downtown set them apart. But it's the gated parking garage at the entrance to the dock which puts Roanoke Reef in a class of its own.

So how did a houseboat dock end up with a parking garage?

"It's a long story," begins Bob. "As I understand it, years ago there were a lot of rather marginal houseboats moored here in Roanoke Bay. The property owner ran into some financial problems and sold this property to some Texas developers who planned to build a five story 112 unit condominium across the Bay. They evicted all the houseboats and tore down the hanger where Bill Boeing had built his first airplane. But before they'd gone beyond the garage and the first story, the State Shorelands Management Act as implemented on Lake Union limited construction on the lake.

"After seven years the issue was finally resolved and the giant concrete platform towed away, but thank goodness they left the uncovered first story parking garage."

"Even though as relative late-comers our parking space is in the landed condo across the street, we really value the convenience," says MJ, "especially when we already have a roughly five hundred foot walk to our house. On a dark rainy winter evening it takes real motivation to leave the coziness of our home."

TREND SETTERS

"We were trend-setters," says Gary. "Linda and I bought the first moorage site in Seattle's first brand new houseboat dock, built specifically as an architect-designed floating homes community."

Gary and Linda Oman married while still in college, but even then they both dreamed of living on the water some day. Linda's days as a student stretched out considerably when their daughter Heidi arrived during her junior year.

"I took evening classes and correspondence courses to complete my degree; whatever it took," says Linda. "It wasn't easy, but I'm so glad I did." Once they both began their teaching careers and making a little money in 1967, the couple started looking at some of the older houseboats which could be had for between $5,000 and $10,000. By this time the houseboats had hooked up to the new sewer around Lake Union and began teetering toward respectability.

While on their treasure hunt, they heard of two brothers, Gary and Grant Copeland, who had built a new houseboat moorage they called Portage-at-Bay.

"We tracked them down living in a funky houseboat on the ship canal just west of Fremont. They were about our age and agreed to take us over to see the dock they had built. We walked to the end of the dock, dangled our feet in the water, marveled at the panoramic view of the Seattle Yacht Club, the Montlake bridge, the University across the bay. We thought, wow, wouldn't this be great to live here? Right then we decided to buy the end moorage site. We put down $200 as a deposit, and signed the paper work."

Linda's brother-in-law and a friend, both newly minted architects, drew up some house plans for them, and Gary confidently headed for the bank with the plans under his arm. But first one bank, then another, and another, and another turned him down. He realized no one knew much about these new houseboats; they'd never heard of a loan on a houseboat.

The Omans almost gave up. But about a year later Grant called to tell them about a new bank just opening up in the Seattle area that might help them. He was right. Northwest Bank was relocating from Spokane and more willing to accommodate potential customers. The Omans borrowed $20,000 to build the house and used the $3,000 from the sale of their starter home in Shoreline to pay for the Ferro-cement pontoon float. Linda and Gary still cherish a 1969 photo of their new

Contemporary Portage Bay

houseboat, with Gary on board, as it was towed under the Fremont bridge en route from Salmon Bay, where it was built, to their moorage site.

"But," says Gary, "our $20,000 only bought a shell. We had neither dry wall nor insulation. Linda and I became relatively adept at cutting dry wall, nailing it to the studs, taping and painting it. With our five-year old daughter and my $6,000 a year salary, we went Mexican on furnishings with a hammock and a swinging chair. We camped out for a while."

"For a looooong while!" declares Linda.

Shortly after Gary and Linda moved in, Linda's parents also bought a houseboat on the same dock. "It was wonderful," says Linda. "Heidi would stop there for breakfast and then her grandmother walked her up and over the hill to kindergarten at Seward Elementary."

The Omans will never forget the day when Heidi was squatting down on the deck, absorbed as only a child can be, in feeding some bread chucks to the passing ducks. Gary heard a splash as he was doing dishes in the kitchen and rushed out to

see her arm above the water where she had tumbled into the lake. He instantly retrieved her and Heidi began swimming lessons at the local Y the very next day.

The following summer, a national magazine heard about the innovative new houseboat and contacted the Omans for an article featuring their new home. Gary and Linda pointed out that they still didn't have any wallboard, only plywood floor and marginal furnishings. The magazine offered to take care of the finishing work. They hired a wall board crew, painted the walls and floor, and brought in some tatami mats, potted plants and furniture.

"We loved it," says Linda. "A little over a year after we moved in they had finished at least the down stairs portion of our house for us. It was thrilling to see our house on the cover of the June, 1970 issue of American Home."

As an urban planner, Grant Copeland wanted to build a sub-community that not only blended with the watery environment, but also fostered interaction among the residents. Although there were regulations for the materials used, such as all natural exteriors and shingled roofs, and paint colors limited to earth tones of brown, tan, or gray, each home differed significantly from its neighbors.

Gary explains, "Our home was more or less designed from the outside in. For example, our living room was designed with the fireplace opposite the view, so especially in the winter you sat looking at the fireplace rather than the view. We moved the fireplace next to the front window, enclosed it faux Santa Fe adobe style, and surrounded it with a stucco wall so we could enjoy both its warmth and the delightful view. About the only thing we haven't changed on the main floor is the open cantilevered spiral stair case."

While the original homes have gradually evolved into various bright colors with mostly metal roofs rather than the less durable shingles, Linda's pet peeve has continued.

"I don't understand the spiders down here," she declares. "The warm weather brings a plethora of newly hatched insects that attract hungry spiders. We're happy to have them trap the insects, but I swear, if the spiders leave their mark on light surfaces, the droppings are dark, while if it's a dark surface, they're white."

Linda's concern about spiders is reflected in their sparkling clean, superbly maintained home which continues to evolve. Their latest project, a new paint job with a Mexican purple-blue color called *anil azuelea* on both their front and back doors, now protects the house from evil spirits, according to legend.

In their remodeling the Omans have made clever use of their limited space. A built-in Mexican sofa has a large oven-shaped hole scooped out of its cement base for storing firewood right in front of a heatalator that helps dry any green wood. A string of Valentine *papel picado* (elaborate Mexican cut-outs) hung from the ceiling separates the living and dining areas. A small door opens to a pantry adjacent to the kitchen that also includes brooms, vacuums and the forced air furnace. The immaculate kitchen includes a toaster oven on the counter, a microwave over the stove on a shelf, sparkling white side by side refrigerator and freezer, and a collection of tiny animals above the sink with a back up light. Mexican marigolds in the window box below the kitchen window above the sink add a splash of orange during the summer.

Upstairs, an extensive walk-in closet includes double half-length racks, shelves above drawers, and access to a small extension to the right that houses a variety of tools. In the center of the upstairs landing a ladder slides out to provide access to a third floor storage area for seldom used items such as Christmas decorations.

"It wasn't until we both retired from teaching that we needed a storage space for all our school supplies. Don't ask me why we want to keep them, though!" exclaims Gary.

Daughter Heidi's room, in addition to the built-in desk and bookshelves, has another ladder up to a double bed perpendicular to the head of her bed. All the beds include drawers underneath and the usual built-in book and storage shelves are mounted on the walls.

Their favorite remodeling project is a bay window added at the head of their bed. "We can see the stars at night, watch as the rain splots down above us and occasionally see a great blue heron or an eagle perched on our roof line," says Linda. "It doesn't get much better than that."

On their large outside deck the Omans claim to have the only orchard on a houseboat: a fig, persimmon and nashi (Japanese pear/apple) tree. "As the daughter of a Navy doctor our family spent time in Japan so I really enjoy the nashi" says Linda.

Gary adds, "The only drawback to the orchard is the rats it attracts in the fall. I don't like to kill animals, not even rats, so one year I set out a live trap baited with peanut butter. In the middle of the night I heard a snap. The next morning I went out and sure enough, there was a little rat in it. I figured if I were a rat I'd like to live in the Arboretum, so I took the trap and brought it all the way over there. Wouldn't you know that little fellow made his way back to our orchard? He had an unusual color so I recognized him when he reappeared."

Just this past summer the Omans finally completed their remodeling when they installed decent flooring in their upstairs bedroom.

"For over thirty years it was just painted plywood," says Gary. "I have a button from a friend who had gone through a similar prolonged remodeling. It says, 'House finished; man die.'"

Although they're officially retired, Gary continues to substitute as a Spanish teacher and Linda currently works part time as a librarian in a Bellevue elementary school. She also volunteers at the Woodland Park Zoo and the Seattle Art Museum "I'm as busy as I want to be," she says.

One might say that each of the Omans have had two careers, their work and their house. As Linda says, "We've surrounded ourselves with artifacts that bring back memories of our travel experiences: a Masai throwing stick from Africa, a mirror cloth from India, miniature hats from Peru and Boliva, prayer beads from Nepal, and a collection of masks from different counties. Since Gary's Master's thesis was on the Day of the Dead observances in Mexico, we also have lots of skeleton images. Mexico's version of our celebration of Halloween and All Saints Day includes laughing at death with lots of playful small skeleton figures engaged in every thing from playing in a band to getting married."

Gary and Linda may have retired from their professional careers, but they'll no doubt continue to enjoy the home that will always be their second career.

Too Handy?

"When it comes to living on the water, we've done it all!" jokes Natalie Handy.

"And then some...." adds her husband Bill.

She and Bill first lived in a slightly overgrown beach cabin on the northeast shore of Lake Washington near Juanita. In the late 1960s the $40,000 price included an adjacent lot along with the aging house.

"We seem to have this character defect," quips Natalie. "We can't live in a place until we do all sorts of remodeling, but we begin various projects only after we've moved in. I remember when we added a second story to our Lake Washington house. We all had to bathe or shower in the evening before the workmen showed up at seven in the morning. We were temporarily without a roof when work began on the second floor; so anyone above could easily see into the one bathroom below. Our evening ritual was further complicated when we didn't 't have water in the kitchen and I had to wash the dishes in the bathtub."

Once the second story was added, with much more space for growing children Ted and Lisa, the family savored their life on water. However, there was a growing problem.

In 1968 Natalie had begun working at World Cavalcade, a company that offers a series of travel films in Seattle, Bellevue, and Auburn. The commute from home to the office usually took less than thirty minutes. Bill was spending only slightly more time driving to his job with American Steel. But by the early eighties both were pushing three hours on the road.

By the time the kids headed for college the commute was consuming more and more of each day. One of their neighbors on Lake Washington decided to move to a new houseboat on Lake Union's Roanoke Reef. When daughter Lisa and her new husband flew off in a seaplane to their honeymoon following their lakeside wedding on a stunning August day, Bill and Natalie decided it was time to check out life in a Lake Union houseboat.

The Handys found the only lot still available at Roanoke Reef was located right next to the large gated concrete parking garage. Hardly the most desirable site, yet the location offered the opportunity to literally live **on** the water, and the garage would be less than twenty steps from their front door. For the first time they could design their home from scratch, actually hire someone else to build it, and wait until it was all completed before they moved in. And they could commute to their jobs in less than ten minutes.

"It was an easy decision," says Natalie. "We sold the extra lot on Lake Washington, paid $150,000 for the moorage site, and hired an architect who specializes in floating homes. Then we sold the house, packed almost everything away, and took a six month lease on a Queen Anne Hill apartment.

"We'd been told that all the necessary shoreline and construction permits for houseboats on Roaoke Reef had already been filed and assumed we could begin building right away. But there was a slight problem. That had happened ten years ago in 1978 when most of the lots had been sold and houses built. The permits were out of date, so we had to start all over again.

Bill and Natalie spent six months in the apartment learning

to live minimally: four place settings for meals, one card table, a borrowed couch, and their bed. Due to the now infamous oil spill in Valdez, Alaska, the Foss tug site where they'd planned to have their concrete float poured was no longer available.

They found a new site but its height above the water meant weight constraints on the size of the float. Consequently, the float had to be poured in three separate sections.

When contractors lowered the large basement section into the water, the heavy structure slipped in the ropes and cracked. Anticipated costs soon doubled from $40,000 to $80,000. Realizing their new home would take far more than six months to complete, the Handys bought a spacious fifty-two foot Chris Craft, which they christened Handy One, and were able to moor it right on the Roanoke Reef boat moorage dock.

"And of course we had to do some reupholstering and upgrades on the boat," adds Natalie. "However, it was worth it, as we were there over a year. I don't think the moorage owner expected us to stay so long; she very tactfully kept asking us how much longer we'd be there."

"Next," says Bill, "we worried we wouldn't be able to occupy our new house within the two year limit for avoiding taxes by reinvesting the capital gains from the sale of our Lake Washington home. We researched the housing code and learned our new house had to have a closet, a locking door, and a bed to be considered a legal dwelling. So we made certain those three items were finished and then slept in our houseboat exactly two years from the date we closed on the sale of our Lake Washington home."

"If we'd had to pay taxes on our capital gains it would have been a major sum. Thank Heaven we didn't have to" adds Natalie.

Once the Handy's settled into their spanking new home they realized the copper sink in the family room section was a bother to clean and the planned triangular hot tub on the channel side wouldn't fit. But the dumb waiter that carried groceries from the sheltered entrance on the lake level up to the kitchen (and also hoisted food and dishes up to the deck for summer time enjoyment) helped immensely. With their former neighbor from Lake Washington already on Roanoke Reef, Bill and Natalie found the same supportive community they'd experienced on Lake Washington on their Lake Union houseboat moorage.

Even though they didn't need to work around contractors while furnishing their new home, in ten years they never found the right chandelier for the living room or the additional chair they wanted there.

"It was a different experience," says Natalie, "and I've come to realize that it never really felt like our home. We hadn't had a hand in it. We didn't pound any nails, plant any shrubs, or paint any walls. Someone else did all the work. It just didn't seem to fit. And we always regretted that we'd never had the opportunity to travel in the Chris Craft when we lived on it. We decided to look for a similar boat so we could both travel and live on the lake."

They found their boat in Sausalito, CA, a sixty-six foot fiberglass Pacemaker. Even better, they also located a moorage site on the north side of Lake Union east of Gas Works Park.

Bill hired a Captain to pilot the "Handy Too" from Sausalito to Seattle, and along with two other crewmen they headed north at five pm on Memorial Day weekend. A severe storm that broke the bow sprit came up that night. One of the port windows leaked onto the toilet paper in the one working head and made it constantly wet. Severe waves knocked the refrigerator door open leaving broken beer and pop bottles along with their contents spread over the main salon. It was the night from Hell. The captain decided the crew would work three hours on and three hours off shifts traveling up the coast, leaving no possibility of a decent night's sleep.

"I swear," declares Natalie, "when they finally arrived in Seattle Bill's eyes literally looked like those of a zombie for almost the rest of the summer. It took him that long to get back to normal."

Once recovered from the trip north, the twosome started remodeling their new acquisition. The bedroom level of their split level boat was torn up until November, so they slept out on the aft deck until workers finished the room. "It had gotten really cold at night, and we were so glad to finally move in down below." says Natalie. "It's been five years now and we really feel settled in. It definitely feels like home."

After their various mishaps, the Handy's had a real break when the Handy Too was at a near-by boat yard for routine maintenance the night a major fire broke out on their dock in the spring of 2002.

"Even though we were some distance from the inferno, it was the scariest night of my life," says Natalie. "Bill manned a hose to put out any sparks that landed on our boat and to minimize the effects of the heat. The isinglass curtains on the bow deck never would have survived if we hadn't been home."

Once Dunato's finished the maintenance on their boat, the Handys were able to rent the end moorage site on their main dock. Natalie notices a lot more activity on the lake from their new location. "And we hear more noise," she continues. "We hear everything from the early morning coxswains shouting orders to rowing shell crews to the microphone commentary of the amphibious "Ride the Duck," tour boat drivers."

The couple has actually run out of projects for their current home, or at least they don't have any urgent ones.

"I just hope if we ever move again, whatever we find will be just the way we want it." says Bill.

"I'd agree with that," adds Natalie, "but could we make it feel like home without a little hammering, sawing and painting?"

Home at Last

"I grew up in one of those "little boxes, little boxes, little boxes made of ticky-tacky" described in Malvina Reynolds' song about Daly City tract housing," says Roland March.

"I felt like a gerbil running around in a cage. I didn't fit in socially, especially during high school; I rebelled against the not so subtle California pressure toward conformity. I didn't realize right away how much the house of my childhood affected me, but I've never lived in a normal house since then."

The five-level house barge Roland and his wife Nancy live in definitely would not qualify as ticky-tacky. Whimsical mailboxes reflecting the personality of the various owners cluster just outside the locked gate of their short dock in Fremont east of the Aurora Bridge. Inside the cyclone fence a proliferation of assorted unpainted bird houses, created by a neighbor who lives on a fishing trawler at the end of the dock, soften the harshness of the metal fence.

The master bedroom, a spacious walk-in closet and the bathroom dominate the lower level. Unlike most houseboats, the bathroom includes a bathtub with jets, but it's the washer and dryer located directly behind the tankless toilet that catch your eye.

"I have to remove the toilet if we need to replace or repair the washer or dryer. It's the price you have to pay for maximizing available space," explains Roland

Near the bathroom a door opens under some stair steps to access the actual barge that supports their home. Shoes are stored on the inside of the door and various other typical basement items cover much of the available space.

The next level is the office and guest bedroom, then up to the living room and kitchen. A window above the sink provides views of marine traffic at the west end of Lake Union and Roland installed a small corner window to frame Mt. Rainer when it's visible. The next level above the office and guest bedroom takes you outdoors, where stairs lead to a slightly higher second deck above the living room.

The decks need to be well maintained to prevent any moisture leaking into the structure of the barge and rotting it. "One of my annual fall chores," says Roland, "involves two or three coats of paint on the cap-rails, the top of the posts on my barge, and securing everything up here."

Before arriving in Seattle Roland lived in a log cabin on Lake Shasta. Then a draft notice arrived during a stint in Modavo, California. "I got an early out," he says. "I had an 'attitude problem.' But I played my cards right and received an honorable discharge." Next it was on to San Quentin Village, right next door to the prison.

"I sent a letter to my Dad, and when he saw the postmark he called immediately. He thought I was in San Quentin prison. He asked how I managed to get a private phone in there, and I prolonged the ruse by telling him I was a telephone maintenance person and had connections. After about a year there I moved into San Francisco where I found space in an industrial section where I ran a wood shop. I bought an eighty passenger Gillig school bus and totally remodeled it. I put in a custom floor and retrofitted it with a hot tub, a fireplace and a generator so it was totally self-contained. Then I moved into an RV storage lot on

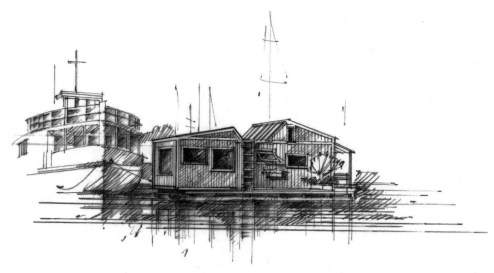

House Barge

Pier 57 in downtown San Francisco where I paid $60 a month rent for a million dollar view.

"Next I drove a Norton motorcycle through Nevada, Utah, Montana, Idaho and finally into Washington and Seattle. Heading north on the I-5 Freeway I saw an exit to Lakeview Drive and I headed toward the water. I ended up at Terry Pettus Park on the east side of Lake Union. I huddled under a tree when a deluge of rain started. 'Oh, this is great; I think I'll come live in Seattle.'"

When Roland first moved to Seattle in his school bus, he alternated between two state parks where you could camp for up to two weeks. After several months of switching back and forth he moved to a trailer park in North Bend, where he eventually bought some property and opened an electrical contracting firm.

"I'd often come back to Lake Union when I needed time to think and sort things out. I enjoyed it very much and finally realized I needed to live here rather than in the rain forest. One day I came to Seattle on my motorcycle, saw a For Sale sign on the barge, called the number on the sign and three days later I'd bought it. I'd never made such a large purchase in my life and felt so right about it. The realtor took a picture of me as I ran through the barge fully clothed and jumped into the lake to celebrate my new home."

One day Roland had a call from Nancy, an Alaska Airlines flight attendant who was remodeling a house on the south side of Seattle's Three Tree Point on Puget Sound. Nancy needed an electrical contractor and a neighbor had recommended Roland. Their courtship began when Roland asked Nancy to go sailing with him. Roland figured if she could take his yelling at her on the sail boat as in "No, no, no! That's not a rope, that's a line!' then she could handle him.

Nancy laughs as she says, "We made it through the sailing. I think ever since I was in my early twenties I wanted to move down here. People would say, 'Oh, you don't want to live on a houseboat, there're logs that have to be replaced all the time and how do you know you're going to get a good one?' When I tell them we have everything we need down here and it's not just a temporary arrangement, they can't quite believe it.

"But moving here was hard. Roland had a compost toilet that had to be cleaned every month, and if it was not properly maintained it smelled like an outhouse. And I'd just put my heart and soul in to my little house on Three Tree Point. I knew I loved Roland but I struggled all the time as to what I wanted to bring down to the barge and what I needed to leave in storage. It's still an issue for both of us. We seem to switch stuff every month or so."

The early years of their marriage were made even more difficult when both found themselves caught up in major political struggles. Nancy was involved in a work-based issue regarding the quality of air in planes and its effect on the health of the flight crew, while Roland was caught up in a struggle to save their home from eviction.

"I didn't have any problem with cleaning up the lake," says Roland, "but when the Department of Construction and Land Use ordered the elimination of all live-aboards due to the grey water they dumped into the lake, we stood to lose our homes. If we couldn't remain on the lake, where could we go?"

Carol adds, "Some of the landlords immediately rolled over to the Department of Land Use and sent out two-week eviction notices. We were lucky to have a large property owner in Fremont as our landlady; she didn't roll over easily."

"I'd been pretty apolitical most of my life," says Roland, "figuring there wasn't much you could do to change big government, so I wasn't plugged in. But because this threatened my home it brought out some good old American revolutionary tendencies I didn't realize I had."

The threatened barge owners formed an *ad hoc* committee shepherded by several folks experienced in working with bureaucracies. The barge owners all agreed to deal with the big issue of black water (untreated sewage) by putting in holding tanks and having them pumped on a regular basis. But the Department of Ecology stood in the way of such a compromise.

"So I went off on my own," says Roland. "Bureaucracies are Goliath the giant and they don't move very fast. I found the man who makes decisions at the Department of Ecology. Then I went down to Metro where they had this beautiful eleven-by-seventeen inch map of all the sites where the sewers overflow during heavy rains and dump about three billion gallons of sewage into the lake every year. The man was thrilled that I wanted one of the maps; he said they had hundreds of them and couldn't give them away.

"Then I went to the Seattle Sewer Department. I connected with one of their "Officers Friendly," as they called themselves and asked how many fines they had processed in the past five years. He told me they hadn't issued any fines as they try to work with the violators to solve the problem.

"Next I went to another Department of Ecology office and heard the same thing. So then I went to the man who makes the decisions and pointed out the unfairness of evicting the house barges when they're not going after the major polluters.

"I told him I think I'll dig a little further and see if I find more relevant information. Just remember if you evict me from my house, I'm going to have a lot of time to dig deeper."

"Is that a threat?"

"You bet it's a threat. You've threatened my house; I'm going to threaten your department because I know you're not doing your job."

Three months later the city registered thirty-two houseboat barges who'd installed holding tanks and gave them official legal status on the water. Roland went on to assemble a book from materials given to him by Seattle's Metro called Best Management Practices. It serves as a guideline for live-aboards on how to minimize the impact of their gray water on the lake.

"I realized after putting my heart, body, mind and soul into this, I appreciated democracy. I'd become aware of what one individual can do. Nancy and I also came to understand the difficulty of maintaining a relationship when you're consumed in fighting for your health and your home. We managed to weather it and the past five years have been wonderful."

Roland relates one more aspect of life afloat. "I was down in my office on an early Saturday in November of 2002. Suddenly I felt a wave hit our barge so I looked outside. Here with our connection to the water we have an instant weather check. You look at the water and you know exactly what's going on. But I didn't see any other rollers. That shocked me; it was very odd. Then another wave hit and there still weren't any other rollers. Usually when someone is speeding there's a police boat screaming through here with its siren going chasing the offending boater. I went outside where I watched as three very strong rollers threw the barge back and forth. I checked my lines to make sure they were all taunt at the same time and not just one was taking all the force.

"The hits got more and more violent and I was amazed the way the barge was tossed, but then it settled down. I know physics and mechanics and such and was frustrated I couldn't figure out what was happening. I was really perplexed, so I stood outside for about fifteen minutes groping around. All of a sudden there was another big roller, and then I realized it was an earthquake.

"We learned later that the shock waves from an earthquake in Alaska had taken about an hour and a half to get to Seattle. None of our land-locked neighbors noticed the quake, but here on the lake it was like being shaken in a cup of tea. If you take a pan of water and move it around you'll notice that if all of a sudden you give it a quick jerk, the water sloshes back and forth. So I realized the first hit was the first wave of the quake. The waves went down to the south end of Lake Union and then came back. They morphed into a really larger wave on the east and south side of the lake where they did a lot more damage than we had here. Those shock waves must have traveled about 600 miles an hour."

Whether it's rain, sleet, snow, eviction notices, or earthquakes, Roland and Nancy doubt they'll be leaving there unique barge home any time soon.

HOOKED ON BOATS

Seaton Gras enjoys one of Seattle's most interesting moorage sites. His true love, the sixty-foot yacht Merry Maiden, floats almost at the entrance to Seattle's hands-on Maritime Museum, The Center for Wooden Boats. In return for his moorage site, Seaton serves as the off-hours presence at the Center and helps set up for various events while painstakingly restoring the Merry Maiden.

This ketch rigged yacht was built in 1946 by Palmer Scott of New Bedford, Massachusetts and designed by Phillip Rhodes for Commodore Irving Pratt of the New York Yacht Club. Almost twenty-three years later Seaton's father, Ranulf, bought the yacht to fulfill his life-long dream of sailing around the world.

Ranulf had graduated from Massachusetts Institute of Technology and worked at MIT's Draper Laboratory. As the children grew he decided that his young crew was old enough to begin the adventure of a lifetime—a sailing trip around the world. In the middle of 1969, when Seaton was thirteen years old, Ranulf bought the Merry Maiden while it was moored in Florida. His father took an unprecedented three-year leave of absence, the family drove to Florida in a rental car to claim their boat and after just three days of preparations and provisioning they were sailing to Boston.

"Dad had never sailed in the ocean before this adventure.

But he had sailed extensively in Vermont's Lake Champlain and had taught sailing in various small boats on the Charles River with the MIT Sailing Club. He knew how the ropes worked."

Seaton and an older brother and sister set sail with their parents, but his oldest brother continued at MIT since joining his family would risk being viewed as a "draft dodger" during the Vietnam War.

The family left Salem, MA, on Oct. 26, 1969. "There are times when a teenage boy doesn't want to be with his family, but the trip itself was fantastic. We were more connected to family than you can ever imagine. When there are no neighbors, a family either becomes very well connected or very fragmented. My parents are both gone now, but they lived such a rich and robust life it's hard to be sorry for them. They dreamed, they fulfilled their dreams, and they did the unthinkable. They traveled and had four healthy kids."

As for the perils of the sea, Seaton recalls, "I was never really scared; hurricanes, fifty foot seas, surfing down a wave with a twenty-five ton boat, it was just part of the territory. That was the lay-of-the-land, so there was not much you could do about it. Acceptance is automatic since you don't really have any options."

After three years at sea, Seaton's father wasn't ready to go home yet. His request for a longer leave of absence from MIT was turned down, so he chose to retire early and continued his odyssey for a total of five years and eight months.

Recalling the experience, Seaton says, "When you're cruising from island to island, the time between is so long that you have time to reflect on where you left and anticipate where you're going. By the time you get there you're ready for another experience. The time between ports is sort of like cleansing your palate."

Seaton recalls the time when they were at sea for fifty-six days between Indonesia and South Africa. Provisions included water for two months and a lot of canned food. "Sometimes in preparation for a long stretch we'd tear off the labels and varnish the tin cans so we could store them in the bilge. We always marked them as to the ingredients, but when the time came to use them you'd see "LB" on a can and couldn't always remember what that meant. As for meat, it was almost uncanny how we'd catch fish every day, or maybe the meal always followed the catch. I'm not sure, but there's nothing like fresh fish at sea."

After his five plus years at sea, Seaton spent about a year on land. "I sort of had my identity pulled away; all of a sudden I was uprooted. I was expected to go to college and all that." He took correspondence courses during the world cruise and considered going to college when the family moved ashore. Then one day during the cold New England winter, after a lot of time reflecting on his prior life at sea and the wonderful tropical weather, Seaton finally decided to have a conversation with his father.

"Hey Dad, I'd like to borrow the boat.

"What do you want to do?"

"Sail around the world"

"But you've done that already."

"Yeah I know, but I want to do it my way."

"Well, I'll think about it."

So about a week later I asked him, "What do you think?"

"About what?"

"About the boat."

"Are you *still* thinking about that?" Perhaps hoping it was just a whim.

"Yeah."

"Well, let me talk it over with your mother."

And then a few days later his father asked,

"How are you going to pay for this?"

"Take on people who are willing to pay as crew."

"Well, okay, if you think it will work."

It definitely did work. Seaton spent seven years at sea heading for Seattle by way of Australia. "It's on the way, isn't it?" he asks playfully. He took on crewmembers that paid $10 to $20 a day, which included room, board and a great adventure. "People signed on for a week, a month, a year, and in one case a fellow joined me for five years. I'm still in contact with some of them. Many tell me the trip was a defining experience that added value and perspective to whatever path they chose."

On his way to Seattle, Seaton met a woman in New Zealand who joined the boat in Australia. He wanted to go west from Australia, but he couldn't find a crew wanting to go that direction. So the two of them, and the new crew of greenhorns, sailed on across the Pacific to Hawaii, and arrived in Seattle in 1981. "I figured if she could endure that much of a voyage she was my kind of gal. So we married, had a little daughter and then moved ashore. I left the Merry Maiden in Port Orchard; we moved back East and I tried my best to have a career.

"When you've sailed the oceans you become very aware of environmental issues. My dad had designed his own house with passive solar heating in the 1950s; he built one of the first privately funded solar houses in America. So the family started a business where I designed, built and sold alternative energy systems. In 1989 I started a company that pioneered building Chlorofluorocarbon (CFC) recovery machines to help save the ozone layer. I tried living ashore, creating a business and making a marriage work, but I don't think I'm well suited to it. I'd left conventional life when I was too young; it wasn't my community anymore. I was a square peg in a round hole.

"There's a different sense of life values when you live on the water, there's a certain tranquility in this cruising life-style. After all, our bodies are mostly water.

"My dad is a role model for me of living life to the fullest and not waiting for tomorrow. You've got to do some things when you're young enough to enjoy them. I took that idea to the extreme and retired at twenty.

"I think the ideal thing is to spend one's life doing something that is really important to you. I've been blessed and so very fortunate; I've seen a lot of people that say they want to sail around the world. They envy my adventurous life but they're pretty much convinced they have to retire before they can do it."

Seaton returned to the Northwest in 1997 to begin the tedious work of restoring his beloved Merry Maiden. He brought the boat into Lake Union where he lived on it while working at a boat yard. Then, an acquaintance suggested he moor at The Center for Wooden Boats, which specializes in putting people on the water in a fleet of classic small wooden boats, both rowboats and sailboats.

After more than five years, Seaton has found it's not an easy thing to restore a boat that's traveled well over one hundred thousand miles. "It's a huge job, especially while living on the boat. When you're sitting onboard and everyone else is living in a house with a dry bed you're thinking, "Why am I living on a boat in the winter with the deck torn apart and the wind blowing through and my wardrobe stuffed in the spaces in between?"

A casual trip to visit a friend who was teaching at a Montessori School on a beach in Thailand triggered a major detour from his renovation project. Seaton discovered the Royal Barges of Thailand, used by kings, queens and princes and princesses for over six hundred years along the Chao Phraya river that runs through Bangkok.

"I was so impressed by these elegant and historic barges covered with exquisite details that I bought a whole array of postcards to share with my friends at The Center for Wooden Boats. The barges were being restored to exacting detail for use during the closing ceremony of the Asia Pacific Economic Conference held in Thailand during October of 2003. The Royal Barge Procession had fifty barges with 2,080 men on board all dressed in traditional costumes and singing ancient boat songs. It was a wonderful spectacle to see and hear. At the end there were fireworks followed by hundreds of small hot air balloons powered by candles that decorated the sky.

Seaton submitted a proposal to the Ed Monk Scholarship Program of The Center for Wooden Boats to help cover the cost of more detailed research of the Royal Barges and was awarded a grant to proceed. He returned to Thailand and began his research. "It was amazing," says Seaton, "the research kept expanding and growing. I learned so much about the Thai culture itself. And the Thai community here in Seattle has embraced what I'm doing. In Thailand they're busy throwing away their ox carts, their old culture, and driving SUVs at ninety miles an hour. So they're amazed to see me engaged and interested in their history.

"I was able to bring two Thai boat builders to the CWB. They had created their own museum, the "Thai Boat Museum" in Ayutthaya, Thailand. They managed to bring twenty-five exquisite teak models of various traditional Thai boats in their suitcases. It was a heartfelt pleasure for me to see how amazed they were to discover how interested Americans are in their ancient traditions."

While in Thailand, Seaton put together a mockup of a book about the Royal Barges. Only the top third of the screen on his laptop computer was functioning. "Probably," says Seaton, "because the heat and/or ants of Phuket, a hot tropical island in southern Thailand, had done some serious damage to it." He used the local Internet cafes for printing the material; then he organized the research material with a glue stick and a sharp knife. He managed to produce a simple cut-and-paste example of his book.

He already has many people eagerly waiting for their copy.

"My book will illustrate the elaborate figureheads and graceful lines of the most prominent barges. The whole experience has taught me so many things. It's been an absolute joy."

As for restoring the Merry Maiden, Seaton says, "When I decide to focus on it, it will happen. Besides, it's the voyage that's important. You can't just arrive, you have to do it."

THE SALLY S.

White tie-back curtains in the three windows and the glossy bright green and white paint on the tugboat MV Sally S. hint at something more than a working tug. The seventy-five foot somewhat stubby vessel is clearly visible on the south side of the ship canal just east of the Ballard Bridge both from the water and the bridge.

The Mallorys found their home by accident in 1996. Their earliest experiences with boating were in Wisconsin on Lake Michigan where they both grew up. "I never was on the water at all until I meant Greg," says Betty. "We met on a blind date shortly after high school graduation, and Greg wanted to buy a sail boat. I like being on the water but I didn't like keeling over in a sail boat; I prayed for rain every weekend."

But once their children, Pam and Eric, came along, both wanted them to enjoy family outings on the water, learn the skills of sailing, and experience the discipline involved. The Mallorys eventually tired of long Wisconsin winters and headed for the more temperate climate of the Northwest. Boat-less once again for a few years, they purchased a forty-two foot sailboat after their move to Anchorage, Alaska in 1984.

When the children were grown, they sold their home, moved aboard the boat and set out for the adventure of sailing down the coast to Mexico. "Cruising in Southern California is not as much fun as cruising in the Pacific Northwest," says Greg, "so after four years, we reversed course and sailed back to Seattle.

By that time, with the addition of two rambunctious tabby cats on board, the sailboat seemed too small. "We began looking for a bigger boat that we could live on without playing musical chairs when we had visitors," says Betty.

They spotted the Sally S. at a Northlake moorage, with a "For Sale – As Is" sign forlornly propped in the window. Betty was impressed with the large galley, and both liked the beautiful lines of the boat. They bought it and hoped that they wouldn't regret the "As Is."

"When our friends came to look at the boat, they would shake their heads and say, 'Boy, you've got a lot of work to do,'" Greg says. "Little did I realize that they were indeed telling the truth."

There was much to be done to restore the Sally S. After many attempts to patch the foredeck leaks, Greg decided to just replace the entire deck. Rather than continuing to use many of the ineffective, old-fashioned ways for sealing decks and walls, Greg researched new and innovative materials to use. This resulted in a deck that is impervious to water and will last many years with very little maintenance.

Greg spent the best part of two years working on the boat. "Our son Eric, who was working at Boeing, helped a lot," adds Greg. "He found an aluminum repair tape they used at Boeing that was incredibly strong. We would use it to patch places where water was leaking in until we could make a permanent repair. In the military you'd call that damage control."

Betty adds, "One of the last places we used it lasted for four years."

Greg comments, "If I'd known what I was in for, I probably never would have done it. I've probably spent half a million in

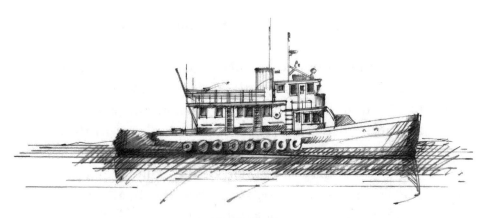

The Sally S.

terms of time and material, but restoring the Sally S. has been a labor of love. She deserves to spend her last years looking beautiful. She is part of the heritage of the Seattle area."

That love is apparent from the moment you board the Sally S., where a small step stool on the deck eases the step down for short legged folks like Betty. The bright green step stool matches the three steps up from the dock which has flower pots on either side. Starting on the varnished foredeck you see a scuttle with access down to the front hatch where a cozy bedroom with shower and head accommodated son Eric. A specialist in electric generation, Greg explains in detail how he rewired everything.

Betty shows off the living area that has been reconfigured from the original layout. "Originally all the staterooms, the galley and the heads were all accessible only from the outside deck. We made it easier by opening up the living area so we don't have to go outside." She points to a coffee table book in the living room, "Spring Tides, Memories of Alaska Tugboats," written by Ed Larson. In it there is a photo of the Sally S. taken when she worked as a tender for net pens in Southeast Alaska in the early 1930's. Along with her sister ship, the Doris E, the

Sally S. was designed by Ted Geary and built for the Skinner family, a prominent Seattle family in the early 1900's. The Sally S. was built on Bainbridge Island at the J C Johnson Shipyard in 1927 and named for one of the daughters of the family. The only structural difference between then and now is the original mast that was used for lifting the fish nets over to the barge where they were emptied has been taken off. Seamen on other tugboats often teased the captain of the Sally S. about being such a perfectionist and insisting that the boat be properly cleaned and maintained. They dubbed her "silly Sally."

"Perhaps that is why she is still around and in such great shape," observes Greg.

The cheery renovated galley is complete with a modern spotless diesel stove, microwave oven, refrigerator/freezer and lots of hickory cabinets. Pictures of lighthouses decorate the walls and lacy curtains adorn the windows. The main salon is complete with an easy chair, built in sofa, bookshelves and TV/stereo. A walk-in closet with a wardrobe, built in shelves and shoe racks provide plenty of storage. The master stateroom is small but cozy with a mahogany captain's bed with storage and drawers below. The master bathroom has a full size shower, tile floor and a full size head.

Greg delights in showing off the bright and shiny engine room below the stern deck. He points out the Caterpillar main engine, two generators, a water maker, and numerous other pieces of equipment. Like the Captain of the Sally S. when it worked in Alaska, Greg maintains an exceptionally ship-shape shop and work area, with all his tools neatly organized and easily accessible.

The stern deck boasts an area big enough to have a large market umbrella, table and deck chairs for entertaining or just enjoying the never ending changing scenery of life on Lake Union.

Now that their labor of love is coming to a satisfying end they can begin to enjoy all their hard work. "We can take our home with us whenever we want to take a cruise. All we have to do is untie the mooring lines. Once we are away from the dock, our expenses go down. We store up to three years of diesel fuel on board so it costs us very little to go on vacation.

Greg and Betty have brought new life to the Sally S., and she in turn has enriched theirs.

FLUKE'S FOLLY

It was perfect timing. Only a few days before the July Fourth fireworks on Lake Union, two tugs towed an enormous three-story boat house onto the north shore of the lake where it moored in an industrial location.

Land based neighbors at Dunn Lumber and the new Palisades Condominiums suddenly saw a massive gray wall instead of their view of the lake and downtown skyscrapers. Lake dwellers questioned the legality of such a high structure. Boaters and neighbors wondered where the latest shoreline addition had come from and who owned it.

Houseboater Tom Stockley, ever sensitive to encroachments on the size limits that maintain Lake Union's open views, discreetly passed the word on to his work associates at the Seattle Times. A little sleuthing revealed the owner was well-known civic figure, John Fluke, Jr., one time president of the Chamber of Commerce, faithful participant in major charity balls and fund-raisers, and heir to the company founded by his father which specializes in measuring instruments.

Clearly Lake Union had done a 180 degree turn from its past as both a literal and figurative cesspool, where only those with no other choice lived.

When queried about the legitimacy of the 120-foot structure, the Flukes explained that the structure, built to house his eighty-four-foot yacht, the Excalibur, was an entirely legal boat repair facility.

But where were the permits? What about the three-bedroom, three and a half bath living quarters? How come they could live at the end of the lake when houseboats couldn't? And what about the height limit on the lake? Concerned neighbors alerted the Department of Construction and Land Use.

When an investigator promptly queried the Flukes, they replied that it was a vessel and consequently not subject to the Shoreline Land Use Requirements.

The inspector challenged Fluke to demonstrate the boathouse was indeed a vessel by taking it through either the ship canal or the locks under its own power and navigation. Surprise! that never happened, so the boathouse was cited for five violations of both land use and shoreline codes and required to move by July 18 to avoid a $75 per day fine.

A mere $75 hardly broke the bank of the multi-millionaire, but Fluke's attorney asked for a hearing. She maintained that the structure, as a covered boat-repair facility, is allowed on Lake Union. As for the living quarters, the attorney explained those were for the crew of any boat being repaired.

In the meantime, Don Dally, whose company had built the Pacific Palisades condominium just north of the boat-repair structure, was dealing with a lot of flak from his now view-less condominium owners who priced the view in their $600,000 investment. He personally queried Lynne Fluke, who had married the Seattle civic leader after his 1993 divorce, wondering how they could live in the boat house when houseboats were not allowed. She answered that it was not a home, but a business. Dally reminded Lynne of the glowing article he'd recently read about their new home in one of the first issues of "Seattle Homes and Lifestyles" magazine. Color photos featured the professionally decorated three-bedroom multilevel home with three and a half bathrooms, living room, workout facility, and hot tub on the spacious deck.

At that point Lynne acknowledged that they were indeed living there, but only temporarily until their boat, the Excalibur, was repaired.

By the time of the requested hearing on September 12, Fluke had already incurred $1,800 in fines imposed by the Department of Land Use. The City duly submitted clarification of their previous decision in writing although the Flukes were absent from the hearing. They also requested an interpretation of the applicable land use code from the city.

It was early October by the time the city completed its interpretation of the land use code; which with minor exceptions, was exactly what had been stated previously. On hearing the decision their attorney stated, "we have not yet decided what the next steps will be. My clients simply want to provide a place where boat owner, skipper, and crew can have lodging while their vessel is under repair."

Finally one bright November morning white collar neighbors in the condo and the blue collar workers on the waterfront woke up to find their view had returned. The elegantly decorated "boat repair shed" was located tucked away just east of the Ballard bridge on a dock where it blended in easily with similar hulking big vessels; no longer a blunt reminder of the extent to which Lake Union has become respectable, even for a multi-millionaire.

WHOSE LAKE IS THIS?

It's not differences in race, social status, religion, sexual orientation, politics, external home maintenance, or income level that triggers divisiveness among Lake Union's water dwellers. No, it's the no longer migratory Canada geese that strain typically cordial neighborly relationships.

On the one hand, rumors circulate periodically about a mildly subversive splinter group actively lobbying the City Council for legislation entitling each home owner to one annual Lake Union goose for their Christmas dinner.

On the other, many on the lake make a point of providing and protecting nesting places for the geese in everything from a hanging basket or flowerless whiskey barrel to a specifically built smaller version of a dog house floating on the lake adjacent to their deck. Offering a nesting area may well be tinged with enlightened self-interest; once the monogamous couples have a home, their noisy territorial battles cease. As one homeowner explains, "Before the geese were nesting, every morning we were out cleaning off the droppings. But once they're guarding those eggs, there's no mess at all; they don't even eat the flowers anymore."

The geese can devour your freshly planted petunias in less than five minutes, typically around dawn before you're even up and about. Water-based flower lovers soon learn to choose non-appetizing flowers for their containers, such as geraniums, begonias, marigolds, and dusty miller or to utilize a variety of defensive strategies. Covering a planter with some kind of securely anchored wire mesh is voted most effective. Thin, tall stakes placed strategically along the outer rim of a container also work. Graceful small dead branches of cork-screw willow trees are more aesthetic, but seem to be less effective. Avid recyclers will use anything from old shingles to the thin metal mesh seats or backs of discarded outdoor chairs to line the edges of a container. Other ploys, such as sprinkling chili powder along side the bedding plants, are considered virtually worthless.

One summer the geese became front page news when a houseboater whose two grandchildren had been frightened by low flying geese decided to take a hand in reducing the goose population. Frank Kloss spied a nesting goose across the channel and walked around to knock on the home owners' door. When it was obvious no one was home, he proceeded to smash the three goose eggs with a wooden two by four. Another neighbor who witnessed the carnage reported the illegal attack and the egg-smasher found himself in Federal Court for breaking the law. A sympathetic judge, who shared the defendant's contempt for geese, dismissed the fine after warning Kloss not to mess with goose eggs again. The story ran on the front page of the local Seattle Times where it generated several letters to the editor, including the following:

"I am writing in response to the article on Canada geese in the May 20 issue. I am a resident of the Portage Bay houseboat community. I, too, like Frank Kloss, have been awakened at dawn, lost flowers, and constantly clean droppings off my deck.

"Geese are not our only "annoyance." There's mildew, low water pressure and frozen pipes (my personal favorite), and let's not forget price. These are the consequences of living so close to

the water's edge and near a wildlife sanctuary. The adjustments that all of us here make in our lifestyles are minute compared to the benefits of living at this edge of land and water.

"Perhaps Mr. Kloss should move to a more landlocked community. Better yet, he should look out his dock and see Portage Bay in its many beautiful faces, at dusk, in a storm, or shrouded in fog and remember why he moved there in the first place.

"By the way, Fish and Wildlife tells me you can rack up to a $2,000 fine for molesting these birds. You got off easy."

Michelle Laccadito

Seattle

There's a sequel to this episode. Kit Willis, on whose deck the goose was nesting, filed a trespassing charge against Kloss. A different judge ordered him to pay a $150 fine, perform 50 hours of community service and refrain from killing birds or face a one-year sentence for breaking criminal-trespass laws.

In spite of the honking, the messy decks, and the clear-cut bedding plants, the geese always seem to have the last word. Around mid-April, adorable high-pitched chirping balls of yellow fluff begin to appear, cruising by in the water with the proud parents jealously protecting them from marauding raccoons, cats, and hawks. Soon the adult geese molt their feathers and are temporarily grounded. Domesticity prevails, and typically all is forgiven, at least until the next year's mating season begins.

ART LOVER IN RESIDENCE

If you cruise, sail, paddle, row, sail-board or swim by house-boat docks on the east side of Lake Union, it's hard to miss the visual feast on the front deck of Charlotte Macmillan and Ray Woodling's end houseboat.

Eight assorted sculptures almost crowd out the plants at the front of their spacious two-story home on the large 35 by 60 foot float.

If you approach their home by way of the dock, a playful tile plaque from Mexico to the right of their front door reads, "Mi casa is **mi** casa," with the Spanish for the second "mi" a definitive red; hardly the usual "My house is your house." Charlotte first went to Mexico in 1965 when she flew down to Puerto Vallarta with her pilot brother. She continues to winter in the southern sunshine, even though one year Charlotte returned from an evening dinner on the beach to find a burglar in her apartment. She attempted to chase the man away, undaunted by her rather formal dress high heel shoes. In the tussle Charlotte ended up falling from her balcony onto the cobble stone walk way twenty feet below.

"I fractured my skull and broke several ribs," admits Charlotte, "and this was in 1971 when there were no hospitals in Puerto Vallarta."

Back in Seattle Ray refers to the art on their front deck as "eclectic, expensive clutter." The clutter includes three metal sculptures by the now well-known artist Dan Kleinnert: a horse and rider, a sea horse, and a pig. Kleinnert, who lives in the shadow of Mt. Rainier near Eatonville, is noted for creating his sculptures from recycled scrap metal.

But it's the twenty foot high totem pole, reaching above the roof of their two-story home, which dominates the outdoor museum.

"I love Northwest Indian art," Charlotte explains, "and I didn't feel I'd have a complete collection without a totem pole"

She and Ray traveled up the Northwest coast seeking the perfect totem pole. They ventured as far north as Alaska, but after numerous references to Bill Henderson, a Kwakiutl carver, they headed for his home at the north end of Vancouver Island near the Campbell River. Once they saw his work, they knew their search was over and ordered one of his totem poles.

The art in their spacious living room with a view of the lake borders on overwhelming. Paintings, sculptures, masks, dream-catchers and hand-woven rugs fill the floor, tables, walls and....ceiling, where five paintings come close to filling it. The largest painting, roughly six by nine feet of dark lush jungle-like colors, reminds one of a darker version of Gauguin's Tahitian works.

The two smaller paintings are attached to the ceiling with L clips. As to how they mounted the much heavier large paintings, Charlotte explains they installed a wooden frame on the ceiling just the size of the interior measurements of the frame on the painting. Then they simply screwed the large paintings to the interior frame already secured on the ceiling.

Ray remembers well how they happened to buy the largest painting. "We were in Amsterdam," he says, "and while Charlotte lolled in bed watching the latest TV news on our invasion of Kuwait, I headed over to the Heineken Brewery Museum just opposite our hotel for a beer. I knew Char wanted paintings for her ceiling that would simulate stained glass windows and I saw one I thought she'd like. Once I finished my beer I returned to our hotel to bring Char over to see it.

"We found out the artist, Bas Koenes, lives in Dardrick," continues Ray. "so we decided to take the train to meet him and see his studio. We found he was an old style very meticulous Dutch art teacher who specialized in paintings of vegetation, simply naming them 'Vegetation #1, Vegetation #2, Vegetation #3' and so on. Char found a painting she especially liked that was about eighty per cent finished. We struck a deal, paid the price, and ordered the painting shipped to us."

The art lover's favorite chair faces inward rather than out toward the lake. "I like to sit here where I can see all my art. In a way it's my history, at least a history of my travels. I've always loved art; as a child I was fascinated with masks."

It shows. Charlotte has forty-two masks scattered throughout her home. Masks from Africa, Sri Lanka, Bali, Mexico, New Zealand, China, New Guinea, and Canada, to name a few. Her favorite, a Northwest Indian transformation mask, hangs just to the left of their wood burning fireplace. Made by the same artist who created their outdoor totem pole, the outer carved face of a woman opens vertically right down the middle to reveal the face of a man. The Kwakiutl tribe transformation mask resembles traditional religious triptychs, including a decorated interior of each half of the woman's face that appears when it's opened.

On the fireplace wall, a large rectangular painting titled "The Murder of Crows" by Alfredo Araguin depicts ten very dark gray crows randomly perched on barren brown tree branches against a stunning bright impressionistic winter sun-set sky in exquisite varied hues of blue, pink and white. On the adjacent wall a contrasting modern painting titled "Sunset" by Albert Fischer seems tame in comparison. Fischer is one of three now prominent Northwest artists Charlotte patronized in the 50s; the two others are Guy Anderson and Leo Kenny.

Charlotte not only enjoys helping struggling young artists whose potential she recognizes, she also became involved when Russian ships celebrating the 500th anniversary of the discovery of Alaska ended up stranded in Seattle. While millions celebrated the demolition of the Berlin Wall and the collapse of Russian Communism, the crew on board the Russian vessels was left with worthless rubles and the clothes on their backs. Their plight made the local newspapers and Charlotte brought some food down for the sailors on one of the boats. When she realized how cold they were without any heat, she bought a generator and gave it to the crewmen so they could have some warmth.

Charlotte discovered life afloat when she rented the Portage Bay houseboat of a good friend while he spent a year at MIT completing his PH.D. "I immediately took my five year old daughter to the YWCA for swimming lessons," she says, "and after that year on Portage Bay, I realized I could never live anywhere else but on the water. I found another rental on the east side of Lake Union and then a year later in 1963 I was able to buy this houseboat. Now all but two of the houses on the dock have been remodeled, including mine. But most people try to preserve something of the character of the old houseboat. We only added a partial upstairs with a small peaked roof set back from the water.

"I love the sound of the water, the gentle gurgle, the plink or plop of raindrops on the roof. I feel a connectedness as the house moves in response to current weather conditions. I love to swim; I was even swimming in the lake long before they put in the sewer."

When asked, Charlotte and Ray cite one minor negative of life on the lake. "The parking has become much more of an issue as neighborhood density increases. We now pay $100 a month to park in a lot across the street. The commercial owners allow houseboat folks to use it after office hours when it's virtually vacant."

Charlotte adds, "We respect neighbor's privacy yet we also look out for each other down here. One of our elderly neighbors can't afford the rising taxes, homeowner's dues and maintenance anymore, so we agreed as a cooperative to carry those costs for him. When he dies his house and moorage site will return to the Co-op."

If you see how much of her art Charlotte shares with the world from the front deck of her house, you know she is happy to be part of such a generous community.

SHOOGUY

Although Phil Webber's license plate reads "SHOOGUY," he doesn't sell shoes; he buys them. Tennis shoes, that is. As Phil explains, "It started out with a pair of regular old tennies, so dirty they wouldn't come clean. So I went and bought some florescent orange spray paint. Most spray paint won't work on fabric, but this one did. On weekends I'd wear these comfortable bright orange shoes around the dock or as I walked along the railroad tracks on our side of the lake. I loved walking along those old tracks. I never saw many trains on them, but my tennies worked well on the old wooden ties. People began calling me the 'shoe guy;' it's become sort of my trademark."

Phil's collection of over sixty pairs of shoes no longer includes the fluorescent orange ones, but the assortment has definitely become more upscale. Phil connected with a cobbler back on the East Coast who makes most of his locally famous shoes. The talented cobbler colors and decorates the leather while it's still flat before stitching it into a shoe. Among his creations are three pairs with a sketch of his two beagles, "Bagel and Milo, my children," engraved in full color, one on each instep. Phil also has a pair he reserves for his assignments as official wedding photographer; the cobbler sketched a ring on one shoe and bells on the other. "When the bride and groom see my shoes, it always loosens them up; they make a great ice-breaker."

Phil almost gave away one pair. The shoes were the same tropical blue as his '65 Mustang with the horse logo on the side. When he sold the car he offered the matching shoes to the new owner, but they didn't fit. Once Phil named his sailboat the "Shoo-Inn" it was only natural that he order a pair of tennies to match his boat, complete with boat soles. Some shoes are identical, but most, like the wedding shoes, are different. His most expensive pair, patterned after the saddle shoes of the Fifties, is blue and orange with each shoe a reverse mirror image of the other. The price included $200 for the wooden last and an additional $600 for the shoes. As for the blue and orange colors, Phil says, "That's the color of the Fremont Bridge and I grew up in Fremont. I like blue and orange.

"I keep threatening to have a pair made with my former wife on the sole, but so far I've never done that. I have to be sensitive where I say that, women don't usually see the humor in it. I figure I don't drink, I don't chase women, but I'm on my feet most of the time as a photographer, so I need comfortable shoes."

Phil's career as a photographer began when he was a mere twelve years old. "I'm dyslexic," he explains, "so I've never been able to read very well. I joined a camera club at the church I belonged to and after about a year everyone lost interest but me. The man that had organized the club encouraged me to continue photography and invited me to come use his dark room any time I wanted. That felt really good, and I didn't have to do anything but buy the paper for printing my photos.

"Then I came up with the idea of hopping on my bicycle any time I heard a siren and chasing it. In those days fires, fender benders or any kind of accidents were big news, so I started selling photos to both the Seattle Times and the Post-Intelligencer. At $5.00 a photo, I was pulling in about $25 a week; that was a lot of money for a ninth grader."

Phil realized his dyslexia meant he'd never receive a high school diploma, only a certificate, so during his junior year he enrolled at the local Edison Vocational School (now the site of Seattle Central Community College) in the evenings. That same year he was hired full time by the Post Intelligencer. Phil somehow managed to juggle attending two schools and a full-time job. An instructor at Edison realized his skill level already exceeded the courses offered there, and Phil was able to graduate from both Edison and Lincoln high school the following June of 1956.

Phil became Chief Photographer at the Post-Intelligencer in 1980, where he has the distinction of having worked there for forty-seven years, longer than any of the current employees. "I've developed emphysema over the past twenty years," says the lean and healthy looking Phil, "but the paper has been very good about recognizing my limitations and not sending me on assignments that involve much physical effort."

As for his houseboat, Phil matter-of-factly declares he bought his Westlake house shortly after he completed treatment for having been a practicing alcoholic for over twenty years.

"I realized I was killing myself with alcohol, so I drank every last ounce of liquor in the house and then asked a friend to drive me to a treatment center. I'm proud to say I've never touched a drop since then. My annual AA birthday is more important to me than my biological birthday.

"At the time I was also between marriages, so when I was released from treatment I was free to make decisions for myself, I didn't have to negotiate or discuss my actions with anybody. I decided to sell my house on Queen Anne hill and buy a really dilapidated old houseboat.

"I've always loved the water," explains Phil, "and I'd had a sail boat moored down at the old St. Vincent de Paul dock at the south end of the lake. I know it's not good to go sailing when you're drinking, but I'd take the boat out on the lake and think to myself how nice it would be to live on the water and have my sailboat right in front of my house. If I wanted to go someplace on it I wouldn't have to load up my car, drive to my boat, and then unload everything from my car onto the boat, because my boat would be right there.

"When my mother saw the houseboat I'd bought she thought I was absolutely crazy. I'd paid $75,000 for a home on a leased moorage in the mid '70s. But I was on the west side near Fremont with views of both the Aurora and Fremont bridges, Wallingford, the University and Gas Works Park. Once I gave the house a fresh coat of paint, that made an enormous difference."

Not exactly known for his reticence, Phil soon became active in the dock community and was asked to run for election to the Floating Homes Association Board. He was elected and continued as a Board member for twenty-five years. Phil not only enjoyed getting to know his fellow Board members, he also heard horror stories of his houseboat neighbors being evicted from their moorage. When he first began on the FHA Board, house boaters were not protected by the current Equity Ordinance from arbitrary evictions. He also knew most banks would not loan money on any houseboat that didn't also own its moorage site, for the simple reason that if a houseboat were evicted, it was virtually impossible to find another moorage site and the house was worth little more than its salvage value.

Phil realized the wisdom of working with his six dock neighbors to become an owned moorage and convinced them to give it a try.

Even though everyone knew the seldom visible owner of the dock wasn't interested in selling, Phil began working with another Phil, Phil Miller, an attorney experienced in the various issues involved in houseboat real estate transactions.

"I never worked so hard on a project in my life," declares Phil. "I can't write, but Phil Miller was really helpful. We worked well together and he didn't charge us for every little thing. We were finally able to convince the owner of the financial advantages of selling due to the increased value of Lake Union moorage sites. Except for the end moorage site, which was obviously the most valuable, we each paid $47,000 for our water. We named our new co-op Nesika Chuck, the Chinook trading jargon for Tranquil Water. At the time we thought $47,000 was a lot of money; our previous monthly moorage fee had only been around $150, but owning our sites brought us security. Now our moorages alone are probably worth $250,000 on average."

Several years later, Phil married his fourth wife, Brenda, and they decided to remodel within the lines of the existing frame.

"We didn't want to change the look of the houseboat, but we totally updated the inside with a new kitchen, new cabinets, new bathroom fixtures and so on. But that marriage fell apart, and I got involved with another woman who really loved houseboats. She wanted to live with me, but we both felt the two of us would need a bigger house. So she agreed to sell her house and put the money into a second story."

The former shack-on-a-raft evolved into a spacious two-story lavender colored home with an upstairs master suite. It included a bedroom, a hot tub, a big walk-in shower, separate space for the toilet, a bathroom window where you could see out but no one could see in, and even a separate little closet for Phil's assorted tennis shoes. The striking remodeled house was selected for the next bi-annual houseboat tour sponsored by the Floating Homes Association.

Unfortunately Phil's significant other blew all the money from the sale of her house on her children.

"That was supposed to go into the house;" says Phil. "I wasn't going to put another dime into the house. We weren't married, and I ended up having to spend $75,000 of my own money on the remodel. I also discovered that in addition to being a smoker she was a practicing alcoholic. I moved out and she lived there for about a year and a half. Neither of us could afford to buy the other out, so we finally ended up selling it for $400,000.

"My life's dream went down to the bottom of Lake Union just like that. I would have had a hard time making the payments, especially since we'd rolled in the costs of the initial remodel. I threw away that $30,000 remodel job to remodel it again four years later. Love is strange. I feel no need to apologize for my five marriages; I look on each as a learning experience.

"I felt really bad about leaving it," admits Phil, "but I love having a bigger house with room for my two children, Bagel and Milo, and lots of space for even more shoes."

Clowning Around

Bob Newman lives on what people typically envision when they hear the word "houseboat." He and his second wife, Beverly, bought the forty-foot twin engine Cruise-a-Home in 1976 strictly as an aquatic recreational vehicle. They were living on Seattle's East Side and active in the Yarrow Bay Yacht Club. Each summer they'd spend a month or so on board the "Zaba Zaba" cruising with ten to fifteen other boaters in Canadian waters. Bob recalls watching a group of whales cavorting in Phillips Arm, a bay at the northeast end of Vancouver Island.

Beverly worked as an accountant for Safeco and traveled throughout the country auditing various Safeco subsidiaries. "She was known as "Nails Newman," brags Bob. "She excelled at finding accounting errors and saved Safeco a lot of money. Beverly was also a very good housekeeper, so when we divorced she kept the house, pun intended, and I ended up with the Zaba Zaba."

Bob found a moorage for his "house" just west of Seattle Pacific University along the ship Canal connecting Lake Union to Salmon Bay and the locks. He describes the Zaba Zaba as a fishing boat with a box on top of it. The stocky gray-haired Bob boards his home at the stern end where bold black letters spelling "Zaba Zaba" on the bottom side of his attached dingy substitute for house numbers. The boat itself measures 13 by 31 feet, but the living space occupies about half that amount. Consequently, his dirty clothes, awaiting a trip to the Laundromat, greet you on the stern deck before you enter the front door. Inside, a standard double bed with dresser drawers underneath fills the left side opposite a deep narrow closet with a pull-out clothes rod that holds two and a half feet of jackets, shirts, pants and such. A typical nautical bathroom, where he stores the vacuum cleaner, lies opposite the bed just beyond the closet. Beyond the bed and bath are the kitchen, sitting room, and bridge. A comfortably worn dark brown upholstered chair that faces the stern blocks access to the Captain's wheel. The chair is opposite a small sofa along the forward side of the bed-room wall. Beside the brown chair Bob's raised wood-burning fireplace includes a glass window so he can see the flames. With some help from an electric wall heater, the fireplace heats the entire boat. The miniscule kitchen stretches along the starboard wall, equipped with a small refrigerator, a four burner stove, a microwave oven stashed on top of a regular oven and an extensive set of the high tech Calphalon cookware.

The many pots, pans, lids, and skillets are either piled on the stove and counter or hanging from hooks on an improvised metal strip screwed into the ceiling. The kitchen space is duly acknowledged by a narrow strip of linoleum tile running along the length of it. Assorted cleaning agents are "stored" at the bow end of the ten inch strip. Four wine glasses and four champagne splits hang upside down from racks on the ceiling awaiting any festive occasions. A TV and CD player, along with almost 300 CDs in three separate racks, are neatly stored opposite the kitchen. "All jazz," he comments, "I don't do anything but jazz."

There's barely room for a token of Bob's land-side passion, a narrow two foot long vertical plaque which holds four nose emblems from the four Corvettes he has owned, beginning with '53, '90, '96, and 2000. Bob has reserved space for the emblem on his current Corvette, an intense Millennium yellow car with an equally intense deep black convertible top.

Bob admits, "I bought my first Corvette when the salesman told me, 'This is the same kind of car that John Wayne drives.'"

His current Corvette has an engine so clean you could eat on it. Bob has installed Millennium yellow covers on both sides of the 350 horse power engine, vast amounts of chrome, and a mirror on the passenger side of the lifted hood to signify the year 2000. The car's interior is basic black, and the large, thick steering wheel sports a glaring yellow cover on both the top and bottom. Bob protects his treasure with a matching Millennium yellow version of The Club anti-theft device, custom coordinated by Bob himself. The license plate, FABULS, matches a tattoo on his left arm declaring, "Fabulous Bob Newman" enclosed in a long rectangle outlined in dark blue.

Bob explains the moniker, "When I was at Garfield we had to take turns introducing the assembly speakers. The usual format was something like, 'I'm John Q student and I'm here to introduce John Q Public, our guest speaker.' When it was my turn all of a sudden I found myself saying, 'I'm fabulous Bob Newman and I'm here to introduce....'"

Bob's attraction to the water dates to his childhood days growing up on the west side of Mercer Island, where his father purchased 250 feet of water front across from the Stan Sayers' hydroplane pits just north of Seward Park for around $10,000. At that time the island lacked not only a bridge to Seattle but also a high school.

"My father" says Bob, originally came to Seattle to teach English at the University of Washington, but he ended up becoming a lawyer. Lawyers were always the last to get paid, especially during the Depression, so we were a do-it-yourself family whenever possible. My two brothers and I grew up digging ditches, laying pipe, pulling Scotch Broom from the yard, (I've hated it ever since) and pushing a make-shift wheelbarrow/fertilizer spreader through the garden. We used free cow manure from the two nearby dairies, Luca's and Person's.

"My mother, born in 1896 to share-croppers near Greensboro, North Carolina, was one of ten children. She had extraordinary parents. They believed so strongly in education that all ten of the kids became professionals: four nurses, (my mom being one) three doctors, two accountants and one clergyman. She knew how to grow almost anything; her chrysanthemums were the size of basketballs. One time a rather socially prominent lady in the Chrysanthemum Society asked her how she did it. When my mom told her she used cow manure, the lady replied, "Thank you so much, Ruth, for telling us about man-your-ray!" Not to be outdone by his wife, Bob's father at one time had the largest private collection of orchids in the United States.

The floating bridge connecting Mercer Island to Seattle had been completed when Bob finished grade school. He went to Seattle's Garfield High School where his father, who worked in Seattle, dropped him off every morning.

"When I encountered all these city kids, who didn't have to shovel out the horse stall, fertilize the plants or any other chores except to simply go home and eat dinner, I decided the city was definitely the place for me. After school, I'd hitch hike south down 23rd Avenue, then climb down underneath the overpass to what is now I-90, then hitch a ride east to West Mercer Way. I'd walk toward home and usually someone driving by would give me a lift. Lots of us hitch hiked in those days."

After graduation, Bob spent a year as a Marine Corps drill

instructor, two years during the Korean conflict in the Pacific with the Third Division, Force-RECON Company, and a final year at the Marine Barracks in the Bremerton Shipyards doing Guard Duty.

When he completed his military duty, Bob enrolled at the University of Washington. He was so struck by all the cameras and action taking place in the new Communications building he immediately switched his major from Architecture to Communications. Once he graduated Bob started working at Channel 7 as a weekend film editor and floor Director. "I loved messing around in the studio. Channel 7 had a pre-Sesame Street show for kids featuring Chris Wedes as the irrepressible clown, J.P. Patches. Various characters were never on camera, such as Gertrude, the City Dump telephone operator. One day when we were on camera, J. P. called to order a ham sandwich, some fries, and a Coke. I couldn't resist the temptation to reply 'Okay, I'll send it right down.' by way of the overhead microphone."

Not long after Bob's impromptu comment, the Director's wife, who was a seamstress, made a Raggedy Anne dress and a mop as a costume for Bob so he could go on camera as Gertrude. Before long the prominent Animal Man position became available. Bob pointed out they couldn't have a show for kids without an Animal Man, so he also began playing Animal Man.

"I made a hefty $7.50 per show for playing the parts of Gertrude, Animal Man and a few others," comments Bob. "It was certainly different in those days; we'd meet at the studio about half an hour before the show, rough out what we planned to do, and then jump in."

Although the days of J. P. Patches are long gone, Bob can't stay away from the action of a TV Studio.

"I still do the make-up for Channel Nine's Serious Money show and the ever present pledge drive (or as he describes them, 'Beg-a-thons.') I also do the make-up for all the hosts and hostesses that are on screen during any pledge drive. I look at it this way; who would ever give money to an ugly person."

The fabulous Bob Newman has also starred in a recent TV commercial for mobility equipment, a clear acknowledgement that his own youth is long gone. Most who remember television's distant past would agree the J P Patches show, in which Bob was a key player, was indeed a "fabulous" one for its time.

A Benevolent Bachelor

Shortly after James Whiting moved into his first houseboat, an unusually high daytime temperature lingered into the night, so he decided to sleep out on his deck. James found the episode so delightful, he's continued to sleep *al fresco* ever since. "With today's high tech outdoor equipment I've slept out when the temperature has been near zero. It's incredible what I've experienced...raccoons romping on my deck, tug boats trailing log booms through the late night mist, kayakers and canoeists paddling by, and even an occasional beaver swimming past within a few feet of me."

James bought his first houseboat in 1954, on Portage Bay at Burley Moorage, located right between the Queen City Yacht Club and the Seattle Yacht Club. His moorage fell victim to the new freeway connection from I-5 to the Evergreen Point floating bridge across Lake Washington. In February 1961, under eminent domain law, the city ordered all houseboat owners on his dock and another smaller moorage to the south to remove their homes within six weeks. Only a few of these fifty-some houseboats found other moorage; the rest were sold or junked.

"It was not a particularly good year," sighs James. "I had to pay personal property taxes for the entire year on the first of January, yet I lost my boat before the year was even half over. The city did not provide any compensation for the evicted houses, since they were personal property rather than real estate. What's more, because it was not an Act of God, I wasn't able to deduct any casualty loss from my income tax."

Witnessing the evictions and facing an uncertain future, many floating home owners fled in panic. Among the many houseboats for sale in Portage Bay were four end-moorage units going for around $5,000; many boats on interior locations sold for even less. James bought his prime end houseboat for $3,000, less than he had paid seven years earlier for his first floating home.

When moving day came for James, he had help from George Johnston, the houseboat flotation expert, who showed up with a raft and a small outboard motor boat he used for working on houseboats. By mid-day they'd moved everything but the refrigerator. They loaded the refrigerator onto George's raft toward the front, and then hauled his boat onto the back of the raft with only the propeller of the outboard motor in the water—just enough to propel the raft over to James' new home. George's raft was so loaded down, it was almost all underwater, and local lore still recounts the tale of a refrigerator gliding effortlessly across the lake with a boat about three feet behind it.

At his new location James became acquainted with Cliff Perry, a retiree who had worked for the University of Washington Alumni Association. Perry lived in a house that was partially land-bound with the front section on pilings. Toward the end of each month he would frequently need to "borrow" ten to fifteen dollars from James.

In those days the current site of the University of Washington parking lot bordering Union Bay served as a garbage dump. One day Perry returned from a trip to the near-by dump and excitedly showed James a recovered treasure. A bright sparkle in the midst of all the trash had caught Perry's

Bachelor Quarters

eye. He investigated and discovered the sparkling object was a 1875 twenty dollar gold piece.

"I'm going to leave it to you," Perry told James. And he did. James says, "I'll never know whether he actually found it at the dump, or whether he already had it and wanted to give me something for the month-end money I had loaned him over the years."

James also fondly recalls dinner parties at one of the nearby houseboats on his dock. The owner, Richard Morrill, was a geography student whose wife Margi put on a weekly dinner for $1.50 to help make ends meet. A glass of wine was fifty cents extra. "It was always excellent food, with usually six to eight people attending. Good food, enjoyable conversation, and a real treat for a bachelor like me. I probably could have walked there in half the time, but it was more fun to paddle over for dinner in my canoe."

The energetic James has enjoyed Scandinavian dancing, canoeing, and frequent dips in the lake, although unlike sleeping, he limits swimming to the warmer months. As a swimmer he's kept a daily record of the lake temperature for years. He recently began recording the winter temperatures, which have dipped down to forty-two degrees, colder than Puget Sound.

In 1993 Donald Wysocki, a University of Washington graduate student, interviewed James several times for his thesis "The Gentrification of Bohemia," a study of Seattle's geographically unique houseboats. Donald worked under the same Richard Morrill, now a Professor of Geography, where James had long ago enjoyed dinners.

James reports, "In the course of one of our interviews, Donald became very interested in my Keuffel and Esser slide rule, which I had used at Boeing for many years before the advent of the small calculators. I mentioned Donald's interest to my friend, Paul Priebe, who had been one of Boeings's representatives on the B-17 in England during the Second World War. Paul gave me his Keffel and Esser slide rule to give to Donald. I also included a copy of my slide rule manual."

After retiring from Boeing in 1984, James has had periodic spurts of remodeling his home interspersed with a major writing project. James helps familiarize college students with the uses and functions of a scientific calculator through a Boeing program for retirees. During a chance encounter with the program's organizer, he reported that James frequently sends checks to cover the costs of textbooks for his financially struggling students.

The final word on James is that neither James nor Whiting are his real names; this intriguing bachelor prefers to remain anonymous.

TUI TUI

The all important Post Office of the Sovereign nation of Tui Tui posts a detailed rate schedule just to the left of the Grande Tui General Post Office mail box. The schedule lists prices in peace (one thousand peace equal one Nupee) and Nupees, coinage of the Realm, to various locations in the Archipelago of Tui Tui as well as the surrounding territories of Seattle, the United States, and various other countries on planet earth.

"I majored in history," says Robby Rudine, "but I'd make a terrible scholar; I like to give history mythic proportions." Robby's penchant for playfulness shows in his description of his "country."

"Here we have the Usluckgolly of Garn with Garney's house, including its two cities, Upper Garnet City and La Wuhwaas City, the main story. We call the uninhabited area below the main floor Baloops, or Raccoon town. Garney's old work shop, which I still use, goes by Port Garnacle. It actually has its own postal cancellations. We leave Garn and walk across the floating bridge, or the Causeway of Conciliation. The causeway reflects the settlement between Tui Tui and the Suzerain of Garn which ended the war between us that lasted from 1981 to 1983. Just like Seattle, our surrounding potentate, Tui Tui also has a floating bridge."

Garn, a pale yellow house that was evicted by construction

of the I-5 Freeway in 1959, found a new site on pilings on the shore of Lake Union not far from its original location. Beyond Garn floats the first of the two houseboats in Tui Tui, dubbed Isle Regis, the name of its owners.

At the end house a door knocker in the shape of a dragon fly decorates the front door of the Grande Tui, the capital of Tui Tui of the Joyous Lake. Dragonfly is the mythic name of Robby's wife, Janet; his name is Dogfish.

On opening the door a stacked washer and dryer appear slightly behind it. "That's the Industrial Zone of Tui Tui," comments Robby. "For instance, if you wanted to build an aluminum smelter here, you'd have to apply to the Zone authorities, but you'd have to bribe the officials and you'd probably fail because we have a lively free press here in Tui Tui."

To the east the Great Wall of Tui Tui, a Hawaiian turquoise and white concrete wall rising from their concrete float, collects the passive solar rays of the southern sun pouring in through the windowed exterior wall. On a more serious note Robby points out his latest stamp, posted along with the mail rates next to the Tui Tui postal box mounted on the wall. "This stamp expresses my sentiments that we don't mess with Mesopotamia; the issue date reflects the beginning of the War on Iraq.

"The niche in the Great Wall here was intended for the ashes of our cat Doodley Squat, the incentive for our buying a houseboat. Unfortunately, she chose her own way to exit this world, so it remains empty. And this is the hexagram of the I-ching which consists of two trigrams, each called tui, and the combined hexagram is also called tui. The broken upper line above the two solid ones represents a container, and the symbol also refers to lakes. This earth-bound symbol represents the lake above and the lake below.

"The clock up above is on Tui Tui time which is a version of tempus puget; it's usually right twice a day, and you can put a card in it and it will punch the time."

"Moving past the dining area between the Great Wall and the windows, we enter the kitchen/living room area. Pointing to a loft in the barrel arch at the apex of their roof, Robby comments, "This is the Hotel Grand Tui, a registered hotel on the mail art network. To access it we slide the library ladder over where it blocks the entrance to the waters of the Kiva so guests can climb up to it. The Kiva serves as the spiritual center of Grand Tui. In mythic scale the spa in the middle of the Kiva is also a lake, that's why we have a lake above and a lake below. The Legislative body of Tui Tui meets in the spa and all major decisions are made here in the Kiva. The ceiling represents a Chinese compass rose, with all the possible trigrams around it. In the I-Ching, a house with its main entry to the west is called a Tui house. As you can see our entry faces directly west."

Small dark polychromatic iridescent green tiles which Robby made at the workshop of a friend, Uroboros Art glass in Portland, Oregon, cover the wall. As for the somewhat gaudy decorations in the incomplete dome over the center of the Kiva, Robby admits that the Architectural Review committee of Tui Tui thinks it looks like a Chinese Bordello and is considering changing the decor.

Passing on to the bedroom, a sink and toilet, referred to as the "Nether Throne Room of the Hoi Poloi" are tucked against the opposite side of a wall behind the bed. In the bedroom, Robbie explains, "This room is the Embassy of the Isle of Oneiros to the sovereign nation of Tui Tui. Here's where we obtain visas to travel into the world of dreams." Various hexagram shapes, including a window, are sprinkled throughout the room. "We don't like 90 degree corners, so we rounded off the only one in the room. I've heard that in some churches in the Mid-west they did the same thing, for fear the Devil might "corner you."

Robby and Janet's house also includes a Music Conservatory, an upright piano against the wall, and the Biblioteque Nationale de Tui Tui, a floor to ceiling book shelf. Back in the living room Robbie points out the Musee National of Tui Tui, a glass topped coffee table with the shallow museum visible through the glass.

"Here's a four leaf clover, medals celebrating the opening of the Hiram Chittenden locks, the Alaska-Yukon-Pacific Exposition, and our 1962 Century 21 World's Fair. I found these arrowheads in Dallas, and an artist friend gave me the raven sandblasted on a rock. That forty-three cent stamp, a recent acquisition, was a joint issue between Tui Tui and Canada, synchronous with celebrating our 43rd birthdays."

Robby explains the joint stamp came about when Canadian authorities unwittingly issued a public invitation to "make your own stamp and mail a wish." The packet for making a stamp came with stickers for creating a design in the blank circle. "You were supposed to do what they told you to do, but I saw it as a blank canvass, so with the help of some friends on Beacon Hill, we did a letter press print in the circle. A group of us went up to Canada on my 43rd birthday (remember, it's actually a 43 cent stamp,) and we had a big birthday party with lots of my Mail Art friends. We did a mass mailing using my stamp and the postmaster actually let me use the cancellation device on my stamps; it was the highlight of my philatelic career."

The playful couple met as college students in London, where both agree it was love at first sight. Robby had already spent a semester in Rome as part of his studies in history at the Dominican University of Dallas, Texas. He met Janet, who left her native Kennewick, Washington to attend the University of

Puget Sound in Tacoma. She was with a group from UPS taking a brief tour of London, Paris and Rome en route to Vienna, Austria in 1971. From Austria the twosome traveled to Italy where Robby introduced her to some of his favorite nuns at the School run by the Sisters of Notre Dame Convent just a few miles form the Vatican.

"I suppose we were rather controversial," says Robby. "Even though we didn't stay in the same room that night at the convent, they knew we were traveling together. I'm surprised they didn't map out a route for us where we could stay at a convent each night."

Once they returned to the States, both went to the University of Puget Sound, then to Syracuse, New York, where they worked in a restaurant. They tried to unionize their fellow employees until they realized the restaurant was actually owned by the Mafia.

"We knew we were in over our heads and decided it was time to go back to school," says Janet. "After graduation from Evergreen State College we moved to Seattle and rented an apartment on Capitol Hill. One day Robby and I wanted to make some wine, but we needed corn sugar. So we headed for the local wine supply store where there was a kitten that had wandered in and was making itself at home, jumping from one corn sugar bag to another. We learned it was about to go to the pound, and I couldn't stand to see that happen, so we offered to take it."

Robby chimes in, "We carried the little kitten home in a brown paper bag. The apartment we lived in didn't allow pets and Doodley Squat was very active, so we had to relocate before anyone found out we had a kitten. Janet found a dilapidated old houseboat just below the I-5 Freeway on the east side of Lake Union that cost only $8,000. We signed the papers on July 29,

1974, and thought we'd bought something. The seller told us we had to pay a moorage fee of $50 a month to the dock owner, but he didn't introduce us to him or tell us anything about him.

"We learned later that the two of them had crossed swords, so Garney, our docklord, didn't like us from the very beginning.

"Garney didn't like noise or people walking down the dock, so he didn't want us to have guests. He had his buddies, we just weren't among them. The world had done him dirty and he'd been forced to move his house when the freeway came. His brother, a member of the Tyee Yacht Club, had arranged for the Club to buy property right next to us without informing Garney. Suddenly, he found he was living adjacent to a party venue.

"And of course one of the reasons he didn't want guests was that only the layers of tar paper he'd put over the dock were holding it together. He kept raising the moorage rates, and we felt in return for more money, we were entitled to a decent dock. So we told him we wouldn't pay any more rent until he fixed the dock and we would avail ourselves of all the protections against arbitrary eviction provided by the Floating Homes Association.

"We also wanted to remodel the houseboat; it was so unlivable. The house was built on three separate floats, consequently whenever it was windy or a boat's wake rocked our house, it was as if an evil chiropractor were manipulating it. The bathroom roof leaked so much we literally had mushrooms growing in it. Each year May flies would come up from a hole behind the tub, and we'd find thousands of wings, just wings, in our bathtub. We had an oil heater with two settings, Dante's inferno and the coldest circle in Hell. So at night, we'd have to turn it off, and then we'd wake up freezing in the morning. We actually found the water in the toilet frozen several times. We even put up insulated blankets over the windows to keep out the cold.

"We showed Garney our remodeling plans, but he couldn't

handle the idea of workmen bringing their tools and such down the dock; he knew it wasn't safe. I decided to go ahead with remodeling and he slapped an eviction notice on me. I hired Dan Rader as my attorney, now the Attorney Admiral of Tui Tui. He felt we had a good case in terms of Jury appeal, since if we were evicted our house would be taken out to Union Bay in Lake Washington and burned. That's what they did with evicted houseboats in those days. But as for the legal issue, the Judge, Liem Tuai, (pronounced like Tui), signaled that he would declare the Equity Ordinance unconstitutional in our case. If he did so, the ruling would put every houseboat on Lake Union in jeopardy. We were in a crisis. The night before we went to court, Dan asked his wife, Marla Elliott, Seeress of Tui Tui, Order of the Yarrow and Rhododendron and officiant at our wedding, to cast the I-Ching, centering on our dilemma, for help. She drew the fifty-eighth hexagram of the I-Ching, Tui, which was something of a description of our life on the lake. Dan came up with the brilliant idea of offering Garney a life tenancy in his house in exchange for our buying both the house and the moorage. The offer included switching our moorage site with the end houseboat in return for renovating the dock. Our lawyer met with Garney the next morning before the trial and Garney accepted our proposal. The Equity Ordinance was unchallenged and we knew we had to name our home Tui Tui, after both the judge, Tuai, and the fifty-eighth hexagram of the I-Ching, Tui."

Robby's folks helped with the down payment and the transaction was settled on July 29, 1983. Robby then began designing and building the house beginning with the concrete float, which included a lot of ducting to make use of solar heat and also the concrete Great Wall of Tui Tui. He also successfully lured Janet back to Seattle from Portland where she'd been teaching English as a Second Language.

Robby says, "After fourteen years of courtship with some interruptions, we happily married on our still unfinished Tui Tui on May 18, 1985. We actually were able to move in on Dec. 16 of that same year."

In addition to helping Robby manage the two buildings they now own on Eastlake Avenue just above them, Janet plays various percussion instruments with a group called Batucada Yemanja do Pacifico. They specialize in traditional folkloric Brazilian music, along with some Caribbean and Cuban rhythms. The group always performs at Seattle's Folk Life festival and the annual Brazilian Festival at the Seattle Center. They played once a month at Zoka, a coffee house in Wallingford, and are now at El Diablo on Queen Anne. The group rehearses every Tuesday night.

While Janet loves playing the drums, the noise of the nearby freeway drives her nuts. Janet explains, "I've become more sensitive to sound as I've been dealing with some migraine headaches and the noise on the Freeway has gotten much louder. We hear the noise of the Express lanes vibrating down as it bounces off the bottom of the main deck. Those of us affected finally got the city to close the express lanes between 11 pm and 5 am. But if there's a major event they'll leave them open longer."

Robby adds, "We joined a group called NOISE [Neighborhoods Opposed to Interstate Sound Exposure], and now we actually have money in the state budget for a plan, not just a study, but a plan, and the next step will be implementing the plan. I'm also in touch with a Spanish physicist, who has designed a tubular bell system for sucking up noise that can reduce selected frequencies by a significant number of decibels. We have extra insulation and no windows where we're most exposed to the noise, and of course it's much less in the winter with our windows closed.

Both Robby and Janet, sensitive to the original inhabitants of Tui Tui, are learning to speak and write the Lushootseed language. In addition to their involvement in NOISE, both contribute to various community projects in Eastlake, such as the now completed Fairview Park, the annual Eastlake Shake, and the design process of Colonnade Park under the I-5 Freeway.

Robby recently issued a new stamp in celebration of the tenth anniversary of the near-by Pocock Rowing Club Foundation. His printer is Anna Banana, who used to be town fool of Victoria. Her mother is the Communist Tea Party lady of Victoria. Anna now lives on the Sunshine coast and has been very involved in mail art for many years. A book called "Artistamps" includes a section written by Robbie on Tui Tui.

He and Janet complement each other when it comes to their favorite time of year. Janet enjoys the winter months when closed windows lessen Freeway noise. She says, "In winter the people on the lake really want to be there; they're not afraid of rain or cold. In summer it's more a vacation land, with lots of parties and activities. We're more isolated here in winter, we don't have the same neighboring aspect as during the long warm days of summer. We love the Christmas boat parades, with all the glistening decorative lights reflected on the water."

Robby adds, "July Fourth with our fantastic fireworks is somewhat an obligatory party. We always invite our tenants down, and I love them, but there's this feeling that you have to entertain. My favorite thing, along with not having to mow a lawn, is jumping in the lake. Last summer, with my brother-in-law and a dear friend, we kayaked through the locks, across the Sound and paddled to Fay Bainbridge State Park on Bainbridge Island. We camped out there, went to the Old Man's House where Chief Seattle was born, saw lots of eagles, ospreys, whales and boats, and even a blimp. It gives me

Canada goose bumps when I realize we could go from our front porch and connect with all that. To feel your house sits at the threshold of the Pacific Rim and all that it includes gives me such a feeling of connectedness.

"Here on the lake we're reminded all the time by its movement that we're connected to that boat passing by, that seaplane taking off, even those people above us whizzing by on the freeway. Right here in this spot in particular is the active nexus between the water and the land."

AN AIRPLANE
IN A HOUSEBOAT?

Tom Susor bought his houseboat on the dock owned by the University of Washington in the mid-1970s. "I'd just missed getting a houseboat two years earlier, so when I found this one with the doors all open, music playing, reflected light sparkling on the ceiling, and the wave patterns constantly moving across a beaded curtain common in those hippy days, I didn't waste any time."

Tom confesses he hastily returned to the University, where he was developing machinery for medical research, and took down all the other notices about "his" houseboat. He wanted to make sure he got this one.

Once he had purchased it, Tom began replacing decayed stringers, rotten floor boards, and almost totally renovating the vintage sprung roof home. A would-be architect with an Associate degree in mechanical engineering, Tom planned his remodel to include a second story addition. When he was ready to raise the roof, he laid in an abundant supply of food and invited neighbors, friends and associates to a week-end work party.

"That Friday," says Tom, "I discovered a Stop Work order on my front door. I'd done the whole house, one floor section and one wall at a time without a complaint. I called an architect friend who advised me how to handle my problem. I rushed downtown to the Department of Construction and Land Use. That same day I was able to get a permit to replace the existing roof without a major review, something you could never do today."

Tom's most interesting experience with the whims of city bureaucracy came when Ed and Karen Hayes hired him to build a log float for their home. The Hayes had lost their houseboat when the oyster barge supporting it sank into Lake Union. Ed and Karen wanted a classic cedar-log float, like those of their Fairview neighbors. Tom explains, "Ed's job as comptroller of a logging mill gave us access and first pick of a huge stack of large diameter first growth cedar logs."

Tom submitted his building plans to an examiner who had never heard of a floating home built on a log float. Since the 1960s all the new houseboats had been built on floats of Ferro-cement and Styrofoam in various combinations. Although the majority of Seattle houseboats float on cedar logs dating back seventy-five years or more, the city examiner had no data on the engineering characteristics of cedar logs.

Tom had to hire Sentinel Engineers to generate a marine engineering study of the structural qualities of cedar logs and the stability of this house/float combination. As Tom says, "For $3,000 and after a four month delay, we finally convinced the city that cedar logs are structurally capable of supporting a floating home."

Tom's interest in building is reflected in perhaps the largest workshop in any floating home; a 10 by 24 foot room created by knocking out a wall to a second bedroom. He is currently constructing a Kit Fox airplane that will be mounted on floats so he can moor it next to the houseboat. The water side of the workroom has floor to ceiling double windows through which he can move the completed plane, with wings folded, onto the lake.

Tom's interest in flying, along with his romance, blossomed shortly after he met Susan at an EST workshop. He took flying lessons, joined the Experimental Aircraft Association, and bought a plane kit. He and Susan are both active in the Young Eagles Program, which introduces kids to flight by taking them for rides in small planes. Under Tom's leadership, as many as twenty-four pilots from his compiled regional list of over four hundred volunteer pilots, turn out for a flight event. More than 7,000 kids have been flow through Tom's Seattle Chapter of the EAA.

Susan says, "Since we don't have any children, it's wonderful to discover most kids are terrific people. We had one youngster call us to share her excitement at finally getting a decent grade in math. While flying with us, she struggled to understand degrees on a compass, so math suddenly became a relevant and meaningful challenge.

"Another classroom created six by ten foot banners to thank Tom for providing them with the flight experience. We had banners plastered throughout the house for months and months. It's thrilling to see how exposing these kids to fight opens up all sorts of possibilities for them; it also shows them their community from a whole new perspective."

When Susan first saw Tom, she knew he was the man she was going to marry. Three years later at the age of thirty-five and forty-two respectively, she and Tom wed, the first marriage for both of them. Susan is a country girl from Index, Washington, one of the small towns east of Seattle where the railroad comes down from Steven's Pass. She still owns a home in Index and works at Valley General Hospital in Monroe, still within commuting distance, as a staff nurse in Surgical Services.

The first year of marriage Tom and Susan maintained their

separate abodes, but Susan has since discovered that living on a houseboat isn't really living in the city. She grows beans, tomatoes, cucumbers, potatoes and peas in a vegetable garden on the land by their dock, and even finds time for canning. Tom retired at the end of 1995 to concentrate on building his airplane. Susan claims that once Tom finishes building the airplane, she plans to put a loom in the large workroom for equal time on weaving projects.

Susan submitted the following "recipe" to the *Floating Kitchens* cookbook:

HOMEMADE HOUSEBOAT AIRPLANE
13 years of dreams
10 years of saving dimes in a red airplane bank
1 supportive wife
1 supportive wife's checkbook
2 bedroom floating home
5 extraordinary friends
1 vacation in Oshkosh
Patience (mostly wife's)

First, get your private pilot license. Then marry a woman with the patience of Job, who gives you a red airplane bank for your first Christmas together. Buy a lot of things that give you dimes as change so you can put them in your bank. Take a vacation with your wife to the world's largest air show in Oshkosh, Wisconsin. Be sure to forget your checkbook, the depository of all those dimes. Find a Kit Fox (as in "build-it-yourself") airplane that you MUST have and get your supportive wife, who did not forget her checkbook, to pay for it.

Once back home, pay your wife back immediately so she quits calling it "her" airplane! Do not let your jaw drop when the "kit" which arrives is larger than any room in your houseboat.

Just knock out a few walls and windows, sacrifice a bedroom, and soon enough your workshop is ready! Now add the help of your extraordinary friends in moving all the pieces of the airplane puzzle into the "assembly hangar." Spend millions of hours organizing the zillions of pieces, from nuts and bolts to ailerons and wings. Keep promising your patient and supportive wife that this thing will fly, someday! Promise your patient and supportive wife that the house will look like a normal houseboat again—someday!

THE ACCIDENTAL OWNERS

One might say Jim and Barbara Donnette have arrived. They own their end houseboat free and clear, enjoy an adult/adult relationship with three well-launched grown children, retired from respective careers in which each earned the respect and admiration of their peers, can hop in their sailboat at a moment's notice to catch a favorable wind, and now have the resources to travel extensively throughout the world.

It's been a long journey in which each has decidedly paid his dues.

Jim grew up on a rural Ohio farm during the WWII era where he was drafted to pitch in with milking the cows, butchering the hogs, tending the chickens, preserving the meat, and picking and canning fruits and vegetables. After the war ended, his adventurous father bought a house trailer and the family spent three months headed west toward relatives in Torrance, California.

Jim recalls, "In between dealing with twenty flat tires we toured Yellowstone, Yosemite, and Sequoia National Parks. My mother couldn't leave all her canned food behind and the added weight was too much for the old synthetic rubber tires. My father finally bought tractor tires to solve the problem.

"I'll never forget when we arrived at my uncle's house. Nobody ever said anything to me and I finally asked if I could go across the street. They said fine and told me there was a beach over there. So I'm running across the beach in the moon light and suddenly my feet are wet and I'm standing there looking at these big waves come pounding in. I'd been to Lake Erie but it doesn't have a surge like that and I suddenly realized this must be the Pacific Ocean."

Seven years later the University of Southern California offered Jim a scholarship, but he had to pay full tuition if his grades slipped. "I looked at the cost of tuition and knew the amount was out of the question for someone like me."

So Jim enrolled in the local community college and began working at Northrop Aircraft. During the Sputnik era Northrop eagerly helped engineering students obtain a three year degree at the University of Southern California. "Once I finished I found myself working on nuclear delivery systems.

"I really wanted a degree in architecture so I ended up at Berkeley, where this kid from Ohio was exposed to Frank Lloyd Wright, William Teller, Yamasaki and all sorts of Nobel laureates. Their creativity simply blew me away."

It was at Berkeley where Jim met Barbara, a native Californian who had grow up in Marin County and was majoring in anthropology.

"Russian was my first language," says Barbara, "and then I went to kindergarten where I learned English. I remember seeing the teacher hit a fellow student. I was horrified; I'd never seen anyone get hit before and I couldn't understand what was going on.

"What I remember most is during the McCarthy era of the late Fifties my Russian parents were looked on as Pinkos. My dad had always wanted us to retain our fluency in Russian, but to avoid antagonism from our peers my two sisters and I distanced ourselves from anything bordering on Communism. It's

A Crooked Old Dock

too bad, as speaking Russian would have been a great asset if I'd stuck with it.

"At least my very Orthodox parents saw to it that we all went to twelve years of Catholic girls' schools, and I grew up to be a happy little person."

Barbara then went on to Berkeley where she met Jim, who by this time had been married and divorced. The couple dated for several years when out of the blue the University of Washington offered Jim a teaching position. That very evening Jim asked Barbara to marry him. Within a week the two exchanged vows in the basement of her family's Russian Orthodox Church. Since the Church prohibited weddings during Lent, the basement location was a compromise with the family. The very next day the newly weds headed north so Jim could begin teaching in the spring quarter of 1966.

When they arrived in Seattle, Barbara remembers thinking, "Oh my God, what have I done? This is a major jump shift in my life."

Jim recalls, "We went to the liquor store and it looked like the employment office. There was no liquor in sight. You'd place your order, they'd go into a back room and get it, bring it back, quickly lift the bottle out of the bag so you could see it, and then immediately put it back in the bag. Local law required all bars to have big windows so the inside was clearly visible. In restaurants a waiter had to carry your drink from the bar to a dining table. I discovered although they sold beer at the old Sick Baseball Stadium, when I bought a bottle I couldn't bring it into the stadium. No more baseball until I finished the beer!"

The Donnette's did find one thing familiar from the San Francisco Bay area, the Lake Union houseboat community. They began poking around the various docks until summer came and they moved out of their furnished apartment. Jim's two boys, aged six and eight, arrived for their summer visit and the foursome, along with their camping gear, squeezed into a Volkswagen convertible in an attempt to visit all the National Parks.

Jim explains, "As an architect I'd worked seven days a week, ten hours a day, so this was my first summer off. We weren't exactly what you would call flush, but we'd vacated our apartment and had minimum expenses."

When they returned to Seattle and the boys to their mother in Michigan, Jim and Barbara camped out in a tent near Steven's Pass while looking for a place to live. They wandered along Fairview Avenue, at that time a dirt road with nothing but small houseboats between it and the lake, looking for a houseboat. They found the only three houseboats for sale were total dogs, literal shacks on a raft. They met Terry Pettus at the Floating Homes office where he spent most of the day and asked for his help in finding a decent houseboat.

Terry mentioned he needed some architectural services such as a survey of the vacant properties across the street. Jim offered to provide the survey and when he and Barbara returned with the drawings several days later, Terry said, "I found you a houseboat."

"Oh, where?"

"It's on this dock."

"Oh, can we look at it?"

"Yeah."

"So we started walking down the dock and we kept walking and walking until we got to the end."

"This one." said Terry, as he pointed to the small gray house with white trim and a red roof.

"We'll take it."

Jim and Barbara couldn't believe it when the owners, two brothers who were both teachers, said they were leaving because Seattle was getting "too damn crowded."

Barbara sold her Volkswagen for the down payment and Jim was finally able to get a two year loan from his credit union based on his three year contract with the University. As the beginning of classes approached, Jim and Barbara stopped in regularly to tactfully ask when their house would be available.

"Each time they'd ask if we could use something, a couch, a bed, a stove, a kitchen table. We paid $25 for their refrigerator and it's still running. Our own kids have bought three refrigerators during this time."

The lease agreement required a meeting with the dock manager before the Donnettes could move in.

Jim recalls, "We went over to his houseboat, knocked on the door, and were told to come in. He was sitting with his back to us looking out the window. He never turned around to see us while he reviewed the rules we had to live by. When it was over we wondered what we'd gotten into, but our new neighbors told us not to worry, 'just pay your rent and keep your nose clean.'"

Once they moved in Jim recognized the salmon and turquoise paint in the kitchen. "I knew from my time with an architectural firm that specialized in schools at one time the government required those colors for all public schools. That restriction used to drive us nuts. We soon realized the previous owners had done everything on the cheap. The bathroom sink has a broken corner. I'm sure they bought it for next to nothing and carefully put it back together. We've used it for 37 years without any problems.

"I started to do some remodeling in a normal way, for instance I'd start to repair a door and its frame. But I had to stop because there's no real framing in the house. I realized we had bought a "shack on a raft" and would have to settle for the same ticky tacky repairs they had done."

That first year was a busy one for Jim and Barbara. First they learned their stringers, the big beams that rest on the logs and support the sub floor, were in the water and the house needed added flotation. They hired George Johnston to solve the problem, which he did by putting 22 nine feet-long Styrofoam logs underneath the house.

Once they'd moved in Jim and Barbara noticed everybody on the dock had a little boat, so they bought a kit with materials for an eight foot boat.

"We started building it out on the deck,' says Barbara, "but then it started raining. During our first winter in Seattle it rained forty-two days in a row without stopping. We moved the boat into the kitchen to finish it. I didn't mind, I was still so star struck!"

That same year, 1969, the owners of the moorage offered to sell individual sites to the houseboat owners for $7,800 each, but most tenants felt the price was exorbitant.

Not only did Jim and Barbara paint, remodel, and build a boat, Jim became active in the Floating Homes Association and Barbara began gardening. She negotiated an agreement with the owner of the vacant lot across the street. In exchange for cultivating his lot she would share some of what she harvested with the owner. The first year went well and several years later the property owner offered to sell it to them for $100,000. The price was perhaps realistic, but not for a garden, so Jim and Barbara reluctantly turned down the offer.

About the same time a neighbor mentioned the City planned to develop a new P-patch on Fairview Avenue about six blocks north. Seattle's P-patch program uses city-owned or other available vacant properties to provide gardening plots for residents in various areas of the city. Eager to have some space of their own, the Donnettes worked along with ten other families to prepare the site. "We hacked down blackberry bushes taller than any of us," says Jim. "Once we finally finished that chore we had to haul out all the accumulated old car parts, stoves, tarps, rotted boats, washing machines, tires and other junk."

"But the worst of all," adds Barbara, "was the disintegrating moldy ancient carpeting that fell apart as I loaded it into my van for a trip to the dump. The mold was memorable, especially for my sinuses." Moldy carpet or not, Barbara volunteered to represent the Fairview P-Patch on the city's Advisory Council. "I began as a volunteer and ultimately became Director of the program."

Jim found his niche working with a group of fellow houseboat owners testing the feasibility of a trial system for moving sewage from individual house boats to the recently completed city sewer. After monitoring the system for a year, the group was able to convince city inspectors there was no leakage into the lake and the sewer system did indeed do the job.

Jim also chaired the Lake Union Investment group, which was formed so that houseboaters could work toward accumulating funds to purchase their docks when an owner decided to sell.

Barbara, with her very practical major in anthropology, began working at Seattle's then premier Frederick and Nelson Department store. It was a win/win situation. Barbara had summers off when Frederick's could hire a less expensive summer replacement. She could be home when Jim's boys came to visit and enjoy Seattle's summer.

All went well until the year of the big freeze when Jim, Barbara and other neighbors on the north side of the dock were without water for ten days.

"The deal was that whenever the temperature dropped below freezing, who ever lived on the end house had to keep their water running so it wouldn't freeze in the exposed pipe that ran down the dock," explains Jim. "But in spite of our dutifully doing so, the water froze further up the dock and broke a pipe running into a neighbor's house. That dropped the water pressure so much that even though we continued running our water, the entire main pipe froze. For ten days we used lake water to flush the john and our unaffected neighbors on the south side of the dock provided potable water."

Thankfully their daughter Jennifer was born in 1971 after those waterless days. With her arrival the Donnettes built a small second-story room toward the back of their house accessible by ladder for the boys' summer visits. As Jennifer grew Jim built small outdoor areas enclosed with wood and chicken wire outside each of their three exterior doors. One included a sand-box. "They also served as a secondary back-up in terms of preventing any accidents. If Jennifer went out any door she was still in a fenced area. She never tried to breach the boundaries. As they say, 'Little boys come to a fence and climb over it and little girls come to a fence and cry.'"

In 1979 the owners of the moorage wanted out. The nephew of one of them who lived across the channel from Jim and Barbara was offered the right of first refusal. He asked Jim and Barbara, along with the two other end houseboat owners, to help organize a dock cooperative that could purchase both the real estate and the rights to the state lease. Since the dock had been extended into land owned by the state, the moorage sites could not be sold separately.

When the twenty-eight other houseboat owners on the two docks couldn't agree on the many issues involved, the co-op idea died, replaced by a limited partnership that included one other houseboat owner who lived on a different moorage. As Jim says, "There seemed to be three different groups; one simply didn't want to buy for whatever reason, another owned their homes primarily as an investment, and the third wanted to buy. They just couldn't get it together." Jim and Barbara suddenly found themselves among the partnership of dock owners.

In compliance with the current Equity Ordinance, intended to protect both owners and renters, the five families who bought the moorage raised the moorage fees based on their purchase price and projected costs of essential repairs. But the Hearing Examiner who reviewed their case decided that most of the repairs involved maintenance rather than improvements. Since only improvement costs could be passed on to tenants, the Hearing Examiner knocked ten dollars off the proposed new moorage fee. That decision meant from then on the new dock owners were $10 in the hole on each house every month.

Barbara describes one of their first challenges as owners. "The dock had been extended up to the navigable water line in 1963 to accommodate some of the many evicted houseboats at that time. It had been covered with plywood in an attempt to make it last a little longer, which of course made it rot even more. It was my job to pressure-wash and paint the dock every year. It was so bad I sometimes worried I might simply wash the dock away. Our houses were anchored to the dock with mooring chains connected to rings on the dock side boards, but any kind of storm that jerked our houses would pull the rings from the rotten wood. We didn't want our homes to be set adrift, so clearly something had to be done.

"We had to do it on the cheap because we couldn't pass on the costs." Jim designed a replacement for the side sections and Art Holder built the replacement dock in twenty foot segments in the parking lot across the street.

"When Art finished all the sections, he helped all of us owners carry each one into the lake by hand. We'd already lifted all the plumbing from the rotting sides and temporarily tied it to the pilings. We then slide the decaying sides out and one by one replaced them with the new sections.

Their next challenge occurred in the midst of a very cold winter. In the rather drafty old houseboats everyone turned on any heater they could find. Jim says, "The city had provided only one power drop for the whole dock and the wire got so hot it melted the insulation to the point it was dripping off the wire. City Light came out, looked at it, and panicked. They quickly ran secondary wire down the north side of the dock to lower the load. But the line was only temporary and we had to pay for a major upgrade."

Finally, in 1997, a Cooperative formed by the homeowners purchased the two docks and Jim and Barbara could retire not only from their professional jobs, but also from the often onerous responsibilities of dock lords.

Now the Donnettes and the four other owners are free of the need to write notices regarding late rental payments, enforce landlord-tenant agreements, rebuild docks and sewers, replace light bulbs, shovel the rare snow and all the assorted responsibilities of ownership. They can read, travel, and indulge in playful pranks with a new neighbor, an Alaska Airlines flight attendant and graduate of rival Washington State University. Nancy and her Cougar sister Jean began with a frontal assault on the University of Washington Husky leanings of Jim and Barbara. When the Donnettes returned from a trip, they found a photo of their house with a Cougar flag flying from its flag pole. Jim countered with a silhouette of the UW Husky mascot hung in their bathroom window, where it was clearly visible from the loyal Cougar fans' living room. Then Jim and Barbara returned one day to find their-silver toned car spray-painted with bold letters proclaiming "COUGARS RULE." Donnettes were vastly relieved to find their Cougar rivals had first covered the car with Saran Wrap. The most recent chapter in this amiable rivalry occurred when the Husky fans filled the Cougar's bathroom with fifty-one gold and purple Husky balloons and stuffed three black balloons in the toilet bowl. The numbers represented the final score of the most recent Husky versus Cougar annual football game, adding new meaning to the term "bowl game."

Although retired from her position with the City as Director of the P-patch program, Barbara still shares the fruits of her P-patch plot with neighbors and maintains the container garden on their houseboat. She continues to serve on the Board and recently coordinated the creation and raffle of a ninety-nine square quilt as a very successful fund raising project. Her enjoyment of hand work also shows in the numerous flags flying from their flagpole. The newest flag proclaims "S O A R," or "Shack On A Raft," as they refer to their home.

"I feel really blessed," says Barbara. "I not only was paid for doing something I loved, but I also felt what I did had a positive influence."

Jim enjoys his emeritus status after thirty-one years with the University of Washington where he rose to Assistant Dean of the Department of Architecture and Urban Planning. Both can sometimes be found weeding recent city planting strips along Fairview Avenue, walking to Mariner games and hiking with a group from the dock.

No doubt about it, the Donnettes thoroughly enjoy these years as the frosting on the cake.

DOWNSIZING, AND THEN SOME

Once you find a parking place on Westlake Avenue, it's a quick walk down some steps at the side of The Boat World Marina to the dock where Jim and Sharon Doub moor their home and business, a ship-shape thirty-three foot long sailboat christened the Whoodat. A flower pot of whatever's in season hangs from the stern.

With only about 150 square feet of inside space, the Doubs stash their expresso machine in the pass-thru bathroom between the living area and the triangular bunk in the bow. The compressed main salon, galley, and office include one couch, a narrow table for two, a stove, micro wave oven, toaster oven, regular oven, a top opening refrigerator, assorted built-in book shelves, racks for hanging soda glasses, space for the cellular phone, tiny cupboards, and a small electric heater.

"Without a TV, we find we read a lot more. And housekeeping is a cinch," says Sharon, "it takes me about forty seconds to vacuum: ten seconds to get out the machine and hook it up, twenty seconds to vacuum, and another ten seconds to put it away."

Jim chimes in, "And we don't shower; I haven't had a shower in two months. So we smell a lot. Actually," he admits, "we joined the Athletic Club up the street, so we go up there to work out and shower every day."

"Or we just shower," admits Sharon. "I gained a pound and a half after our first month of showers."

If the weather's amenable they've become experts at barbecuing a variety of foods which they then eat on their bow deck. Utensils are kept to a bare four of everything: plates, knives, forks, spoons, glasses, mugs, cups and saucers. As for cooking, they admit to eating out three or four times a week with frequent take out, microwave or crock pot meals at home.

"For our laundry," says Sharon, "we found a local Laundromat that's a gathering place for a whole lot of boat people on Saturdays. We discovered that most of the boat people we know go there and make a party out of doing the laundry on Saturday mornings. So when they opened up the new Krispie Kream doughnut place on Aurora Avenue, I got up earlier than I would have if I were going to work, raced up Aurora, bought about two dozen doughnuts along with a handful of Krispy Kreme balloons and whisked down to surprise everyone at the Laundromat. It was a blast!"

The nautical couple have grown even closer to each other in their tiny space, although each came from a very different past.

Sharon headed for Seattle in '67 as soon as she finished high school in Spokane, Washington. She married and raised a family in the Wedgewood area of Seattle where they lived in the same house for seventeen years. She worked as an office assistant for various dentists, and then ended up living on her son Russell's power boat when the marriage ended. "My kids now all race sailboats, daughter Katie's boyfriend used to live aboard his boat on Lake Union, Heidi's former boyfriend is a Naval architect and Russell once ran a boatyard." For a former Spokane gal, her children are true web-footed water-loving Seattle natives.

Jim took a more circuitous route. "It was one of those things;

I went from the dormitory at Berkley to a remodeled chicken house when I graduated. There were several apartments, then the first home. As I worked my way up at Hewlett Packard the houses kept increasing in size up to one that was 7,000 square feet. Then we moved to Connecticut where we bought an 1812 farmhouse that was on the National Historical Register. Everything kept going up: income, expenses, depression, aggravation, and anxiety. I finally said this has gotta stop. That was fifteen years ago and it's been going the other way ever since. Pretty soon I'll be back to a chicken house."

"I guarantee it will be a chicken house that floats," declares Sharon.

Jim and Sharon connected in Seattle when they had both joined an outdoor group, the Mountaineers. Jim took Sharon sailing with a group from the Mountaineers and the romance of sailing blossomed into a romance for the two of them.

"I lived in a great little bachelor pad just west of the University Bridge that included a moorage space for my sail boat, the Whoodat, that I'd bought in Portland, Oregon. Sharon was living on her son's boat over in Lake Washington at Newport Shores. We had our first date when I offered to take her for a sail.

"After we were married in 1995 we started looking for a place of our own. We found a houseboat we liked on the dock just north of the "Sleepless In Seattle" dock. We knew it was a leased moorage, which meant we would only own the house, not the moorage site, but we decided to make an offer. Then in the process of financing the deal we found out the lease for the moorage site expired in five years, so the whole deal fell through."

"I cried," remembers Sharon, "I was so disappointed. But there were a lot of houses down there for sale so we continued looking around. We went to almost every houseboat open house.

We saw a listing under House Barges in the newspaper classifieds for the "Hot Fudge." I pictured a barge hauling cattle, cement and coal and such, but I said let's go look. The first time we sat on the deck and savored the view from downtown to Gas Works Park, we truly bonded with the Hot Fudge. We thought, 'we could do this.'

"We tried not to look too excited in front of the realtor, but anyone who's seen the Hot Fudge knows it's hardly a cattle barge! Living on it has been all we anticipated; it's magic. Cars get older, new things lose their shine, friends may leave, but living on the water just gets better and better."

The Doubs describe living on the barge as magical and they enjoyed the challenge of living in less space. They even put a small door into the side of the structure on the dock with three steps up to their front door so they could store pots, shears, trowels, and fertilizer in it. "We find solar heat really helps," says Sharon, "and also our propane stove. I rather enjoy going to pick up the propane tank every week when it's delivered; it's somewhat like going to the well for water.

"With the Whoodat moored on the same dock," says Jim, "we came up with the idea of offering sailing trips and sailing lessons and named our business "Sailing in Seattle." While it's never been a full time deal, we get a good steady little income. It's a wonderful way to meet some really fun and interesting people. We've done corporate team building, sales training, and I've recently been licensed to do weddings. We've already had several. One couple we took out from Kansas wanted so badly to spend the night on the Hot Fudge we spent the night on our sailboat and turned the Hot Fudge over to them. They sent us pictures of their farm in Kansas and we still stay in touch."

Jim and Sharon paid a monthly moorage fee of over $500 for a forty-seven foot space on the dock for the Hot Fudge, which included water and metered electricity. A place to park, laundry facilities, and a bathroom were up to them. Boats coming in for repair would sometimes run into them or their neighbors.

Jim reports, "You'd suddenly hear the cry, "Fend off, fend off," and know it was time to rush outside to protect your home." When kids came around Sharon provided them with fishing poles with magnets instead of hooks. "Even though the lake bottom was over forty feet down, it's amazing what they'd bring up. One time they brought up a gallon of paint that had inadvertently fallen off the dock."

Jim and Sharon felt secure on the lake. They knew when they bought the Hot Fudge that in the late 1980s all house barges on Lake Union were threatened with eviction for environmental reasons. Just as the houseboats had done, many people living on barges coalesced to fight their eviction. They all agreed to put in holding tanks for sewage, to subscribe to a code of conduct, and even urged the city to number and assess them. The Hot Fudge was duly taxed and registered as a legal barge. The Doubs have a copy of the code of conduct posted next to their front door.

Then suddenly Jennifer Belcher, the State Land Commissioner, abruptly ordered all house barges, including the registered ones, off of state lease land. Because house barges usually occupy the larger moorage sites near the end of a dock, including the Hot Fudge, most of them were in the state lease land. The growing popularity of living on Lake Union triggered an influx of small, unregistered "turtle" barges, many of them built by Mark Scott, son-in-law of parking magnate Joe Diamond. Scott had purchased the Swift Sure Marina where he welcomed barges, including several transient rental barges operated by Houseboat Hideaways. Permanent residents found the late-night partying of the transients and the loss of parking spaces, not to mention the reality that none of them were legally registered, very frustrating. Apparently Jennifer Belcher decided to deal with the usurpers by forcing everyone on a barge from the state owned property.

Sharon explains, "When we thought of living in an apartment somewhere we realized we just couldn't do that; we'd have to find another location on the water. So we organized immediately, got an attorney to represent all of us on the legal barges, raised a bunch of money and public sentiment, and managed to put the whole thing on ice for about two years. By then Jennifer Belcher chose not to run for office again and Jeff Sutherland, elected as the new State Land Commissioner, dropped the whole thing. We know people who panicked, sold their barge homes, moved on to land, or left the lake and moved into Salmon Bay. You don't know how much you like something until you're threatened with losing it, and then you take a stand."

Jim points out that if no one's allowed to live on the lake in one kind of vessel or another, we wouldn't be able to have the NOAA ships, the Boeing yacht Daedelus, or the beautiful blue hulled boat from the Grand Cayman Islands complete with a uniformed crew that shows up every summer. Even the tugboats that come through would be illegal.

Once the threat of eviction faded the Doubs settled back into enjoying life afloat. But as the economy worsened, Jim "retired from unemployment" and they decided to downsize once more.

"We wanted to try the real live-aboard life style," explains Jim, "so we put the Hot Fudge on the market and moved to the Whoodat. It's worked much better than I expected. We have one fourth the space we had before, but now I'm retired from retirement. I have office space on the shore where I manage the boat yard where we're moored. It's probably one of the shortest commutes in town; all of a hundred feet away, if that."

Sharon explains, "What I love about this is the coziness. I think bigger, bigger, bigger lessens closeness. I'm convinced all of us want some kind of closeness if you can balance it all. I think if we move back on the barge I will miss that. I think the smallness takes you back to when you were a kid and you had your little hidey places and you'd play under the stairs or in a tree house or whatever, but it's your special little space and you can sort of control the smaller area. If you're in a bigger space you're not really connected to it. You're connected to every little thing in a small space."

Jim nods agreeably, "Yeah, I'd go with that."

ROMANCE AFLOAT

"Valentine's Day is my favorite holiday. I do far more for Valentine's Day than any other holiday. I get into it like other people do Thanksgiving or Christmas," declares Loretta Metcalf.

She and husband Jim Healy live a real life romance in the floating home featured in one of 1993's most popular movies, *Sleepless in Seattle*. Actor Tom Hanks portrays a recent widower living with his young son in a Seattle houseboat. The lonely youngster's plea for a new mom on a national talk show piques the interest of an East Coast woman portrayed by Meg Ryan.

Jim and Loretta were both living in Princeton, New Jersey, when they first saw the movie and Loretta exclaimed, "Wow, wouldn't it be fun to live in a place like that; how romantic!" But the Seattle houseboat was as distant for Jim and Loretta as Tom Hanks was from Meg Ryan.

Yet, St. Valentine intervened, and several months later Jim and Loretta flew to Seattle where Jim, who works in wireless communications, had scheduled a job interview. They hunted down the movie houseboat, discovered a **For Sale** sign on it, and found a realtor as curious to see the place as they were.

Despite the $740,000 price tag, it was love at first sight for Jim and Loretta. "I think what impressed me most about it was the window seat and the furnishings," says Loretta. "The furnishings were similar to ours. I could envision endless hours reading the *New York Times* and watching the activity on the lake. We liked everything about it, but the next day we flew back east to real life in Princeton."

When the Seattle interview led to a job offer for Jim, he and Loretta decided to buy either the famous Lake Union houseboat or a place in Madison Park. None of the other houseboats had enough wall space for Loretta's treasured antique family bookcase.

As Loretta says, "In houseboats there's just not as much space. Even though ours is almost 2,000 square feet, what I really miss is a basement or an attic—space to put all the stuff. When you paint the porch and you have some paint left over, you don't throw it away; you put it down in the basement 'just in case' you might need it someday. There's no place like that in a houseboat."

Even though there was no place to put the leftover paint, Jim and Loretta made an offer on the houseboat. It was accepted and they moved into their famous home shortly before Valentine's Day of 1994.

"I know some of our neighbors could do without the curious sight-seers," she adds, "but we enjoy the tourists, as long as they come by water, and not by land."

Loretta particularly remembers all the curious kayakers from her first week on the lake. "I don't know whether you've ever moved anyplace where you don't know anyone, but in the middle of a gray February there was not much activity on the dock. I relished all the action on the water. People out on the water were friendly; kayakers would wave to me, and I felt a part of something, like I wasn't all alone."

Jim enjoys all the industrial activity on the lake. "We saw one of the big white NOAA ships just returning from its trip to

Sleepless in Seattle House

Antarctica, and we were home to see one of the float planes almost sink."

Jim continues, "And once one of the dry docks across the lake at Lake Union Dry Docks got flooded on one side. Both the dock and the ship that was in it listed almost forty-five degrees. It was fascinating to watch all the repair operations.

"And the neighbors here, as you get to know them and what various individuals do, this is a neighborhood that would be hard to replicate. There're a fair number of people here that you normally just wouldn't happen to meet."

One night, shortly after Jim and Loretta had moved in, they heard water running as they walked down the dock after dining out. They discovered the flexible water hose from the pipe line under the dock to their home had broken.

Jim recalls, "So at 10:30 at night I was rounding up neighbors I barely knew, and we all gathered on the dock to brainstorm how to fix the problem, and then get the job done."

Jim also learned how to deal with some other challenges of houseboat living. On the eve of their wedding day he noticed their toilets weren't flushing properly, so, once again, he consulted his neighbors. "A simple, but not obvious, reset of the dock pump solved the problem."

Loretta reports losing a gold earring through one of the cracks between the boards in the dock. "I've learned to hold firmly onto my car keys and to be very careful not to drop anything."

"A sacrifice to the lake god," says Jim, "and well worth it."

CREATIVE HOUSIING
SOLUTIONS

Sandi Lindbeck and Kit Willis' location on Portage Bay dovetails perfectly with their jobs at the University of Washington. Sandy frequently chugs to work in her eight-foot dinghy, which she moors at the University's Water Sports Center. From there, it's only a football field length to her office where she manages the Sports Club Program of thirty-one student organizations. Kit bikes in all kinds of weather to the Husky Union Building where she manages the bowling, video games, table-tennis and pool tables in the Husky games area.

Kit first rented a houseboat as a graduate student in the late 1970s. After her first Seattle summer, Kit gave up her job and sold her house in New Jersey to head back to Seattle. She had met Sandy previously and the two of them looked for a home to share. They found a charming house in their price range on Camano Island, about sixty miles north of Seattle, where Sandy had grown up. Reflecting her Scandinavian heritage, Sandy had opened an Uff Da Shoppe in nearby Stanwood. For the first year they commuted the hour and a half drive each way to and from Seattle.

"It was a nightmare," declares Sandy, "so we ended up renting a very sparse studio in the Ravenna district, only five minutes from work. Then I found an end moorage houseboat on Fairview's Phoenix Dock available for a few weeks during the summer. After my first day on the lake I knew this was my forever life style. I told Kit I was going to find a houseboat to rent year around. I started walking along all the neighboring docks on Fairview and talking to anyone I ran into about houseboats."

One day, Sandy struck up a conversation with a man getting his mail at the Wandesforde Dock mailboxes. When she mentioned she was looking for a rental, he replied, "We have a situation on our dock. That new houseboat down there, the two-story one, some people in Olympia might be willing to rent it out, but it's kind of a crazy thing. They want to rent it only during the work week so they can use it on week-ends, but they'll never find that."

Sandy immediately declared, "I'm the person, that's me; that's just what we want—to be in Seattle during the week and then go to our home on Camano for the weekends."

Sandy quickly wrote a four page letter to the owners, Ed and Karen Hayes, and weeks later Ed called to invite Sandy and Kit to meet them.

The foursome gathered on the top deck of Ed and Karen's new houseboat. As an accountant Ed had drawn up a very through four page contract. They had signed almost every page, and all four were excited the unusual situation was going to work. But then, on the very last page, there it was: no pets.

"Oh my gosh," said Sandy, "we have a blind cat and a little dog."

Karen said, "No, it won't work, we have a little dog, Patches, and it's his house, I can't do that to him." She had tears in her eyes as she added, "Besides, I'm allergic to cats."

Sandy arranged for her folks to take care of the blind cat and after several weeks called Ed again.

"Ed," she said, "my folks will take our cat. So what could our dog Yule do, except maybe piddle on the carpet. Okay, we'll pay for the carpet up front, and if necessary we'll replace it."

Ed answered, "Well, I don't know, let me talk to my room mate."

Sandy got a call from Ed the next day suggesting she and Kit bring Yule to Olympia so he and Karen could meet their dog. Several days later, Sandy and Kit picked up their elegantly groomed and be-ribboned pooch from the local pet beauty salon late in the afternoon and drove to Olympia to introduce Yule to Ed and Karen.

Ed opened the door with, "Oh, is this Yule? Come on in, let's have a drink." Kit remembers that Yule and Patches sniffed each other, pranced around in circles, and then lay down almost side by side. It was an instant friendship.

Sandy continues, "We spent all that night looking at Ed and Karen's pictures of their new home. Their first houseboat had been built on an old oyster barge that sank during a heavy snow. They hired Tom Susor (the same Tom who's building an airplane in his house) to build a log float and built a new house from the water up. Their new houseboat was built on the ship canal and then towed across the lake to their moorage site on Wandesforde."

Kit adds, "We didn't discuss dogs at all!"

Sandy continues, "Ed and Karen's neighbors thought our arrangement would never work, but it just couldn't have been better. When we moved in the following Sunday evening Kit headed upstairs with her clothes and I hung mine in the downstairs closet. That was all we had to do; they provided the sheets, the towels, the dishes, everything."

When Sandy and Kit left for Camano on Friday, Yule left a thank-you note to Patches. When they returned on Monday Yule found a new food bowl from Patches.

They lived on Wandesforde during the work-week for almost

three years, then one day a dock neighbor told Sandy about a houseboat for sale on Portage Bay. It was advertised for $90,000.

"I knew," says Sandy, "at that price it was only the house, not the water, and we'd also have a monthly moorage fee to pay. I knew we should go look."

They motored over to Portage Bay in Sandy's dinghy, found the house, and pulled up just as the realtor was opening the door. It was on the same dock where Kit had lived when she was in graduate school. They knew the house as "Ernie's place." Although Ernie's had once been a machine shop, Sandy found the two most important rooms, the kitchen and bathroom, both up-graded and complete.

"We realized if we were ever going to own a houseboat we'd better make an offer on this one;" says Sandy, "the price was right."

Kit continues, "It was amazing; after we moved in we discovered there were four people on the dock who I had known when I first lived here. I feel like I've come home."

Sandy had mixed emotions about the move. "I was happy at Ed and Karen's, and I didn't need a houseboat anymore, because I had one during the work week. When the time came to move, I put my clothes in my dinghy and headed for our new *Fleetenhus,* Danish for floating home. I was crying all the way."

At a farewell dinner Sandy and Kit gave Ed and Karen a key to the *Fleetenhus,* so even if they rented their houseboat for the entire week, Ed and Karen would always have a place to stay in the houseboat community.

Sandy concludes, "I found new tenants for their houseboat, but they rent it full-time now. They knew they couldn't find anyone like us."

HOUSEBOAT TREASURES

John and Shelley Herron clearly prefer houseboats. Wherever their careers take them, if it's anywhere near the water, they find a houseboat home, as in Almeda and Sausalito, California and eventually in Seattle.

The shore side of their single story white houseboat trimmed in light blue faces a lush green bank, thanks to Shelley's persistent weeding and planting. Several boats, tended by John, languish in the calm water between their house and the shore. A shiny baby blue structure resembling a small dog house, but labeled "Duck Lodge," floats in the quiet lagoon. Every year at least one duck faithfully nests inside until her eggs hatch. Shelly says, "A friend in California built it for me as a farewell gift when we moved to Seattle. Originally the house had only one door, but I felt the ducks might feel a bit trapped inside, so I added a rear door. I think they're more comfortable now."

A large palm tree on the corner of their deck, another remnant from their time in the Golden State, has somehow survived eleven years in Seattle. Abundant honeysuckle spreads over a trellis and flowers spilling out of window boxes and hanging baskets soften the lines of their house.

John and Shelley were each drawn to houseboats before they even met. John grew up in West Seattle where his High School class made the national news with their Senior Prank.

They filled the West Seattle High School courtyard with tires collected during their final year. Ever the prankster, John boasts about his military duty, "After two years in the Navy guarding the shores of Hawaii, I'm proud to report not a single grain of sand was reported missing."

After his rough tour of duty in Hawaii, John returned to Seattle and found a small houseboat at Lee's Moorings on the north shore of Lake Union. He asked his widowed mother, who had recently remarried, for help so he could buy it, but she would have nothing to do with a houseboat.

About the same time Shelly, who had grown up in Bellevue's Lake Hills area, rented a houseboat on Tenas Chuck moorage on the east side of the lake. When the owners decided to sell, Shelly requested help with the financing from her family, but they also turned her down.

In the early '70s, John's best friend, Chuck Quinn, needed help rescuing his new contemporary floating home at the foot of Hamlin Street. Chuck had moved in earlier and finished most of the interior himself. He had just bought the stove, refrigerator, washer and dryer. His architect, Jim Jessup, used Styrofoam logs for flotation so the tall two-story contemporary houseboat had a rather high center of gravity. Knowing he would need additional flotation to balance the placement of the new appliances, Chuck had grouped them all in the center of his house. Then he left for a December business trip to Spokane.

Back in Seattle it snowed and snowed. Chuck's house has a very steep roof on the dock side, and a larger gradually sloping roof on the west side facing the lake The weight of the snow on the larger west side caused the houseboat to tip just enough the tilting appliances slid down the incline. Their added weight caused the house to tip even more, a few Styrofoam logs began shooting out of the opposite side, the house tipped further, more

logs popped out, and the house ended up partially submerged floating on its side.

"It was about a full week's endeavor to raise the houseboat and right it," says John. "You can't just get a crane and lift it up. Chuck hired George Johnston who used his "foam float" to replace the Styrofoam logs. The float had what looked like a giant waffle iron in the open center. He'd place a Styrofoam log in the waffle iron, which had enough added weight a diver could maneuver the Styrofoam under water, and then lower the contraption into the lake. My job as Pull Two on the dock side was to pull the waffle iron containing the log toward the house. Next the diver would decide where to put it, release the lever, the log would pop out, and he'd place the Styrofoam log under the house. Pull One would then pull the waffle iron back to the float for the next log. We did this over and over to gradually bring the house up, one log at a time. We worked slowly, because we had to let the water drain out of the house and add the logs gradually so the house didn't snap in two. A neighbor on the dock often came out to offer me coffee. My hands were so cold I'd pour half of the hot coffee on my gloves to warm my hands and then drink the rest. I endeared myself to Chuck forever just by showing up."

The two wanna-be houseboat owners met when John was hired as manager of the Golden Tides restaurant. As Shelley describes it, "I trained him to be a waiter and two months later he was my manager. We worked well together; within six months we were engaged."

John and Shelley ended up playing Cupid for each of their best friends. When Chuck opened his new restaurant, Charlie's on Broadway, they invited Shelley's best friend, Leanne Gallanar, to join them for the opening night. Leanne and Chuck fell in love and married. As John puts it, "Here they are, our best friends, living on their new houseboat while Shelly and I are still living in our stupid little home in Ballard. At least Chuck let me moor my Cat boat at his place, so we spent a lot of time with them on the lake."

John and Shelley's dream of living in a houseboat finally came true when he was transferred back to Seattle from southern California. When they returned to Seattle, John discovered a houseboat he had looked at previously was back on the market. Shelley relates, "I really didn't want to leave the warmth of California, and here we were huddling in the December cold waiting for the real estate agent. Fortunately for us the sellers were desperate. In mid-December the market was very slow, and we were able to buy at a good price and quickly close the sale. Even though we bought a well built house, we began various little projects, and of course they multiplied."

John adds, "When we moved the hot water tank we found a leak behind it. The previous owners didn't even know about it because the water went right through the floor and into the lake. Our original idea of moving the hot water tank turned into a major remodel of the kitchen floor. Our first year on the dock Art Holder, the stringer man, was practically our room mate; we had so much work for him."

Their spacious house on a 1600 square-foot float includes an office that was once added as a nursery for a baby, the renovated kitchen, and a living room, bedroom and bath filled with an eclectic assortment of treasures. The creative Shelley has salvaged a neighbor's windows and hung several as room dividers, mounted an antique spice cabinet where she stores buttons on the living room wall, and acquired various treasures from the Nordstrom Gift Department where she works. The original living room floor was laid parallel to two adjacent walls and dove tails from the corner toward the center. The wood on the interior walls runs horizontally on one wall and vertically on the opposite one. "And all the water faucet knobs are reversed," says Shelley. "Fortunately, it didn't take us long to realize that hot meant cold and vice versa."

A handsome brass clock framed by a moving Captain's wheel hung on the wall adds a nautical nuance to their living room. The nautical theme is repeated in their bathroom where the seats of a vertically hung tiny dory double as shelf space. Fish at the ends of the curtain rod, a mirror with a mermaid handle, a frog candle, and a mirror standing on duck feet decorate the small room.

If you spend an afternoon at the Herron's you understand why Shelley describes many of their treasures as gifts from various friends. A former employee of John's drops by to describe her new house, another couple launch their canoe from the back deck, a neighbor pops in to announce an informal concert by his European guest, and another friend wanders onto the deck to commiserate with Shelley about her recent bee sting.

A recent playful column titled "Urban Legends" in the local

Eastlake News posed the question as to whether anyone has ever seen a mermaid in Lake Union. Most replies were in the negative, so Shelley plans to report the mermaid she and John found lounging in their water garden when they returned from a trip to California. The elaborate four-foot long reclining statue was bequeathed to them by the son of its original owner, Merlin Proctor, shortly after she died. Her son apparently felt the Herron's garden was the perfect place for the cherished statue which his sister, Valerie, had made for their mother.

The ceramic mermaid, posed on her right side, has corkscrew curls tumbling down over both sides of her shoulders, black eyebrows resembling twisted macaroni, intense blue eye shadow above the bright blue eyes and a large, rather defiant, nose. She seems to look right at you, as if to say, "And who are you?"

"She doesn't say that to me," insists Shelley. "She knows who I am."

The mermaid's lips are the ultimate dark yet bright red, and her bosoms far more copious and anatomically correct than those of a Barbie Doll. Her arms and upper torso are meticulously covered with what must be hundreds of hand-made fluorescent dark blue and green scales about the size of a dime. Below the baby soft watery blue hips her two legs merge into a tail with a playful twist. Shelly has moved the mermaid onto their deck under the sheltering eaves until she can repair the broken right arm and restore the grand gal's original splendor.

Several summers ago John and his friend Mark, "slightly under the influence of Mt. Rainier," as John puts it, were enjoying a casual sail on the lake. John and Shelly's dog, Sumatra, (so named when as a puppy she smelled like coffee) clearly indicated she needed a pit stop. John decided to dock temporarily at the Center for Wooden Boats with its grassy shore land. Once Sumatra's needs had been met John spied a classic dory at the Center priced at $300. Although the boat obviously needed a fresh coat of paint or two, John and Shelly had been looking for a long, narrow boat for several years.

John explains, "We used to be able to get our sixteen-foot ski boat through the channel between our side of the dock and the houseboats on the dock to the south, but with the prevailing southern winds, especially during the winter, the end pilings of that dock are now in a trough. Consequently the length between our two docks keeps shrinking. We're in a constant state of change down here, and sometimes that dock has moved up to six feet in the wind. So I'd been looking for a narrower little boat small enough I could moor it at our house and still get through the channel to go fishing, especially when the Sockeye salmon are running in Lake Washington."

John offered the Center $100 and the Center countered with a $200. "I decided why not? I yanked out my credit card, offered $150, and it was ours. I paid for it on the spot, hitched it to a tow line and took off. I called Shelley from my cell phone, "Sweetheart, I bought a boat and it's following me home. It doesn't eat much; can we keep it?"

Once the Herrons began working on the sixteen-foot Cape Cod dory they found a few problems. The boat took on water, was very heavy to move in and out of the lake, and clearly needed more than "a few coats of paint."

"I love to paint," says Shelley, "but it was obvious this boat was going to take more work than we'd anticipated."

When John began sanding the old wood, he found a small identification plate with the name Elbert Honeycutt. Shelly looked in the phone book, found a listing for Elbert Honeycutt and called. His wife, Ione, answered the phone. Although her husband had died she kept the listing in his name and it was she who had donated the boat to the Center for Wooden Boats.

Connecting with Ione gave the boat a whole new life. It suddenly acquired a history and a personality. The Honeycutts had bought the dory when Ebert was a college student back East where he met Ione. She had family in Seattle where the newly-weds planned to move, so they had shipped it back to Ione's parents who lived on Maury Island, a short ferry ride from West Seattle.

John sanded the boat down to the bare cedar; Shelley painted the hull a gleaming white, the top with four coats of a bright turquoise blue, and the interior a bright yellow. She has mounted two decorative brightly varnished birch scrolls on either side as bow trim, John recreated the original splash barrier from mahogany which Shelley finished by first rubbing teak oil into the wood with steel wool and then applying four coats of varnish after sanding between each one.

Although it was never official, Ione Honeycutt told the Herrons their neighbors usually referred to the little boat as the African Queen, so Shelley has already bought the wooden letters for "African Queen" on one side and "Cape Cod, 1947" on the other.

"Now my dream has come true," says John. "With all the new paint, varnish, brass fixtures and decorative trim it's become a show piece. We're going to invite Ione down as soon as it's finished and next year for the first time we'll have an entry in the annual Wooden Boat Show at the Center."

A Kind Place

"I knew I needed to find a kind place to live," says another houseboater who prefers to remain anonymous. We'll call her Adele.

"I had to move out of my cozy cottage in the Ravenna neighborhood," she explains. "On top of that my car had been stolen and I'd just ended a relationship with a man I truly cared for. Having grown up on the Oregon Coast, it became crystal clear to me I needed the curative power of the water. I drove west along Portage Bay where I'd once looked at a refurbished barge near the University Bridge. After driving under the I-5 Freeway Bridge, I swung south along the water until I saw a small hand-lettered **Houseboat for Rent** sign on Fairview. I parked my car, walked down the steps to the dock, and located the bright yellow little clapboard house. I immediately loved its character."

Adele had found another cottage. The original 12 by 21 foot rectangular home with a peaked roof had become a T with the addition of a bathroom, kitchen and breakfast nook at the back. Her sleeping alcove doubles as a passage from the front living room to the kitchen and bath in the rear.

When Adele first saw the house, Art Holder, the stringer expert, had torn up the deck to replace decaying stringers. Between tenants the owner was painting the burlap walls of the living area an off-white, paneling the kitchen with wood from a ranch in eastern Washington, and had mounted two white pedestal columns on still unpainted six by six upright beams to support the corners of the front porch roof.

"The place was a total wreck, but it had such wonderful historical character. I was immediately charmed by the appearance of the entire dock, especially where it curves just beyond the wide area where we have all our potlucks. Each home had its own configuration and color. At first I questioned whether I could live in such a small space. I even wondered if my books would slide off the shelves when the house rocked, but then I viewed the small inside space as a great challenge."

Adele, a petite brunette with close cropped hair, thrives on challenges. She spent her junior year of college in France, has traveled through Europe, Asia, and Central America, worked in a plywood mill and as a Jobs Corps librarian, and earned Master's degrees in both history and architecture as well as a teaching credential. She worked as an architect in New York City before moving to Seattle, where she's currently involved in long-range planning.

"Because of my design background, I appreciated the design of the old house. It had a seven foot-high ceiling and double-hung windows on all sides that give it a sense of space and openness. And I realized I could create an additional outdoor room on the side deck accessible by the recycled single glass French door off the kitchen."

Inside, Adele has been careful to keep her 425 square-foot cottage sparsely furnished. In the living room, a large teak reading chair with a matching teak ottoman that doubles as a coffee table, two light rattan chairs, and a square pine-wood corner table opposite the corner wood-burning stove encircle a small hemp rug on the original fir floor. She designed her own futon bed which assembles and comes apart with military efficiency.

Betwixt and Between

Adele knew she had found a kind place. Shortly after she moved in two neighbors came to welcome her. "They told me how important they thought it was to have a strong sense of community. Here were these rather straight older women sitting in my house telling me something I've believed in all my life. They also shared all sorts of practical information: when the garbage is picked up, where to put various recyclables, and not to flush anything but human waste and toilet paper into our delicate sewer system."

Adele particularly appreciated a welcome packet that included a brief history and fact sheet about Lake Union and houseboats, a copy of the current Floating Homes Association newsletter, and a map of the two docks showing who lived in each house and their phone number. The map also included the phone number of the Seattle Police Harbor Patrol so she could call if a boater rocked her house by exceeding the seven knot speed limit.

As a renter, Adele particularly appreciated being included in the monthly home-owners' meetings, especially in the winter when folks tend to hibernate.

Adele recalls at one meeting a neighbor mentioned a cellist he knew who believed in playing the cello in unusual places so more people could hear its beauty. She'd played in laundromats, shopping centers and parking lots and had offered to play on our dock. Paige Stockley, a professional cellist, was in town visiting her parents. So the two of them, who had never played together, staged a *Bach on the Dock* concert. We each brought a chair and gathered at the wide place in the dock as the evening eased into a gorgeous moonlit night; it was exquisite.

"The same two women, who initially called on me, often come by to tell me they're going swimming, knowing that even if I've had a hard day at work I'll join them and feel energized as a result. If you live on a street, you just don't go and knock on someone's door and say, 'Let's all go play baseball.' That just doesn't happen. On the dock, it's different."

Another difference on the dock appeared about four years later when Adele realized there was a creature in her cozy cottage. She heard it skittering around at night, didn't want to kill it, and hoped one of the five resident dock cats would solve the problem for her. No such luck.

"One night I discovered droppings behind my cutting board, so I decided I'd had it with this creature. I marched over to Pete's where I found some poison, but Connie, one of the clerks, pointed out that if my mouse died hidden in my house, I'd have a terrible odor. So, I replaced the poison and came back to the cash register with a mouse trap and some cheese. Pat was the cashier that night and he pointed out that peanut butter works better than cheese. I found the smallest, cheapest jar of peanut butter they had, and while I was paying for it I asked Pat how to set the trap. He went into all these details, and I finally said, 'Look, I'm just too tired to deal with it now, would you please help me?' So Pat unscrewed the top of the peanut butter, put some on the trap, and set it for me. I gingerly walked home holding this trap, scared to death that it might snap on my fingers. I put it under the sink and sure enough, Pat and Connie's advice was right on target. The next morning I found the little mouse in the trap. Where else can you find a grocery store where they'll help you catch a mouse?

"What I like best about living here is that we each have our own space, our home, and everyone respects that privacy. We also have this wonderful public space, the dock. In the warm months, I spend a lot of time outside. I can sit on my front porch and visit with everyone who passes by. I can read on a neighbor's sunny back deck, sit at the end of the dock to view the ever-changing lake, or stop to absorb the beauty of another neighbor's extraordinary garden.

"Even in winter, when its cold, wet, and stormy outside, we'll often gather in each other's homes. One year, seven of us on the dock planned a trip to Greece, with the help of a neighbor who once led students from Western Washington University to Greece during spring quarter. We'd meet every Sunday evening in her small, brightly lit home, sip tea, and read Homer's *Iliad*."

Adele also remembers a warm summer night when a full moon prompted about twenty dock denizens to swim out beyond the end of the dock for a better view of the shimmering city lights. Some carried lighted candles and waved at passing boaters, who didn't realize most of the swimmers were without swim suits. After they climbed out of the lake and wrapped themselves in towels, the group gathered on the Stockley's deck, staying until almost midnight to savor the warmth of brandy, the moon-lit night, and their shared escapade.

HINE SIGHT

When Emily Hine decided in 1998 she wanted to purchase her first home, she made it clear to her realtor friends, Laurie and Jim Way, what her priorities were: 1. Real estate, 2. A view, and 3, peace and quiet. Now her former realtor and still friend teases Emily "I use you as an example of the classic real estate cliché: 'buyers are liars!'"

Emily went to an open house one Sunday and simply fell in love with a Westlake houseboat almost under the noisy Aurora Bridge. The old home didn't include any real estate, but the monthly moorage fee was under $250 per month. The only view from inside the house was the greenery on a wooded hillside below the railroad track that once serviced various industries on the lake. The house did have a large open deck upstairs with views of the ship canal, the Fremont Bridge, and Gasworks Park.

The original floats for her houseboat were built around 1918. In the 1940s, more of the downstairs area was enclosed and in the 1970s the owner added the upstairs. "What I find interesting in the history of this house is that the earliest owners did everything improperly because for them it was only temporary housing. Now, because it's rare and it's a houseboat, great and romantic stories were created to justify why things are as they are."

For example, Emily was concerned about a major hump in the kitchen and den floor when she was inspecting the house and deciding whether to buy it. She was told that the hump was there because that room was used as a sleeping porch in the early days and the floor was slumped intentionally so that the water would run off when it rained. To a new, potential houseboat owner, that was just the romantic story she needed to overlook a deep flaw in the kitchen floor. Years later, when she remodeled, that "sleeping porch" turned out to be a poorly cut joist that was wreaking havoc on the entire first floor.

Five years into houseboat living, Emily laughs, "I should have figured it out after I spent two days on a ladder scrubbing the ceiling upstairs because owners in the 70s didn't even put in a chimney for their wood burning stove! They didn't take care of the place; not only was there no chimney for the wood stove, the insulation in the walls was old newspaper and the entire second floor was supported by nothing but a few two-by-fours!!! Sleeping porch, my ass!"

Emily celebrated her first Fourth of July on the Lake by inviting all of the friends who helped her move into her new houseboat. She put the keg of beer on her back porch near the French doors that open into the living, dining, and kitchen area. As the day wore on, her friend Perry commented "I didn't realize your float was so close to the water line before." This was news to Emily, and on inspection she soon discovered that the weight of all her guests enjoying the kitchen and the keg was nearly submerging the back end of her house. Emily instantly directed the keg carried upstairs to the deck on the opposite front end of the house; then both the party and the house evened out in response! Emily still has parties from time to time and if she spies a land-loving guest who looks unsettled when the houseboat leans a little, she simply prepares another cocktail for them and instructs them to move to the high side of the house.

"The temporary leaning doesn't bother me nearly as much as the more permanent leaning that occurs. When I first moved in, I was advised to situate my furniture and then hire someone to properly balance the houseboat. It always leaned a little to the port side." She hired a diver who came out, put a few new barrels in place, and then asked Emily how it felt. She inquired, "What do you mean, how does it feel? Don't you have a level or something you can use to measure that kind of thing?" He told her that normal tools and rules like that don't apply to houseboats. Emily wanted a more scientific approach to this houseboat balancing endeavor, so she found a marble and placed it in several different locations on the hardwood floor. Next Emily noted which direction the marble rolled and relayed the information to the diver. He then placed barrels accordingly until the marble stopped rolling and Emily was happy.

She feels lucky that she had the opportunity to buy on the water in her early thirties when houseboats were still close to the same price as the land-based houses and condos she was considering. Like many who live in houseboats, she has a diverse set of interests and a career that reflects her desire for strong community. Emily majored in communications at Western Washington University, and then began as a fund-raiser at United Way working with corporations to establish giving and volunteer programs. Years later, she took a sabbatical from the "real world," got her commercial drivers license and drove up the Al-Can highway to Alaska. She drove a tour bus during the long summer days. After touring Europe as well, she returned to Seattle and was recruited to run the employee giving and volunteer program at Microsoft. In her tenure at Microsoft, she helped raise over $70 million for non-profit organizations across the United States. Today, Emily runs her own consulting firm, HineSight Consulting, and helps non-profit organizations across the United States with fundraising, public relations and marketing.

Her love for building strong communities doesn't stop with her career. Emily has been on the Board of the Floating Homes Association for three years where she's made a noticeable impact in the Floating Homes community. "I realize what we have here is very special and unique and we all have a responsibility to maintain the community and the lifestyle that we love." She introduced PowerPoint presentations to the Floating Homes Association Annual Meeting – a huge relief to the new, high tech members of the community and an awesome novelty to some of the technologically challenged in the audience.

Part of the motivation for Emily's intense interest in preserving the floating home lifestyle is her encounter with the risk of losing her houseboat. In late 2000 dock owners Mark and Margie Freeman notified their tenants that their moorage fee would be more than quadrupled due to the increased value of Lake Union property. "For many of us, that meant our moorage rental would be more than our mortgage payments," remembers Emily. "It was a real blow. We could understand the increased value, and many of us were willing to pool together and purchase our two docks, but the docks had been part of the Freeman family for decades and they didn't want to sell.

"Sadly, we had to hire a lawyer to argue our case, which involved protecting our rights under the houseboat Equity Ordinance. A Hearing Examiner allowed the Freemans to raise our rent a little, but nothing like what they had originally proposed. Finally, after nearly a year, we were able to negotiate buying the moorage from them. It was quite a process: forming a legal entity to buy our dock, deciding the value of each of our sites as a percentage of the whole, drafting by-laws and the terms and conditions of the sale. That kind of process can make or break a dock. We were fortunate in that we all stayed involved in the process and did our best to negotiate with each other fairly."

There are twelve houseboats in her new Westlake Cove Co-op. They are still learning how to manage the place together; luckily the Freemans still live on the dock to help guide the new co-op. "The process was definitely not an easy one, but I feel like we have a stronger community because of the experience. We all value our lifestyle even more after experiencing the real risk of losing our floating homes."

Today, after five years and one remodel, Emily has truly made her house a home. She converted the upstairs living area into her bedroom so she could wake up to the view of the canal; she created an office space in the former downstairs bedroom and she combined the den and former apartment-sized cooking area into a large well-equipped kitchen and seating area. Emily has a beautiful new Australian Cypress wood floor minus one bad joist! She installed stainless steel appliances and had custom cherry cabinets built to utilize the space under her stairs. She also built in a large granite countertop that doubles as a table for the living/dining area. She put in a gas stove downstairs that heats the entire house and left the wood-burning stove in her upstairs bedroom.

Her compact home office centers on a Nautical Architect's desk that she found at the Fremont Outdoor Market. Her computer and anything else on the desk, all less than four inches high, disappear from view the minute she checks out and closes the attached hinged cover over the work area. "They told me it was a Nautical Architects Desk when I was considering purchasing it; that was before I told them I lived on a houseboat.

So either they were telling the truth, or they thought I'd just rolled off my sleeping porch!"

One of Emily's favorite stories about her houseboat also occurred during the remodel. She recalls coming home late one night from work to discover that her contractor had ripped out half the floor downstairs and all she could see was water and logs where her kitchen floor had once been. She was living in her house at the time of the remodel so just took it all in stride with the rest of the chaos of a remodel. Later that night, camping out upstairs and responding to her email, she heard a splash coming from downstairs INSIDE the house. "That's just wrong," she thought. As she went to explore, she found an old abandoned beaver's nest under her kitchen floor between the currently exposed logs! Like many of us, Emily finally realized that it's all just part of the process of living in a houseboat. You take the tall tales and inexplicable events with a grain of salt and you realize, if you have to share your "basement" with a critter from time to time, so be it. You still have one amazing lifestyle and you'll never be short of stories.

A Touch of Europe

One of the non-skid strips on the short, still temporary gang plank from the dock to the house has come partially unglued. However, once you're on board Heinz Strobl's floating home, everything to the last detail is immaculately maintained and in ship-shape condition.

Heinz' home truly looks like those you see in magazines: no newspapers lying around, no jackets hung over a chair, no glasses left in the sink, no opened mail piled on a table, zero miscellaneous clutter on the kitchen counter, not even any shoes left scattered on the floor. Actually, as one of the newest and grandest houseboats on Lake Union, Heinz' home has been followed on a web-site, appeared in several newspapers and magazines, and will be in an upcoming coffee table book. "Not to mention," adds Heinz, "local TV, King 5, videotaped the house and Josephine Chang interviewed me for a Houseboat special on their home show program."

Although he grew up in land-locked Austria, once Heinz moved to Seattle he succumbed to the lure of the water.

"I lived on Capitol Hill," he explains, "and I like being so close to downtown. I knew I wanted to stay on this side of Lake Washington, but I'm a night person. If I bought waterfront on Lake Washington, I'd be on the west side of the lake. I know myself well enough to realize I'd seldom see the sun if I lived on the west side." So the affable Heinz began checking out house-boats. He finally found a large rather non-descript beige-gray home right next to a steep green bank below Fairview Avenue on the east side of Lake Union.

"I bought it with plans to add a second story," relates Heinz, "but soon learned that the water was too shallow to accommo-date the added flotation needed to support a second story addi-tion. I considered the possibility of dredging the site, but my future neighbors were worried the dredging might weaken the steep bank at the edge of the water. I certainly didn't want to be the cause of the street above crashing down on our dock."

Heinz had seen a site near Lynn Street being dredged to support a larger home and queried the couple who owned it. They recommended houseboat denizen and architect Gene Morris. "He came over and showed me his portfolio," says Heinz. "When I saw he'd designed a home which I'd looked at on the west side and was almost tempted to buy, I knew Gene was the right person. Once the plans were finished, we couldn't find a local contractor who was interested in building a cement float that included a basement. Most declined to even submit bids, and those who did priced them so outlandishly high that it was pretty clear they didn't want to have anything to do with it."

Eventually Gene remembered that a number of years earli-er, International Marine Floatation Systems, of Delta, British Columbia, Canada had developed a houseboat community in the Fraser River delta. The Company had actually designed a houseboat for somebody in Seattle. "Initially IMF was just as reluctant as the rest to take on the project, because it was a complete deviation from their tried and true (and unsinkable) proprietary float system, but they eventually did accept the job. Originally, they were to build the float, which would be towed down here so the house could be completed on site. It soon became clear that it would be infinitely easier and also more economical to build the whole house on dry land. All the standard tools and methods of the trade (think plumbs and levels…) would function accurately and they could use machinery too heavy for water. It just grew from there, and IMF built the entire house to almost turn-key." Construction began in 1998 when the difference in the value of the Canadian and U.S. dollar also made economic sense.

"I was slaving away at Microsoft during all this," explains Heinz. "and I had to travel up to Delta, about twenty-five minutes south of Vancouver, fairly often, but at least once I managed to include some skiing at Whistler."

Another slight complication was the looming question of what to do with the houseboat he'd already bought. His realtor suggested Seattle's famous maritime museum, the Center for Wooden Boats. Fortunately, the Center had moorage available, needed additional office space, and was happy to accommodate the vintage houseboat among their classic wooden boats.

During the roughly three year waiting for his new digs, the Microsoft slave opted for retirement in his early 40s during the summer of 1999. Almost two years later, his future home was towed out of Delta for the trip south into Puget Sound and Lake Union. The ocean going tug, and his house, encountered a weather delay near LaConner, Washington, about seventy miles north of Seattle, but finally his home arrived at Shilshole Marina on Puget Sound where it tied up for the night before its trip through the locks and into Lake Union.

"I wanted to ride in on it," says Heinz, "but I still remember the pain of knowing I'd have to get up at 5:30 in the morning **and** how hard it was for me to actually get up that early! But I jumped on my new house at 6 am and rode it through the locks and the ship canal to temporary moorage at City Boat on Northlake."

Moving day was scheduled for May 31, almost thirty days after its arrival in Lake Union. Sid McFarland and his crew began modifying phone, cable, telephone and water lines for quick disconnection on the seven houses that would have to be moved to create access for his new home. Sid obtained all the necessary permits from the City, notified Seattle Police Harbor Patrol, co-coordinated with City Light to handle the wiring connections, notified the Center for Wooden Boats to expect delivery of their new office space, and scheduled the two small tugs from City Boat that would do the heavy work. Heinz obtained "Perils of the Sea" insurance for all those who wanted it and confirmed the date with his across the dock houseboat neighbors who had agreed to let the six houses that had to be moved tie up to the back of their homes where open water made that possible.

On the day of the move the two tugs arrived at about 8:30 in the morning, one of them with Heinz' new house in tow. It was tied up to a boom log south of the dock and the tugs began moving the houseboats blocking the channel and tying them to the houses on the south side of the dock. At lunch time Heinz took orders for sandwiches from near-by Pete's Supermarket for everyone involved in the move including his dock neighbors temporarily without a kitchen.

Finally the tugs could tow out Heinz' old houseboat, which they moored on the same boom log where his new one had been temporarily tethered. Then, beginning with Heinz' Canadian version of a houseboat, they began moving everyone back into their moorage sites.

By the time the end houseboat, that of Charlotte McMillan with all the sculptures on her front deck, was safely anchored and reconnected to utilities, it was well after eight in the evening. Heinz ordered pizza for everyone's dinner to celebrate a successful move and the final arrival of his new houseboat.

Once his home was duly moored, the heat exchanger dropped in the lake, and all the utilities connected, previously slightly skeptical neighbors, most of whom cherish the low profile of their homes, were pleasantly surprised. The lines of Heinz' house replicate the old-fashioned sprung roofs, the cedar shake siding blends in well with the dock community and it floats lower than the previous home which exceeded the current allowable height limit.

Beyond the gangplank, in the covered area by the front door, a prominent glow-in-the-dark large round almost gem-like deep blue button serves as the doorbell. The typical houseboat Dutch door opens to an entry hall tiled with material resembling slate in shades of golden brown and green and every color in-between. Straight ahead a small open closet comfortably accommodates what appears to be eight to ten practically identical dark colored jackets.

"I know closets here normally have doors," comments Heinz, "but in most of Europe this is far more typical."

The amiable Heinz will also add that you don't need to take off your shoes, although one look at the highly polished tile floor of the vaulted common room to the left and most guests voluntarily do so.

The kitchen, which borders the dock, includes a tall stainless steel refrigerator/freezer, dishwasher, and six burner stove with oven. "The oven is electric, but the stove is gas," explains Heinz. "Since our dock doesn't have natural gas, I have to lug in propane tanks. But it's not that bad, I usually go through only one every two months or so."

A gold-speckled dark green granite counter separates the kitchen form the living/dining room. On the floor, just below the counter's end, a small stainless steel bowl in a black rubber ring almost looks like a connection to something under the floor, but the ring anchors a water bowl for Heinz' two cats, siblings he adopted from Meow, a local animal shelter. "Nala, the female, is quite affectionate and sociable, but Tigger, her brother, is a real wuss," says Heinz. "They are both quite affectionate in their own ways, but while Nala is fearless and intensely curious, Tigger usually needs a bit of time with strangers. It amazes me that two cats from the same family could be so different."

Opposite the kitchen between the channel wall and his couch, Heinz accommodates his feline friends with a small fluffy fur-like bed, which the two of them share, and a scratching post.

"You might call the scratching post enlightened self-interest," acknowledges Heinz, "It's far better they do their scratching on the post than any other place."

On the channel side of the main room an oval folding table with a black lacquer finish has four chairs made of tan leather over a frame of chrome-plated steel pipe. A cherry chest with a black granite top framed in cherry serves as a contemporary version of a buffet.

"Even though it's surprisingly rather hefty, the table is easy enough to pick up and carry outside to the deck if the weather warrants it, and you can see there's space for it," comments Heinz.

He also points out that the windows open two ways; if you pull the handle up, they open at the top to provide ventilation, whereas if you push the handle down, they swing open horizontally from the side. Gene, his architect, was able to connect Heinz with a German craftsman in the south end of Seattle who made the windows which add another touch of what is typical in Europe.

Towards shore, an exceptionally tidy office includes an almost full floor to ceiling bookshelf. A coffee-table quality book with a German title and a copy of the sixteenth century Flemish painter Pieter Bruegal the Elder's depiction of "The Tower of Babel" lies on his desk. "I find it very fascinating," remarks Heinz. "It's about the origin and diversity of language and writing which has always intrigued me. I bought this massive thing, it has four volumes, even though it's very heavy, when I was visiting family back home in Graz, Austria. My home town was chosen cultural capital of Europe for this year and the book is a catalogue to one of the major exhibitions."

His washer and drier are tucked away in a closet near a spacious bathroom with a deep tub, double sink, and separate area for the toilet. The white tiles include a border of unusual somewhat southwest Indian or African motifs that Heinz found in a tile shop in Bellevue. The master bedroom enjoys a view across the channel of a neighboring houseboat with remnants of old Indian designs painted on the isosceles triangle of siding below the slightly peaked roof. "When the previous owner did a major remodel before he sold his house, he left that art as a memento of its previous life; I enjoy it," says Heinz.

The upstairs includes generous deck space, with a small covered portion, and a formal living room looking out over the vaulted common room below. The ceiling dramatically shows the metal slightly purplish red beams supporting the classic sprung roof. Combine a wet sink with the liquor cabinet above it, a first class sound system, a TV with a thirty-six inch screen, and a superbly comfortable couch and chair with a striking night time view of downtown Seattle, and the mix may explain some of Heinz' nocturnal habits. The second story also contains a bathroom and small guest bedroom with a serene view of the green growth on the adjacent bank and the same spectacular views of downtown as the adjacent living room.

Perhaps the most interesting aspect of Heinz' house is the

basement built into the float, where the plywood floor clearly indicates the area awaits its finishing touches. The round underwater window with a view of the bank is believed to be the first of its kind in a Lake Union Houseboat. "The logs of my neighbor's house that you see through the window appear much closer than they actually are," Heinz points out. "The window is made of Plexiglas which is more susceptible to scratching than glass, but it doesn't weep. You can see a little hole in the float at the bottom of the window left over from the original plan to use glass; the hole was for draining the condensation."

The basement level also includes a climate-controlled wine cellar with space for roughly four hundred bottles. "Let's say I like wine," says Heinz, "and it's nice to have some handy." Heinz' comment rates as a candidate for understatement of the year; his extensive collection of "Wine Spectator" magazines and books about wine would rival those of internationally known wine expert, houseboater Tom Stockley.

On the opposite side of the wine cellar a mechanical room includes a heat pump that extracts heat from the heat exchanger in the water for his radiant floor heating. Drain pipes in the room indicate this room also serves the same purpose as the bilge of a boat. While no one expects the float to leak, there's always the possibility of a burst pipe or leaky hot water heater.

"I was here when the earthquake near Fairbanks, Alaska caused big waves in Lake Union," says Heinz. "My house rocked as if it wanted to be beached. I've heard since then some houseboats did get beached and had to wait until late spring for the lake level to rise sufficiently to wash them off the land.

"Although no one on land felt the quake, on the lake it was very impressive and kind of scary. I don't think another quake would break my float," says Heinz.

In the meantime, earthquake or not, the young retiree intends to thoroughly enjoy his unique floating home, leaving it only for travels, skiing, and kayaking. Maybe he'll even have time to finish reading the massive "Tower of Babel" volumes he brought home from his most recent trip.

CAROLINE'S HOME

Former Bellevue resident Caroline Kuknyo had grown increasingly irritated by her daily treks across the I-90 floating bridge to ply her trade as a vitamin and herbs sales representative to alternative medicine practitioners. So shortly after her son moved out she began looking for a place in the city.

An ad in the *Seattle Weekly* for a rental houseboat piqued her curiosity, especially when the owner pulled up on a motorcycle to show her the house.

Caroline recalls, "After about twenty minutes or so I felt an intense feeling of peace, so I decided to rent it. Not long after I moved in, a home on the neighboring dock came up for sale. I wanted to buy it, but the house was on a leased moorage so the bank required a twenty-five per cent down payment. I simply didn't have that much cash."

She started looking at land houses again, found one in Fremont, and made an offer on it. "I went home with an uneasy feeling," she remembers "and that night I woke up crying. I felt like I'd been banished from the lake. The next morning I called the realtor to explain why I couldn't go through with my offer."

Caroline finally found a jerry-built floating home on an old oyster barge referred to as Fort Apache for its peculiar design. Locals joked that whoever built it must have smoked a lot of grass.

Because Ft. Apache was located on a co-op dock where she

would own her moorage space, the bank agreed to finance the houseboat. Caroline laughs now, "I figured for a mere $35,000 I could make it livable, but soon after I moved in I discovered my new house was a living petri dish. Whenever it rained the ladder to the second floor turned into a waterfall. After two months I realized this moldy study in random ugliness had to be torn down.

"It was the year from Hell. I hired Jim Jessup, an experienced houseboat architect, found a place to house-sit, and frantically borrowed money from a variety of sources as my 'mere $35,000' ballooned to over $80,000."

Caroline's son came up from his home in Arizona and installed all of the wiring for her, several friends pitched in with carpentry help, and Caroline herself laid the tile kitchen floor.

"Having grown up in the housing projects of Chicago, I had a real fear of moving back into an unfinished house," she explains. "I have a hard time with chaos, so it was almost six months before I moved back in."

Completed in 1990, the three skylights, open floor plan, lace curtains, taupe carpet, and soft colors of Caroline's 800 square-foot home whisper serenity and peace. Her master suite fills a loft at the back of the house above her small office space and well-appointed kitchen.

Although Caroline was thrilled with her home once she moved back in, she soon learned that the dock's by-laws allowed extensive remodeling. Within four to five years many of the once low profile homes expanded into boxy two-story edifices. Much of the light, views and spaciousness had been lost. She found herself moored close to shore in a canyon with her back-door neighbor, who planned a second story addition, only five feet across the channel. "I loved my home," she declares, "if I could have moved it to a different moorage site I would, but I

An Upstairs Office

felt boxed in, I needed a different space." Once again Caroline began looking for a new home.

When she learned the owners of the leased moorage where she first rented a houseboat were selling, she found several homeowners who were planning to sell their homes rather than buy their moorage space. Excited at the prospect of moving back to her first dock community, Caroline somewhat reluctantly listed her home for sale.

She set the price high enough to enable her to purchase both a home and the moorage site on her former dock. She was stunned when her house sold within a matter of days to an eager buyer who wanted to move in within the month. On the plus side of the quick sale, it enabled her to buy a house next to the prime end-moorage site; she would be almost kitty-corner from her first rental houseboat.

But it was several months before Caroline could occupy her new home on her old dock. Her realtor found a houseboat listed for sale on the architect-designed moorage Portage-at-Bay that she could rent temporarily. Caroline reports, "It was a spacious, elegant home, but I didn't know anyone there, I missed the convenience of Pete's grocery, and there was very little activity on the dock. It all seemed so different from the Fairview neighhborhood I loved."

Finally Caroline moved into her own single-story classic houseboat. "And this is my last move," she insists, as she sips tea in her spacious wood-paneled living room with a view of Gas Works park and the Aurora Bridge. "It's good to be home. They will have to carry me out when I die in bed at 103."

Journalist to Professor

While Fendall Yerxa won't detail his career as a journalist, he'll readily describe how he obtained his first newspaper job.

In 1938, when the Great Depression still lingered on, resumes were rare and few companies could afford a Personnel or Human Resources Department. Fresh out of New York's Hamilton College with a basic Bachelor's degree, Fendall returned to his home town of Minneapolis.

"I took up residence on a daily basis in a big old leather chair in the lobby of my local newspaper. Finally one day the Managing Editor, Mr. Adams, spoke to me as he walked by."

"Are you still here? What are you doing sitting there day after day?" he asked.

"I'm looking for a job, Mr. Adams, and I'm going to get one."

"Well, what do you want?"

"Whatever you've got," answered Fendall.

His persistence paid off. Mr. Adams hired Fendall as a copy boy for the astronomical sum of $60 per month.

"I got along all right," says Fendall. "I brown-bagged my lunch almost every day and finally got promoted to the staff. I covered the police beat and various other assignments. I worked on a variety of papers in the Minneapolis area as one newspaper after another folded and was eventually absorbed by John Coles. We all became slaves of his empire, which included the *Des Moines Register* and the *Minneapolis Star Journal.*"

Fendall married and the first of five Yerxa children, Rusty, arrived when Europe was already involved in World War II. Fendall registered for the draft and was ranked as A-1, but his status as a married man and a father exempted him from military service. However, one day a draft notice arrived at the Yerxa house.

"So I went to my Draft Board in Hopkins, MN and respectfully informed them that as a married man with a child I was not subject to being called up.

"Well, Mr. Yerxa, we don't want to take exception to that, but some of us here do feel that you probably got married to avoid the draft."

"Well, I winced, there wasn't much I could say; that's what they believed. I finally realized I could demonstrate otherwise. I pulled out my wallet and handed them our engagement announcement from the society pages of the newspaper. 'Mr. and Mrs. John C. Hawkins announce the engagement of their daughter, Florence, to Fendall Yerxa . . .'

"Then I assured them they didn't have to worry about me. I was not a draft dodger, and if this war got serious I would join up. The next time I heard from my Draft Board I was in the middle of the campaign in Okinawa, one of the bloodiest battles in the Pacific. Their letter informed me they hadn't heard from me in a while and asked me to get in touch with them and tell them where I was.

"I'm damn lucky I'm still here," exclaims the tall and lanky white-haired Fendall. "I guess I learned how to keep my head down in Okinawa; I ate a lot of sand."

After Okinawa was secured, Fendall was flown to Guam where he waited two weeks for "the first available transportation" to Pearl Harbor on board the Long Island, a baby aircraft carrier that was once a freighter. After that trip, which took about thirty days, it was on to San Francisco.

"I'll never forget that day we arrived. There were banner headlines in the paper, "TWENTY THOUSAND TONS OF TNT," a quote from President Harry Truman. We had just dropped the first atomic bomb on Hiroshima.

"We were billeted in the ball room of the Sir Frances Drake Hotel in rows of single canvass cots with a footlocker at the end of each one. But we all had as good a time as you can when you're waiting to get home; there was a good bar on the main floor of the Sir Francis Drake."

Finally the soldiers got their orders, trains came along, and Fendall, along with thousands of other war-weary G.I.s, returned home to his wife and son.

Not long after returning home and resuming life as a civilian, Fendall accepted a job back East with what he describes as the best newspaper in the world, the New York *Herald Tribune.*

The family left Minnesota for New York where they spent much of their time on a farm purchased by his father-in-law after World War I. Fendall maintained a pad in the city as he often worked late at night on stories for the morning paper. He rose to Managing Editor of the *Tribune,* did a stint with the ABC Network, and served as Executive Editor of the major paper in Wilmington, Delaware.

"They wanted to change the name of the paper, the *Journal-Every Evening* and I wouldn't let them do it. I thought it was a great name for a paper."

Eventually the prestigious *New York Times* offered Fendall a position. Although Fendall was happy with his career, a call from Bill Shidell, a friend from his days at ABC, triggered a change of direction.

"One day Bill Shidell called me when I was working for the Times."

"What are you doing?" he asked.

"Nothing," I replied.

"I'm over here at the Statler Hotel, come on over and we'll have a drink."

So Fendall went on over to the Statler.

"I'm working for the University of Washington where we have a couple of openings in the Communications Department. We'd like to get some good working journalists; can you give me names of people at the Trib or the Times?"

Fendall gave Shidell a few names and forgot about it. Then about a year later he had the same call from Bill.

"What are you doing?"

"Nothing."

"I'm over here at the Statler Hotel, come on over and we'll have a drink."

"I went over and he told me he'd gone through the list of people I'd given him and he didn't want any of them.

"What are you looking for?" I asked.

"We want you."

"Me?"

"Yes, you."

"So we sat down and talked and sure enough that's what came to past. We decided to give Seattle a try. We caravanned from New York to Seattle in two cars in 1965. Our daughter Julie had a little red Triumph.

"We lived in Bellevue for a while then Florence and I went our separate ways and we each moved. I found an apartment on Queen Anne, which was convenient to my sail boat at Shilshole Marina. I didn't like Shilshole; I felt it was too paternalistic. So I found moorage for my boat here on the ship canal. One day I was walking down to take out my boat and I saw all the work going on at the houseboat at the beginning of the dock. The former tenant, who everyone called the Troll, had really trashed the old houseboat. Mike, the owner of the dock, had kicked out his messy tenant and was remodeling the house. He was putting up these French doors and this cedar cathedral ceiling, so I asked him what his plans were."

"I'm gonna rent it when I'm done, you want to rent it?"

"You betcha," I said, "and I've been here ever since.

"I found I really enjoyed teaching," says Fendall, "so I taught as long as I could, until 1984. We could work until we were seventy and we could continue through the academic year of that birthday. I managed to squeak in almost another whole year because I fell inside that window by three days. I wanted to teach in summer school, which I'd always done, but they wouldn't let me work that last summer."

Fendall is currently quite content in his roughly 20 by 40 foot houseboat with a bedroom across the back, living room in the middle, and a well furnished kitchen/dining area with the bathroom cut out along the side. He doesn't have a washer or dryer, so takes his laundry to his favorite Laundromat in Ballard.

His houseboat differs from the floating homes located on Lake Union which are all in residential zones where dock owners agreed to hook up to sewer. Fendall's houseboat is moored on a multi-use dock on the ship canal connecting Lake Union to Salmon Bay and the locks leading into Puget Sound.

"I'm on sewer," he adds, "although it doesn't always work as it should. Mike, my landlord, put in a pump and all of us here, boats, barges, and houses, are connected."

His house has baseboard heat in addition to a wood burning stove, which Fendall declares will heat the entire home. It's also handy if the electricity goes off.

A contemporary computer dominates the large desk by the dock wall opposite the sunny western window behind his large comfortable couch. "I only use the computer for word processing and email. I love being able to keep in contact with my far-flung kids, Rusty in Alaska, Rufus in Geneva, and John in Australia. It's great to be in touch with them."

Fendall also has a TV on one of three TV trays in the living room, "I get all over the world with my TV dish; I get a lot of stuff, including a lot I don't want."

On another TV tray an extensive sound and entertainment system includes a DVD player which one of his children installed for him.

"I like it here. I have my application in at University House, which is a very nice retirement place. My son Quentin set it up for me. They get in touch with me once in a while when they have an opening. I could go there right away, but it's for full assisted care, which means I would have to eat three meals a day there, and I don't want that. I eat out some, but I also cook a lot.

"So I tell them 'no thank you, I'll pass.' I've got my down payment there, so any time there's a limited care apartment I might consider it, but I might not.

I have a philosophy about that. I think you've got to force yourself to keep doing things for yourself, otherwise you lose the capability to do it. So I do a lot of things that I probably shouldn't, like carrying big loads of laundry in and out of here.

"I'm happy here. I'm left alone, which I want to be most of the time. My cat Sparky jumps out the window the minute anyone arrives, even my daughter Julie. I'm free to have people come down, which I enjoy doing. I'm quite contented."

"I get my paper every morning from an independent carrier, Li Qwon Quock. He gives me an envelope every once in a while, and tells me how much I owe him. Li Qwon Quock is a very enterprising Vietnamese refugee. He must start off about two o'clock in the morning when he picks up his papers He never fails me; the paper's on my porch every morning."

Maybe some day Li Qwon Quock will learn about Fendall's newspaper career.

WHY WOULD I GO ANYWHERE ELSE?

Ethel grew up in Zamboanga, a small town in the southern Philippines, where her father had fought during the Spanish American War. After the conflict ended, he began publishing a weekly newspaper featuring balanced reporting for both the local Catholic community and the many Muslim traders. Ethel helped with the editing aspects of the family newspaper until her father died when she was eighteen. At that point, her mother, four sisters and two brothers, and Ethel decided to sell the newspaper and move to Manila.

"In Manila I applied for a job with Della Rama, a large steam ship company," says Ethel. "The manager, Enrico, was a flamboyant Italian who had married the daughter of the Philippine owners. Enrico liked to manage by frequently writing various notes and memoranda to himself and others. 'I need someone who can read my handwriting,' he told me. Then he handed me a sample. 'Can you read this?'

"I was able to correctly read his somewhat distinctive English back to him. He hired me right then. It was one of the nicest jobs I ever had. He gave me my own secretary to do most of the typing; that made my job much easier."

Shortly before the bombing of Pearl Harbor, Ethel's husband, a young Navy Lieutenant, was assigned to a ship on the East Coast of the United States. When she said her final good-byes to Enrico, he told her to go to the Della Rama office in San Francisco where a gift would be waiting for her. True to Enrico's word, the San Francisco office handed the young couple a modest check but large enough to buy a small used car for their trip east.

"We were lucky," says Ethel, "at that time many people were fleeing the Philippines and there was a waiting list for space on ships heading to the United States. We were able to get passage only because of my husband's military orders. Once the United States declared war on Japan, all the rest of my family were sent to the Santo Tomas prison camp. The first year conditions were not too bad for them, but gradually the amount of food dwindled. My very resourceful brother John, who always related well to the locals, managed to buy peanuts which my mother made into peanut butter. Then John would sell or barter the peanut butter for other goods."

Meanwhile, back on the East Coast Ethel's husband had left for sea duty in the Mediterranean and she began working for a small firm in Rockerfellow Plaza. After work she volunteered as a nurse's aide at Roosevelt Hospital. "I'd hurry home to my studio apartment for a quick supper and change into my uniform; then I'd walk back to the subway station for the trip to the hospital. I usually worked about three hours, helping get all the patients fed, toileted, bathed and settled down for the night. I'd ride the subway back home and briskly walk the two blocks along the lighted street to my apartment. Once the doorman let me in, I'd quickly go to bed and sleep very soundly until the alarm rang the following morning."

The next twenty years or so Ethel's life revolved around her role as a Navy wife and mother to their three children. The family was stationed in Hawaii when she and her Navy husband parted company. Mutual friends introduced Ethel to Belding Scribner, who was vacationing in Hawaii, and a long distance courtship followed. The two were married in Hawaii and Ethel moved to Seattle where "Scrib" was teaching at the University of Washington Medical School.

"He'd bought a small Portage Bay houseboat just across from the Medical School. Between us we had seven children, mostly college age, so we bought a three bedroom house just a short walk up the hill from the houseboat. That house and the houseboat were two of the best investments we ever made. Assorted children in our blended family stayed in the house at various times. As they became independent, we often hosted visiting professors, graduate students studying at the University on fellowships, and occasional foreign fellows. Scrib has had people drop by that remember spending time in our land-based house twenty to thirty years ago. They want to revisit their former home."

Scrib had grown up an only child in the Chicago area. His father was a builder, always very handy, who seemed to be able to do most anything. Scrib was definitely his father's son, he loved to tinker around and make things. He even built a radio when he was a child.

Scrib's childhood experiences came in handy when he struggled with the inability of the new artificial kidney machine to treat patients with chronic kidney failure. Patients could only tolerate a limited number of treatments, since each treatment damaged veins and arteries. Suddenly, in the middle of the night, Scrib came up with the idea of creating a U-shaped shunt with one end stitched to a vein and the other to an artery. Tubes from the artificial kidney machine could be plugged into the shunt to route blood through the dialysis machine and back into the patient. Working with Wayne Quinton, a medical engineer at the University's School of Medicine, and thanks to Dr. Loren Winterscheid's suggesting the recently invented Teflon for the shunt, the Scribner shunt has kept thousand of patients, with chronic kidney failure, alive for years.

Shortly after Scrib and Ethel married they began a major remodel of the small houseboat. They moved into their land house while their architect's brother handled most of the reconstruction. The moorage owner, who lived just up the hill with a view of the dock, became so exasperated with the continuing mess on her dock she sent the Scribners an eviction letter. Not long after that news, Scrib was trimming the bank at their land house, when a neighbor told him that Carrie Stafford was planning to sell her moorage. Scrib and some fellow evicted houseboaters organized to buy the three docks now known as Houseboat Harbor, one of the earliest co-ops on the lake. Three of the eleven houseboats on their moorage are partially on land leased from the State, so the buyers formed a Corporation to buy both the actual real estate and the rights to the State Lease. The co-op chose to leave most of the middle dock of the moorage partially vacant, so everyone enjoys a view of the lake. Owners also can swim between their docks well out of range of the boat traffic.

"We always seem to live close to architects with all sorts of ideas for remodeling our house," says Ethel. The front of their houseboat now looks like an almost continuous window, with four major panels, the better for viewing the traffic and activity on the lake. An extensive array of indoor greenery thrives just inside the window and a five-foot long red and gray remote controlled plane hangs from the living room ceiling. "Scrib really enjoyed building remote controlled airplanes," says Ethel. "One day someone called the harbor police to report a small plane down in Portage Bay. After a few questions the caller was assured that the "downed" plane was just Dr. Scribner playing around with one of his remote control airplanes."

A sliding barn-style door of blue and yellow canvas increases privacy on the deck at the front dock corner of the house. Just behind the deck a long narrow room stretching along the side of their house functions as what most houseboats lack, a basement. The washer and dryer, shelves with pantry type items, a computer Scrib used in his workroom, stored Christmas decorations, an extensive long workbench with all sizes of nuts, screws, nails and other small items carefully labeled and stored in small containers, and tools hanging from the wall fill the narrow room. The Scribners added a partial second story to the original house which now includes two full bathrooms—not very common in older houseboats.

In addition to their "basement," the Scribners had another treasure actually under their house. "One year we had a family of river otters living under our swimming dock," says Ethel. "They were very playful and we spent a lot of time watching them. We often noticed the remains of crayfish on the dock, so we decided to buy a crayfish trap at Doc Freeman's Marine Supply store. We were able to trap a lot of crayfish back then. One year we had some dinner guests from Sweden. When I served them crayfish, they were terribly impressed, especially when we told our guests we'd caught them right here in the lake. We learned crayfish have to be imported into Sweden where they're considered a definite delicacy.

"Scrib was an ardent fisherman and taught me how to cast. One day when I was casting off the dock I caught a three pound bass. My only problem was that I'd forgotten to bring a net. Several men on the other dock were watching me and obviously amused by my dilemma. I kept gradually reeling in the fish, all the time wondering how I could land it without a net. I wasn't about to ask the men watching me for help when they wouldn't offer it. Finally I got the fish close to our adjacent small swim dock that has a ladder. I was able to 'walk' the fish up the steps and onto the dock where I immediately pounced on it. We had it for dinner that night; it was delicious!"

With her husband's growing fame, the Scribners traveled extensively all over the world. Ethel always accompanied him and became known as "the woman who turns her hotel room into a kitchen."

Ethel explains, "After his lecture or presentation Scrib wanted peace and quiet. He needed some private time. So we'd come back to our room and have our dinner there. Our meals were very simple; Scrib loved soup so I made a lot of that, or one-dish meals, usually with a salad. I always attended Scrib's presentations so it had to be quick and easy; sometimes I'd pick up takeout food at a local restaurant. At first I spent a lot of time preparing for a trip, but I eventually learned just what equipment and staples to take. Our luggage was always quite heavy. I used to take a small gas stove; I'm sure you could never carry one on board a plane now!"

Ethel found Scrib's association with the University opened doors to meeting all sorts of interesting and different people. She especially enjoys two groups sponsored by the University. One is Seattle, Seattle, which organizes trips to different parts of the city, and the other is Gallery Goers, which plans similar expeditions to local art galleries and museums.

She also enjoyed volunteering for the Health Sciences Open House and conducting students on tours of the University Hospital and Medical School. "They were generally nice kids," she says, "but they always wanted to ride the elevator rather than walk up the stairs. I felt the elevators needed to be available for patients and staff, so I insisted we walk. I figured if I could climb the stairs, the young people could certainly handle them."

Scrib died over a year ago when he apparently stumbled or lost consciousness while walking down the dock and fell into the water. Ethel's children on the East Coast suggest she might want to come back there to be with them.

"I'm staying here," she declares. "why would I go anywhere else? All my doctors are here; if I need to I can even walk to their offices. My friends are here and I know all my neighbors."

Not only would her friends and neighbors miss Ethel, the Canada geese would sorely miss the only known person who doles out popcorn for them every day.

It's Magic

Dan and Becky Graves first saw their Mallard Cove floating home on a television newscast during the summer of 1993—on fire! Sam, the owner at that time, had been working on his motor boat and left some oily rags on the float attached to his front deck. As the afternoon sun eased into the western sky, it reflected off large windows on the front of the house causing a spontaneous combustion that ignited the rags. Moments later a propane tank, only a few feet away from the burning rags, exploded and blew out all the windows. Next the whole front of the house caught fire.

Worried neighbors manned buckets, hoses and fire extinguishers, a pump-equipped Harbor Patrol boat sped from across the lake, and a fire truck raced down from the nearby Roanoke Fire Station. The mid-afternoon drama was just in time for the local early evening newscast. Becky, who along with Dan had been considering moving to a houseboat, remembers saying, "Wow, maybe we'd better rethink this houseboat idea."

It was Dan who first discovered houseboats when he left Indiana in 1971 for graduate school at the University of Washington. The maverick community tempted him, but once he and Becky married they wanted a quality home on dry land rather than one of the shabby shacks on the water. Dan and Becky settled into a spacious home on Magnolia Bluff close to downtown Seattle. They had two boys, and Dan acquired his own communications and public relations firm.

Shortly before their younger son entered high school, Dan and Becky attended an Intiman Theater benefit auction. When the auctioneer described a week-end on a Fairview Avenue houseboat, the lure of the water loosened their purse strings and they placed the winning bid.

"We had the most wonderful time," says Becky. "Friday night when we carted our luggage down the dock Dan was stiff as a board; by Saturday he'd loosened up considerably, and by Sunday he was as relaxed as a rag doll. It was magic. When we told the owner, Jan, what a wonderful time we'd had, she encouraged us to come again whenever she was out of town. We ended up staying at Jan's place seven times; we were hooked on life afloat."

In the fall, Dan and Becky began working in earnest with Elaine Eigaman, a realtor who specializes in houseboats. Thus began a series of serendipitous incidents. They initially made an offer on a shore side houseboat next to the parking lot at Mallard Cove. The purchase was contingent on the sale of their home in Magnolia.

They put their house on the market in late October. Then on the day of President Clinton's first inauguration, a storm came through with ninety-mile-an-hour winds that literally peeled the roof off their Magnolia Bluff home. Once they took their house off the market, Becky and Dan had second thoughts about the Mallard Cove houseboat.

Dan says, "In Jan's place we could see various boats coming and going, Queen Anne Hill across the lake, and the city lights reflected in the water. We didn't have that on the back row of Mallard Cove where we faced the parking lot. We realized the house was a compromise. I had agreed to it because it was the

A Mallard Cove Houseboat

nice house Becky wanted, and she was doing it for me because it was on the water. So when the Mallard Cove owners offered to extend the contingency on selling our Magnolia house, we decided to pass."

They kept looking that summer of 1993, when interest rates dropped so low they found they could buy twice as much house as they could handle before. They came within an inch of buying a home on Magnolia's Perkins Lane they'd never dreamed would be within reach.

"We were crushed when we didn't get it," Becky says, "but the very next day our realtor took us to see Sam's house, the one we'd seen on fire during the evening news. Elaine explained the fire damage was not completely repaired, and Sam was hesitant to have it shown, but she'd persuaded him to let us see it.

"I'll never forget it," says Becky, "The carpet was not installed, appliances and ladders were in the living room, and there were no interior doors yet. Then I saw the three good-sized bedrooms, the open upstairs living area, and the view west towards sunsets, open water and the Olympic Mountains. `This is it!' I exclaimed. `I want to live here forever!'"

"I don't see how we can possibly afford it," replied Dan.

"Somehow we'll find a way," declared Becky.

They talked Elaine into holding an open house for their Magnolia home the following day, a Sunday. A couple saw their house, fell in love with it, and sent their agent to Dan's office Monday morning with a full price, no contingency offer. By the end of the day, it was a done deal, and Dan and Becky ended up in one of the few houses on Mallard Cove with an open water view.

"And we've had more social life in one year here than we ever had during our seventeen years on Magnolia," exclaims Becky.

"People do things here," adds Dan. "Shortly after we moved in a neighbor hosted a black-tie Christmas party. Now we're part of a floating wine-tasters group on the dock that gathers once a month."

"Shortly after we moved in," says Becky, "we had our version of a house-warming, only we called it a boat christening. A hundred people watched us break a champagne bottle on our concrete float. At Christmas, we invited about sixty people to come see and hear the kayakers that paddle around the lake singing Christmas carols. Every night for eight days we saw boats festooned with Christmas lights head toward different neighborhoods to share the holiday spirit. It was absolutely magic."

Dan adds, "When I think of all the time we spent on the yard in Magnolia, doing something neither one of us enjoyed, my only regret is that we didn't move sooner. I would have moved into a funkier place much earlier to be on the water; that's where Becky and I differ.

"Maybe the one disadvantage here is a lack of covered parking for my convertible. Yet, I enjoy experiencing the rain on my cheek, the cold wind in my face, or the warmth of the sun as I walk the fifty-some yards to my car. I feel more in touch with nature. During the summer my office gets really hot, so I'm completely withered by the time I get home. I shed my clothes, put on my swim trunks and jump into the water. I'll greet neighbors, maybe stop for a drink with one of them, and if it's Tuesday, I'll swim out to watch the sail boats racing in the Duck Dodge. That swim just totally rejuvenates me."

"And when Dan's gone," adds Becky, "people on the dock know it. I'll inevitably get a couple of knocks on the door, `Would you like to come down for dinner? Is everything okay?' They look after you."

Becky concludes, "We used to feel we needed to get away from it all, we'd go down to the beach at Ocean Shores, east across the mountains to Lake Chelan, or up north to Victoria. Now we have absolutely no desire to leave this idyllic setting. We recently took a trip to Spain. But even before the trip was over we were eager to get back home to our panoramic view, our ducks and geese, and our neighbors. It's magic."

Circumstances change and at this point Dan and Becky have gone their separate ways. But each still treasures memories of their days in the Mallard Cove houseboat.

SHE'S COME A LONG WAY

"I don't know why I love the water so much," says Caroline Culbertson. "I was born on Lake Michigan and in the summer we went to the lake every day. Even though I knew my mother didn't like me, she taught me how to swim so she'd have someone to join her. I adored her so much I loved those times on the lake. Swimming was one of the few things we did together."

A gracefully aging slender blond, Caroline recalls memories of her mother, dressed in a black and gold sequin dress, standing in front of a mirror putting real gold dust on her eye lids while waiting for her father to come down the stairs in a top hat, tux, and scarf looking like Clark Gable. She also remembers their growing wealth coincided with an increasingly hostile relationship between the two.

"My parents fought frequently, with screaming and physical abuse. I've never associated wealth with happiness, so it was easy for me to become poor, and not care about making a lot of money. Our first Christmas in the big new house (it was so big I still remember the holly on silver wall paper in a third story room where I got lost) they told me I could have whatever I wanted for Christmas. I got a big hollow feeling in the pit of my stomach because I knew that none of it meant anything. I don't even remember what presents I got, because it meant nothing compared to the one teddy bear I received when we were poor and they were still happy together."

When her parents finally divorced, a sensitive judge gave custody of Caroline and her brother to their father, unusual for the 1930's.

"I didn't have a mother to teach me how to behave, how to play the game, so I was very academic. I went to Chicago's New Trier high school where I was in a super-advanced English class with professors from Northwestern University. I'd eagerly raise my hand, but the Professor was very cruel to me because I was too bright for a girl. During the forties it was a male world. I'll never forget the day I'd raised my hand and he finally called on me, only to say, "It's all right, Caroline, you can go to the bathroom now; we'll let you go." That did it; I was the last of three girls to withdraw from the class."

Caroline first came to Seattle when she spent a summer visiting her mother who was working as a riveter at Boeing during World War II. "It was a magical, wonderful summer with Mt. Rainier out every day. I met a group of kids I could identify with; they took me into their group and I had a social life."

As a drama major Caroline returned to Seattle again, fascinated by the University of Washington Drama Department's innovative theater-in-the-round. She played the part of "Aunt Sue" in a children's show on pre-rock KISW. Next she enjoyed various adventures in Europe and then settled in New York, where she became a full-fledged member of Equity, the actor guild. Caroline permanently returned to Seattle in the mid-60s after a disastrous love affair. "I just wanted to heal," she says, "so I came to put my back against the hills and my toes in the water. That is, I had my back up to the Cascade Mountains and my toes in the Pacific."

She began working in the University of Washington Radio

Department and found a little house on pier pilings on the lake's northern shoreline between the I-5 Freeway and the University Bridge.

"The houseboat in front of me was owned by a policeman who had been killed in a hunting accident, so it was tied up in the courts. The policeman had been a really big tall man, and the house had a marvelous long and very comfortable claw-footed bath tub. The attorney for the policeman's Estate had rented out the houseboat, but the tenant, a Seattle University student, was extremely mentally disturbed.

"He punched a hole through the bedroom wall, had ducks walking in the front door, ruined a beautiful oil stove by burning drift wood in it, had no money, and never paid any rent. The pipes had broken during a winter freeze, so there was no running water. When he was pressured to pay some money, he did a flit. I knew exactly when he left. The sounding board of the dock reverberated in my ears and I knew it was he leaving in the middle of the night. I felt like a spider in the middle of a web.

"I also knew the Estate was about to be settled, the policeman's kids were back East, and the lawyer wanted to wrap it up. A friend of the attorney came down to the dock and took me for a dumb blonde."

"You know," he said, "I could get you a really good deal on that houseboat, I could get it for $400 to $500 dollars for you."

"I knew better. I consulted with several of my neighbors, one of which was a contractor who kept back hoes on barges right next to me. He told me the houseboat had arrived in 1950, was a former logger's home, and wasn't worth anything. It needed additional flotation, a new deck, insulation, new plumbing and heat.

I called up the Estate lawyer and asked, "What would you consider a good price?"

"Well, I'll have to come down and look at it."

He never did, but I guess he had somebody check it out. He called back and said he had to have some money for it.

"What about $200?" I asked.

"Well, I gotta have more than that."

"So we dickered and came up with $250."

Caroline then rented out the houseboat and used the income to begin fixing it up.

"I was able to hire Art Holder to put in new decking. We had a keg party for repairing the roof, somewhat like an old fashioned barn-raising, and I hired George Johnston to put in Styrofoam logs for supplemental flotation.

"But with my location just west of the University Bridge and the channel under it, I was rocked a lot by all the wakes from passing boats. The Styrofoam logs kept floating out. It's a very vulnerable spot, so I finally got this crazy guy who liked to dive and he came up with using polyurethane barrels to equalize the weight.

"Next I found a journey-man plumber, I took out all the required permits, drew up the plan for my plumbing, and basically "supervised" while he did all the work.

"As for the electrical, I had a wonderful inspector who loved the houseboats. He pointed out the narrow paneling in my bathroom was typical of the 1930s so I knew the houseboat was built then. The inspector was about to retire and I told him I wanted to do what was right and needed his help. Other people were always fighting with him, so he loved helping me. I brought everything up to code and even replaced the flooring."

Then in 1972 Marjorie, the dock owner, pressured Caroline to either move in to the houseboat or go somewhere else. With a better income at that time Caroline moved in and continued making improvements, such as the loft she put in on top.

"Finally Jay, my next door neighbor who owned the property out to the channel, decided he wanted an interest in Marjorie's property to secure his own property line. He suggested that since neither of us could afford to buy all Marjorie's property, we all three go in on it. He told Marjorie, 'Caroline has been down here for thirty-five years and she's always paid her rent without fail; she's a good tenant.' Actually, I'd even paid for the sewer connection; she didn't. Marjorie wanted money coming in, but she didn't want any going out.

"The dock was a total disaster; it was like a rotten tooth in a mouth full of scurvy. I finally said, 'Marjorie, you've got to come down and look at this dock, it's dangerous. I've been responsible down here and this dock has got to have something done to it.'

"I was polite, but I was firm. I kept calling her and she kept me waiting for months.

"Marjorie was from a southern finishing school, so the day she finally came floating down the dock she was wearing stiletto high-heeled shoes and carrying a parasol. The minute she set foot from the land onto the dock I said 'See!'

"'Oh, yes, Ah do see what youawl mean about this dock; Ah think we're gonna have to do something about this. Ah'll get a man down here, ah'll get Clay to come down here and do something.....'"

Caroline not only managed to get the dock repaired, she's equally persistent about swimming. She'd swim every morning, often into November, before heading for her 1 to 9 pm shift at Harborview Hospital in the Emergency Room.

"I had the Harbor Patrol pretty well trained," she says. "At first they were very upset with this woman swimming out in the channel from Lake Union to Portage Bay. But I explained that I was always legally within the twenty feet parameter from the shore and not in the actual channel. Every morning I'd swim down to the red buoy that marks the entrance to Lake Union from Portage Bay, circle around it, then float and contemplate the Universe for a few minutes before I'd turn around and swim back home. In early November when the water turned really cold, I'd leave the hot water running in my claw tub so I could enjoy something like a sauna when I came out from the chilly waters."

One day in late October Caroline was swimming along under the I-5 Freeway when she heard the Harbor Patrol Boat. It was one of the senior officers reporting he'd just got a call on his cell phone and needed to check in with her to see if she'd seen a jumper off the I-5 bridge. The patrolman told her the incident had happened about seven minutes ago.

"No hurtling bodies coming down," she answered.

"Finally, it dawned on me. Someone had seen me while driving on I-5 during my float routine before I turned around and headed back home. The driver couldn't believe a live person would be swimming at this time of year!"

Gradually over the years Caroline turned the once trashed houseboat into a real home. Unfortunately, by then both Jay and Marjorie wanted to sell the property. Caroline was a minority of one, and when the property, including her houseboat, finally sold in 1996, the prices had sky-rocketed to such an extent she couldn't afford to buy out her share.

"The last week I was there I was feeling very sorry about all the wildlife I was going to lose: the beaver that swam by, the raccoons, and especially the great blue heron. In all the years that I'd been there I'd never seen river otters, but that last day as I was heading out through the living room I heard all this commotion. Right on my covered front deck davenport were two juvenile otters, cavorting with one another, diving over, in, and around and totally enjoying themselves. I was so close I could feel their wildness. They are not tame critters, they had a wild look, but they were so free and beautiful.

"When I came out, it startled them of course, but they didn't leave right away. It was as if they knew I was a friend, so they played around a little bit more and then they just slid into the water and away they went. It was the best goodbye I could have had, something I'll never forget, and it will probably never happen again."

Caroline spent three years on Echo Lake while her realtor sought out waterfront that she could afford. The realtor finally found a site in a Kenmore Trailer Park right next to the Sammammish River with an adjacent wetland.

"I didn't think I wanted to be in a trailer park, but she coaxed me to take a look and I realized it was one of the better trailer parks. It's lovely here and I have good neighbors, but I still miss being part of the houseboat community. However, just yesterday I saw two blue herons alight right in front of the river bank. They were courting each other; it was magnificent to watch. I still have my connection to the water and the wildlife."

ANN OF LAKE UNION

I was born in Beaufort, South Carolina," says Ann Prezyna, "and moved with my Navy family to Buffalo when I was still in the single digits. My Sundays, as far back as I can recall, were spent outdoors in the woods, fishing, catching snakes, or hiking with my father. As cradle Catholics my parents attended mass every Sunday, but they both agreed my sister Carol and I would be closer to God enjoying nature than sitting in church. That's when I first developed my life long interest in the environment."

When it was time for college, Ann chose Cornell University based on its strong natural resources program. It didn't hurt that her cousin, Joanne Trifilo, was also attending Cornell and the in-state tuition was only $400 a semester.

After deciding the best way to impact the environment would be as a lawyer, Ann went on to graduate from the environmental law program at George Washington University in Washington, D.C.

"I was in D.C. at the time of the Watergate hearings and dating Steve Jacobs, a producer for CBS News. I could get sneak previews of the latest developments before they went on the air. It was clear to me the whole city was about power. People were amazed that the Washington Post went so far out on a limb with their Watergate investigation. It was a remarkable time.

Needless to say, there was never a dull moment in my Constitutional Law class as history was being made right before our eyes."

After law school, Ann obtained a Master's Degree in Water Resources Management from the University of Wisconsin to provide a more solid technical focus beyond her undergraduate work in Natural Resources. Her added studies paid off when only a few days before graduation, she got a call from Brent Petrie in Anchorage, Alaska, offering her the opportunity to rewrite the state's water use regulations.

As Ann says, "The position was mine if I could get to Alaska and obtain residency *tout suite*. Sure beat looking for work, so I packed my bags and drove cross country in my 1972 Toyota Corolla to Seattle, Washington, where I caught the Alaska ferry. It was Alaska or bust!

"What was I thinking? When I arrived in Anchorage, I didn't realize what a change it would be from the city life I had previously led. Anchorage was a bit behind the rest of the U.S. in many ways. I recall Walter Cronkite's news program arriving on videotape in a can flown in from the lower 48 overnight, quite a change from the instant news reporting I was used to receiving. The lack of goods and services compared to the variety I had experienced below was daunting at times. The last frontier with all its scenic beauty and seemingly limitless opportunities proved irresistible over time. I intended staying only a couple of years and ended living there for almost ten.

"Alaska was a terrific place to launch my law career. I was twenty-something working in the Attorney General's office on a large variety of cases involving issues of water rights, air and water quality, wildlife, commercial fishing, mining, forestry and oil and gas. It was a very heady start. One of my first cases was defending the state sale of timber near a reserve for bald eagles in Haines. The city of Haines, which supported the sale, was so doubtful of my abilities as a young lawyer that they hired their own counsel to represent their pro-sale interests. The sales tax they passed to pay for the lawsuit exists to this day, even though their lawyer was largely confined to bench warming. The judge had ruled early on that the city's interests were adequately represented by the state, that is, me. We went on to win the case. I graduated later on to oil and gas work, which included helping collect the billions of dollars in oil and gas revenues generated by their sales."

With the long daylight of summer days Ann slept only three or four hours a night. She remembers long summer days when they'd start an overnight hike at 9PM and not set up camp until midnight because the sun was still up. During the first winter she made up for lack of sleep, hibernating for as many as sixteen hours a night. The following year she joined a basketball team made up of women from the AG's office. Their games started as late as 9 or 10PM, which cured her of the urge to go to bed at 6PM. Local judges, the attorney general, and other notables cheered on the side-lines. As Ann says, "Alaska was that kind of a small town.

"On the plus side of the long dark nights were the Northern lights. They could be so bright it was like someone finger-painting the entire sky in reds and greens and yellows right above our heads. At times we could even hear them crackle and hiss. The aurora was easily viewed from the log home I bought with my partner, Gordon Lewis, in Stuckagain Heights, a subdivision carved out of a homestead in the Chugach Mountains near downtown Anchorage. Stuckagain was so named because of the poor condition of the dirt access road: narrow and steep and twisty. Although only about a twenty minute drive to downtown in the best of times, in the worst of times we'd never get up, or down. Ice on the road coupled with rain would turn it into an inclined skating rink. Hence the name, Stuckagain. The positive side of our rugged location was that we could don a backpack or skis, step out our back door, and be in the wilderness. We also had a variety of wildlife in the yard, including black bears and brown bears attracted to the suet feeder we'd hung for the birds. It was an ideal setting for a person who loves the outdoors as I do."

In the mid 1980s a precipitous drop in oil prices forced a reduction in state employees. After ten years in Alaska Ann and Gordon decided to make a break and head for the lower Forty-eight and more secure job prospects. They sold almost every-thing and bought a Winnebago LeSharo, a small diesel-powered motor home that made forty miles to the gallon and could fit in a standard parking space. Since neither Ann nor Gordon had taken a break between school and work, the two elected to take a year's vacation on the road and bravely headed down the AlCan highway in December of 1986. This time it was "the lower Forty-eight or bust" for Ann and her partner.

"The fates were with us. Our destination was the Alaska ferry terminal in Haines. Winter was ordinarily not a good choice for traveling the highway: too much snow and cold driv-ing in a vehicle with bad winter traction. But that winter was one of the few on record with no significant snowfall by December. We made it thorough the last large mountain pass the day before the first winter storm arrived and dumped sever-al feet of snow there. Right outside of Haines we saw hundreds of eagles gathered to fish for salmon: the Haines eagle preserve. I'd come full circle."

After the Alaska ferry completed the trip to Seattle, Ann and Gordon spent a few days visiting friends and then headed south on their great American road trip. They marveled at all the sights they'd never seen before, camping and hiking as they dawdled along. About mid-way through their journey Ann realized she'd have to return to work someday, so they headed back to Seattle. With a climate and natural beauty similar to that of Alaska, as well as an easy jumping off point for visits up north, she and Gordon decided to spend the summer there while Ann studied for the Washington State bar exam.

"We scanned the classifieds for a summer residence and were attracted to the "Houseboats for Rent" listing. The owners, Gary and Linda Oman, were both teachers and heading south for their traditional summer in Mexico. We fell in love with the place when we saw it, but learned there was a long list of interested renters. How to get to the top of the list? Linda and Gary had a couple of pet rabbits and a cat that might need to be boarded while they were away. One of the rabbits, Keiko, had a fondness for wall board and needed to be dosed daily with papaya medication, no easy task unless you have a knack for getting bunnies to swallow large pills. 'Oh, we love animals,' I volunteered with great enthusiasm. 'We'd be happy to attend to their every need.' Our willingness to share a house with three animals that had the run of the place plus Gordon's past experience with getting bunnies to swallow pills cinched the deal.

"Gary and Linda gave us a quick course in houseboat living. We'd swim in the bay every morning and rented a rowing shell for daily workouts to the University of Washington Arboretum and back, particularly delightful when the morning sunrise lit up the bay with color like the aurora would light the night sky in Alaska. Life on the water was idyllic."

When summer ended and after Ann had taken the bar exam the adventurers lingered in the Southwest, then hugged the coastline through Texas and Louisiana. They sought out small restaurants with local pickup trucks so they could spin tales of

Alaska in exchange for local wisdom. After reaching Key West, Florida they once again followed the coast line until heading west to Buffalo for a visit with Ann's family.

"Shortly after we arrived in Buffalo I received a phone message from Deborah Gates, an attorney with the U. S. Environmental Protection Agency in Seattle. I had worked with Deborah on some oil and gas matters when I was representing the State of Alaska. Deborah let me know of a couple of positions for attorneys in the EPA's Seattle office and invited me to apply, which I did. I was not going to spend any money for an interview outfit for a job I wasn't certain I wanted to have, or had much chance of landing. To my surprise, I was offered a position about two weeks after the interview. (I was told much later that my outfit did raise a few questions, like 'wonder if she'll come to work dressed like that?') But somehow my credentials overcame the casualness of my attire. They wanted me to begin work in one week, on December 14th. 'Give me two weeks,' I replied, 'and I'll be there.' Again, it sure beat looking for work."

Ann and Gordon arrived in Seattle homeless, car-less, and wardrobe-less. Ann raided her savings and bought all three in a week. Lured by fond memories of Portage Bay, Ann and Gordon worked with Elaine Eigaman, seasoned houseboat realtor, until they found a 400 square-foot studio with a wide open view toward the Montlake cut leading into Lake Washington. Having lived in an eighteen foot motor home for the past year, and with Gordon's continuing work as a land use consultant in Alaska, the small house seemed quite large enough for two. The house had begun life as a chicken coop which the dock owners, Fred and Roberta Fischer, had installed on a log raft. A former Boeing engineer had remodeled the original chicken coop to optimize the use of space; creating a very nautical and ship-shape house.

After three years of cohabitation Ann and Gordon decided to buy a larger home and convert the Portage Bay residence into Gordon's office and impromptu guest quarters.

Once again, with the help of Elaine Eigaman, they found their current home on the east side of Lake Union. "The previous owner, Jan Hart, had to vacate the premises because she owned two cats, which were prohibited by the lease when the dock was still a rental moorage."

Their current home has an upstairs bed room that you step down into with a computer desk, double closet, and windows on the north and west sides, a shower across from the toilet and sink, a family room with lots of windows, a couch, table, stereo system, television, built in book shelves, knotty pine ceiling, cork floors, and a spacious outside deck looking out over the channel with a partial view of downtown Seattle. A circular stairway leads downstairs where a similar pattern with the addition of a washer/dryer and a shower with bathtub and a kitchen/living room area replace the upstairs family room and deck.

Several years after Gordon and Ann moved onto the dock homeowners were able to purchase their moorage sites. The longest term resident on the dock, who had purchased his home for about $4,500 forty-five years ago, couldn't afford the price of his moorage. Ann couldn't imagine the dock without its unofficial "mayor," so she bought the moorage with his home and rents his house to him on a long term lease.

Gordon used any of his spare time to put together a small dinner raft, complete with an electric trolling motor and officially licensed as a vessel by the State of Washington. The small raft, pictured in a *Seattle Times* article about the relatively new phenomena of such dinner rafts, accommodates a small table and four chairs for dinner guests along with an ice chest. As

Ann says, "For those of us who live on the street end of house-boat docks, it's an inexpensive way to get a view and costs only a few hundred dollars versus the large sums end moorages command these days."

Ann and Gordon recently married after their twenty-five years of courtship. "You know, you can never be too sure," quips Ann. It was the first marriage for both of them. "When I went downtown to apply for a license," reports Ann, "I was old enough to be the grandmother of most of the others in line. When the man doling out applications asked whether I intended to change my name, I responded: 'Not on your life. I've had the same name for over fifty years, and I ain't gonna change it now.'"

Daunted by the idea of a formal wedding, Ann and Gordon timed their wedding with a previously scheduled dinner with friends Gloria Lamuth and Dave Justad. Tina Cohen, a friend of Ann's since age three, served as the surrogate family member and another friend, Elizabeth Cook Hastorf (the Reverend thanks to having become a minister of the Universal Church of Life at Ann's request) presided.

"We dined, then once dinner was over we turned to our friends and asked them whether they would witness our marriage."

"You're joking!" they exclaimed.

"No joke."

"Where's the ring?"

"Oh oh."

"Fortunately, we had on hand some gift wrap from Christmas which included one of those fancy twist ties with stars and other ornaments of various colors. An ideal make-shift ring. I'm not much of a jewelry person and felt money for a ring would be better applied as down payment on a house in Arizona. So we signed papers, clinked glasses, and were married without nary an 'I do.' I didn't tell anyone about the ceremony, letting word get around through the grapevine. It took several months before word reached my family on the East Coast."

Two days after the non-ceremony Ann, who continues working as an attorney for the EPA, left for a business trip to Washington, D.C. and Gordon, now retired, headed for their second home at Rancho Gulag in Arizona, where there's no end of things to repair and maintain.

Ever the environmentalist, Ann recently discovered a nasty sheen on the water around her home. A worker at one of her neighbor's homes had spilled deck paint into the water. Fortunately she had a house guest who was a veteran of the Exxon Valdez oil spill. Ann contacted Jeff Rodin, an oil spill cleanup expert in her office. He recommended making pom-poms by shredding plastic trash bags into strips then raking the water with them. Ann and her guest spent the next hour or so cheerleading for the environment with their pom-poms.

"Our efforts greatly reduced the sheen on the water. Given the urban wildlife in the neighborhood, such as turtles, bass, beavers, muskrats, and otters, we're glad this simple trick worked."

CREATURE COMFORTS

An ancient willow tree almost hides the steps down to the dock where Thom and Oy Laz moor their houseboat. Beginning in mid-summer, the Army Corps of Engineers uses the spill gates at the Hiram Chittenden locks to gradually lower the water level of Lake Washington and Lake Union by twenty-two inches. The lower water level lessens the impact of winter storms and also causes the five houses on either side to float several feet below their stationary dock. On the way down the dock, a house with a gleaming white porcelain urinal mounted on the front designates the owner's trade. He's planted a thriving orange begonia in the basin.

At the Laz home on the end of the dock, visitors taller than five feet five have to stoop to enter through the mahogany brown semi-circular wooden front door. Inside, a large open area has an abundance of hanging plants in front of ceiling-to-floor windows facing the water. A fireplace has replaced the wood-burning stove that stood against the opposite wall with a kitchen tucked around the corner. The thick door to Thom and Oy's bedroom doubles as a book case on the bedroom side. Daughter Pudchaa sleeps in a loft above the bathroom that also has floor-to-ceiling windows on the water side.

"It's pretty different from when I first bought it back in July of 1968," muses Thom. "I'd come down to Seattle from my family's home in Snohomish, an hour or so northeast of Seattle, and started looking for a boat. The first houseboat I was ever on was Belding Scribner's over on Portage Bay. His son Pete and I had mutual friends. As we sat out on the deck with our feet dangling in the water, I decided this would probably be about the only way I'd want to live in the city."

When Thom saw a houseboat priced at $1,200, he offered half the listed price. He was stunned when the seller agreed. Then Thom learned why. "The owner of the moorage for my new home had agreed to sell the property to Mr. John King, a developer. Mr. King planned to buy up docks, evict the houseboaters, and build condominiums. I'd just bought a houseboat on a dock where Mr. King was planning to build a condo. Fortunately, the implementation of the Shorelines Management Act stopped him from doing so; I lived there for two years. When they decided to rebuild the run-down dock, I had to move."

Thom found a new location on the western shore of Lake Union where he could moor his house in dead storage, which meant no utilities, for $75 a month. Although City code prohibits living in a houseboat without electricity, it does allow working on the house.

Thom admits, "I had quite a few visits from the Seattle Police Harbor Patrol just across the way on the west side of the old gas plant. Every time I'd hear a police boat coming by, I'd get out my hammer and saw. They'd come in and see me working away, so there was no problem. Actually, those guys ended up helping me get a lot of work done."

Thom always felt the houseboats were doomed, so much of his work was make-shift. "I originally built that whole wall with the leaded glass windows facing the water without any nails. I fit everything together and built little joints to hold everything in place. Since that was my stereo wall, I wanted to take it with me when I had to leave."

During his houseboat's two years in dead storage, Thom met Frank Granat, the man who eventually offered him the choice end moorage on Fairview Mooring where he, Oy, and Pudchaa now live. When Thom asked Frank the price, he answered $160 a month. That settled it.

"That was back in the summer of 1972. When a friend offered his boat to tow me back to the east side of the lake I invited about a dozen other friends along. We trolled for fish and after we caught enough for everyone I fried them on my wood-burning stove. It was a great day."

Thom survived electricity racing through his body when he accidentally became grounded into Lake Union while wiring his houseboat at its permanent location. Once he got both electricity and water hooked up and settled into his now floating houseboat, Thom became active in the houseboat community. "That's when I met Terry Pettus, joined the Floating Homes Association, and even bought some stock in the Lake Union Investment Corporation. The Corporation hoped to buy moorages as they became available, but that never happened."

Thom's hands that built the nail-free wall also created original designs which he printed on fabric. Next he designed and sewed a shirt from the fabric as a pattern for workers he hired to sew identical garments. Thom developed a thriving import-export business which took him to Thailand where he met his wife, Oy. Marriage and the arrival of Pudchaa led to a regular job as a machine shop manager.

"Life on the lake is a lot more secure now," says Thom, "but we've paid a price for our security. Houseboats have gotten more respectable and much more expensive. I don't understand some of the new people who have come into the houseboat scene. They supposedly come here for what it has and then they immediately want to change it."

The usually mellow Thom is adamant as he says, "If you want to get a look at what houseboat living is like, it's not two-story houseboats. Because to me, one of the best things about houseboats and Lake Union is living in small little homes, very close to each other and close to the lake creatures.

"I like the idea of living out in the wilderness. I guess it goes back to growing up on Flowing Lake near Snohomish where my Dad operated a small, rustic resort. People could come to picnic, fish, swim or boat on the lake. One of the reasons I put so many plants on my deck is to encourage the animals to live among them. I had a beaver that I considered my cheap gardener; he did all my pruning. He had a great affection for willows, roses, and rhododendrons. One day I discovered he'd taken my big willow tree down and I got so angry I decided I was going to put an end to this. I located my bow and arrows and then put little bells on almost all my plants as an alarm. Sure enough, it wasn't long before I heard some of them tinkling at about five in the morning. I went out with my bow and arrow to find the beaver had just taken down my rose bush with about 300 buds on it. I drew the bow and was about to release the string when I thought, `Death penalty for eating roses? That seems pretty harsh.' So I put down my bow and I kicked him instead. The beaver turned around and gave me a funny look, then jumped into the lake and swam off.

"I grabbed my canoe," Thom recalls, "and threw the rose-bush in it. I followed that beaver as he headed for Portage Bay. He swam all the way through the Bay, then through the Montlake Cut, and finally out to Foster Island. He climbed out in a little bay where his mate and pup were waiting for him on the bank. I threw the rose bush up on the bank and yelled, `I know where you live.'"

Thom adds wistfully, "Pudchaa says she's seen the beaver

since then. Whether it's the same beaver or not, I'll never know. But I'll always know I made the right decision when I put down my bow and arrow. Animals are part of houseboat life. This lake belongs more to the creatures of the lake than it does to the humans and their houseboats."

A Cast of Characters

"I arrived in Seattle on March 1, 1971 and drove directly to the Space Needle," declares Elliott Wolf. "I took the elevator up to the observation deck where the bright sunshine offered picture postcard views of the area. Being from Colorado, I assumed it was always sunny here. I dropped a quarter in one of the available telescopes and lo and behold, I saw the houseboats on Lake Union."

From the observation deck of the Space Needle, Elliott studied the roads and charted a course to the houseboats he saw on the east side of Lake Union

As he drove along the lake, he saw a man knocking up a "For Rent" sign at the head of one of the docks. Elliott parked, queried the man about the rental, took a quick look and signed an informal rental agreement with the owner, John Southern. He ended up buying the small sprung roof house on the south side of the dock less than four months later.

"It's a lovely place; I've lived here happily every after.

"The first week I was here, John showed me how to sink a refrigerator. First of all he put rocks inside of it, but that didn't work. Next, he took the door off and poured water inside, but it still didn't sink. So John went inside his house and came out with a rifle that had to have been made sometime between the Revolutionary and the Civil Wars. It was the hughest gun I've ever seen in my life. He's standing at the end of the dock above the unsinkable refrigerator and he lifts the enormous gun and shoots the refrigerator. The next thing I see is John plastered against a wall about thirty feet away.

"I actually don't think he ever succeeded in sinking it. As a matter of fact, that refrigerator may be a navigational hazard today; it's gotta be still floating. I've heard there are a lot of old wringer washing machines on the lake bottom, but I've never heard of any refrigerators.

"The dock had an interesting cast of characters. Ruth Foss, who married the old man Foss on his death bed, was one of them. She was in line to receive everything owned by the founder of Foss Tugboats, but the family came down and said you know, we don't think this is appropriate. The Foss family negotiated an agreement that gave her ownership of the dock."

Elliott points out that the houseboats on his dock were the first to connect to the new sewer; they were the test case to demonstrate that the gravity flow system with a sump pump under the dock would work. His dock was also the first to own their moorage sites. The gun-shooting John Southern rallied his thirteen neighbors to from a corporation that bought the real estate and the rights to the state lease.

"On our dock we have only fourteen houseboats," explains Elliott, "so that if we ever lose the land leased from the state we could push evicted houseboats back onto the owned real estate and still accommodate everyone.

"Although he had as much business sense as a slug, John became the manager of the dock. But he was a very nice guy and probably the innovator of the concept of running electricity under the dock rather than strung up above on wires. When our dock was built it was unthinkable to run electricity so close to the water.

Fairview Dock

"We had a nice old guy who was a mailman. He and his wife lived a reasonably ordinary life at the end of the dock. Then there were these two little ladies who ran a restaurant that actually was a brothel. When I met them they had retired. They were the perfect Mutt and Jeff; one was a bean pole and the other a butter ball. Actually, the two women were quite interesting; they were fun neighbors to have.

"Then there was Dr. B and his red-haired wife Bubbles. He was an anesthesiologist who had two of the largest snakes I'd ever seen as pets. These were huge long babies that I think were boas that could live in the water. I used to have nightmares of them wrapping themselves around the sewer pipe, breaking it and then coming up the toilet. Dr. B was the biggest guy I'd ever seen; probably about six-foot five or six. He practically had to get down on his hands and knees to get in and out of the house. He was president of some medieval group and used to walk around in armor just like a knight. One day he left the armor on the dock and I tired to pick it up; it weighted so much I thought he must be inside it. Bubbles was a midget, compared to him, but she was no push-over. He had a library of paper back books. The largest I've ever seen. You know on houseboats, you measure things in pounds. When they vacated the house it rose about seventeen inches.

"On the other end of the dock there was a school teacher who reminded me of a second grade teacher I never liked. We weren't very close. On the other side was Ed Locke. Ed used to play the bag pipes at 5 AM on Sunday mornings when he came home. He was truly a wild and crazy guy. He had a patio on his house about ten feet above the water. He would stand on the top railing around his patio wearing his water skis and hanging onto the tow bar as his friends gunned the ski boat. He took off on his skis from the top of that railing. Once he took off carrying his bagpipes and they didn't survive; that ended the 5 o'clock Sunday morning concerts.

"The next neighbor was a recluse. Hers was the only houseboat I was never in. She kept it very dark and had bars on her windows, but every day she'd go to the Senior Center. I trust she had friends and companionship there; maybe she just felt we weren't her type. She was cool and passed away about five years ago.

"Another neighbor, Gary, lived in his shop; his whole houseboat was a mechanic's shop. Gary was about thirty years old and a Rube Goldberg who made some great art. Gary and John Sunderland used to get plastered. Those guys were true alcoholics.

"The architect who owned the house across the way used it as a rental unit, so I never met him until a couple of years ago. His renters were usually interesting folks."

When asked where he grew up, Elliott replies, "I can't answer that because I haven't grown up yet."

In spite of never growing up, the tall man with his white hair in a pony tail shares a few specifics of his early days and a very successful career.

His formative years were spent in Denver until he enrolled in the University of Colorado where he lived in the basement of a sorority house as a houseboy.

"It's was an economy move," he insists, but admits it was the best deal in town.

The summer before his senior year, he and two girls worked together designing a calendar funded by advertising and modeled after the old desk blotters. When students returned in the fall they bought enough of the calendars to pay for the originators' last year of college. After he graduated, Elliott visited a buddy in Phoenix who had taken a desk calendar and stapled it on the wall. Right above it he had put his college calendar that listed all the important dates and special events during the academic year.

Elliott thought, "Wow, I could do twelve pages of advertising! I took that idea back and we made calendars for all the schools in Colorado. The following year we got even larger, and then we did it all over the country, and then I retired. It was fantastic."

After two years of retirement, Elliott began doing a restaurant guide and ended up doing them all over the country. He came to Seattle where his business evolved into the oldest small press in the country.

"The world needed another publisher," insists Elliott.

Classic Day Publishing has offices in Denver, Scottsdale, Minneapolis, Vancouver, and Portland, as well as the home office in Seattle. Chances are almost a hundred percent that Elliott can also claim the distinction of being the only publisher who kayaks to work.

"My houseboat is a Chinook shack. I once found sort of a

diary by the man who had built it; he'd used egg cartons and newspapers for insulation. Fishermen built curved or sprung roofs where they'd put the fish nets to dry. I'd never heard they had to dry their nets, but I've learned since that the nets can rot if they're not dried properly. Not what you want to have happen to a rather major investment.

"I like life on a houseboat; it's almost like living in a resort. I've never found any place on the face of the earth that is nicer than Seattle during the summer. During the winter it really doesn't get a whole lot better unless you're in Phoenix or where it's sunnier. I've often asked people why they like to live on a houseboat; there's definitely an attraction to it. I know every one of my neighbors; I chat with them all the time. When somebody moves on the dock, they're duly welcomed. What could be better?

"I Couldn't Believe It"

Ozell Gaines credits the United States Army for sending him to Seattle where he lives on a Portage Bay houseboat. Although he grew up in Sweet Water, Tennessee, Ozell spent the summer between his last two years of high school with an aunt who lived just outside of Detroit in Hamtramck, Michigan.

"Hamtramck was a clean, respectable ghetto of Blacks, Poles, and Ukrainians who mostly worked at the local General Motors plant. I'd come there looking for a summer job but it was tough going. I couldn't find work anywhere. One day I saw a bunch of kids walking along in a group and decided to follow them. When we came to a school I suddenly realized summer vacation was over. I followed them into the building and went straight to the Principal's office where I told him I wanted to enroll in his school.

"The Principal told me I'd first have to furnish my records from Sweetwater. My parents knew the Principal there so I called them and my records arrived in less than a week."

After graduation, Ozell enrolled in the Pre-med program at Detroit's Wayne State University. At some point during his first year a friend convinced him that eight years of school was too much. Ozell decided to join the Army if they would train him as a food inspector in the Army Veterinarian Corps. After a training period in Chicago, the Army sent Ozell to Seattle where he worked in the cold storage area south of the city.

He didn't discover Seattle's houseboat community at that time, but he did marry Danielle, a woman he'd met at Wayne University. She came all the way to Seattle to marry Ozell, but she barely had a chance to see the city. Six days after their wedding the Army sent Ozell to Japan. Fortunately, she soon joined him where he was stationed in Zushi on the Miura Peninsula south of Yokohama.

"We were practically on the water," he reports. "It was very much like the Oregon Coast. We went swimming every morning and I graded beef the rest of the day. I went to work in a white lab coat with the medical insignia. I didn't have to wear a military uniform. I think that's what got me through the whole thing, nobody knew what I was doing."

By the time his tour of duty was over in Japan, the Vietnam War had begun. Although Ozell was tempted to re-enlist for training as a helicopter pilot, the couple decided to return to Seattle where Ozell entered the University of Washington's Public Health Program.

Before long, Ozell and Danielle were invited to a party by one of their professors who lived on a houseboat below the Red Robin restaurant just east of the University bridge. The party turned out to be an announcement by the professor that he was leaving Seattle for a new job. He added that his home would be available to rent.

The timing was right for Ozell and his wife. Environmentally sensitive Seattleites had voted to fund a major clean up of both Lake Washington and Lake Union, which included constructing a sewer around Lake Union. Since houseboat owners knew the City would evict them if they didn't connect to the sewer, the value of houseboats plummeted and the professor didn't want to deal with the sewer issue. He was willing to sell his houseboat for next to nothing. Danielle and Ozell decided to buy it, moved in, and began looking for a moorage site that would be connected to the sewer. At about this time Danielle's parents came for a visit to Seattle.

"I'll never forget it," says Ozell. "One time Danielle's mother had just finished washing the dishes and happened to notice soap suds floating at the back of the house. On the off chance that they might have come from the kitchen sink, she used a lot more soap on a few more dishes. When she went to the back of the boat and saw even more bubbles; she couldn't believe it. She just laughed and laughed."

In his quest for a new moorage site, Ozell met fellow houseboaters Ken Kennedy, Belding Scribner and Bob Kerr, who were hoping to buy a Portage Bay moorage with sixteen sites. They invited Ozell to a meeting where they discussed possible financing for purchasing the dock. The next day Ozell went to Seattle First National Bank where he invited the banker to come take a look at the moorage site. Apparently the banker was favorably impressed; he agreed to loan Ozell $50,000. The initially loosely organized group evolved into twelve people who not only were able to come up with $60,000 for their moorage site but also their share of an equal amount to cover the costs of installing and connecting to the new sewer system.

The previous dock owner, Carrie Stafford, was in her mid-nineties and happy to enjoy the rest of her life on the dock free of the responsibilities of ownership.

Danielle served as the first secretary of "Houseboat Harbor," one of Seattle's earliest floating homes co-operatives founded in 1965. Ozell himself spent many years on the Board rotating through various positions.

"When it came to connecting to the sewer, we were lucky," says Ozell. Our neighbor, Ken Kennedy, is a Master plumber. He designed a gravity flow system from the pipes under each houseboat through what looks like the venting hose of clothes dryers. The sewage goes through the individual hoses into a wide concrete cylinder about fifteen feet deep under the dock. A sump pump in the concrete cylinder carries the waste to the sewer on the edge of the lake."

Ozell settled into houseboat life and worked with the Federal Health, Education and Welfare Department. He was also involved in a study measuring the effectiveness of the Carter era Income Maintenance Program, which provided income and work training to laid-off workers.

When Congress failed to fund the Boeing Super Sonic Transport, the Seattle economy took a nose-dive and that skewed the study. Those were the days when billboards announced. "Will the last one leaving Seattle please turn out the lights."

The study moved to Denver so Ozell began teaching at Seattle Community College. Life was good in the houseboat until the late 1990s when a freak fire destroyed most of Ozell's home. Neighbors offered him temporary housing while he tried to decide whether to rebuild on his still intact log float.

Since his home had been so cheap initially, Ozell had never gotten around to insuring it. Although Ozell's various jobs had paid well, the costs of a brand hew houseboat had changed radically since he bought his original one.

Fortunately, George Johnston, houseboat handy-man, knew a couple who were building a brand new houseboat in Vancouver and needed to find a home for the original houseboat they were replacing. George told Ozell he thought the dimensions of the old house would fit Ozell's moorage site.

George checked out the measurements, confirmed the house was the right size, and arranged for the owners, Susan and Rune Carlson, to meet with Ozell.

"I just didn't believe it." says Ozell. "They were sincere about actually giving me their house once the new one arrived from Canada. And Susan worked for the City of Renton so she knew how to negotiate through all the bureaucracy involved in getting the required permit to move it."

Ozell submitted his plan to the Department of Land Use in September, but it was months before the approximately $2,000 permit was granted. The Vancouver house finally arrived in April of 2001 and Sid McFarland handled delivering the Carlson's house to Ozell's moorage site. Ozell especially appreciated the Carlson's gift when he learned how expensive it was to dispose of his burned house.

"They used to just take old houseboats out into Union Bay and burn them, but no more. I ended up having to pay Lake Union Dry Docks to destroy it."

Another cost was dealing with the raft for his previous home which was left unscathed. He'd moored the raft temporarily on a street end while he listened to various suggestions as to what to do with it.

"I spent a small fortune advertising the raft," says Ozell. "I didn't want to sell it to someone who was just going to tear it apart and sell the cedar logs; I felt it deserved to be used. But no one seems to want to build on cedar logs anymore. I finally found an Everett buyer who planned to build a house on it. He towed my raft to Everett with a fishing boat headed for Alaska."

Ozell currently savors being once again "at home" on his Houseboat Harbor moorage, where he's been the dock manager for the past nine years. Although he's getting close to retirement age, the large gentle giant with graying hair plans to continue both as dock manager and as janitor at Seattle's popular Jazz Alley.

"I love to read," he declares, "and although I was raised a Southern Baptist, I've explored many other religions, beginning with Zen Buddhism when we lived in Japan. I'm back at Seattle's First Baptist church after the previous pastor helped me synthesize all that I'd learned."

With the stress of losing his home behind him, this something of a Renaissance man once again can simply enjoy life on the lake in his very own place.

STRINGERS ART

A college degree in English rarely leads to crawling around under houseboats, but that's the official background of Art Holder, the indispensable stringer man. Since 1976 Art has been replacing the rotting or damaged wooden beams aligned on cedar logs to support the subfloor of an entire home. Art also proved himself capable of building log floats when he replaced Ed and Karen Hayes' sunken oyster barge on Wandesforde dock.

Soft-spoken and slight in build, Art single-handedly lifts homes that average forty tons. "I use salvage fire hoses that I buy by the pound at Pacific Industrial Supply," he explains. "I make what I call a hydraulic sandwich by putting the fire hose between two planks. After the sandwich is placed properly under the house, I fill the fire hose with water to make a hydraulic jack. The water pressure provides between ten to forty tons of lift per jack."

Seasoned houseboaters know that when their floor begins to sag at the edges, it's time to call Art. With about eighty percent of Seattle's houseboats built on cedar logs rather than concrete floats, there's plenty of work for the man known locally as "a beaver with a chain saw clenched between his teeth."

Art explains his solo business, "Historically, it's been diffi-cult to get the people on the lake to pay the substantial added costs of Harbor Workers insurance; a small business person like myself simply can't afford that. Houseboaters used to have stringer repair parties. A bunch on the dock would get together and get the job done over the week-end. But now, more people are working full time plus, so they're happy to pay me to replace their stringers."

Art completed an internship in architectural photography after his college days and still maintains a darkroom in his home. He worked as a photographer and in the film industry for ten years. He reassessed his life's work when he went through a divorce. "I'd been involved in numerous stringer parties, knew something about structures from my interest in architecture, and started doing stringer work in response to a basic need for the safety and future of the community.

"I've always enjoyed eclectic architecture and like getting to know the different houseboats on the lake, especially some of the older homes that were towed over from Lake Washington. Some of the houses with sprung roofs were built by shipwrights, and it's a treat to see the craftsmanship in those homes."

Art has run across some intriguing vestiges of houseboat history while crawling around under houseboats.

One home had a fence or "skirt" between the deck and water level, typically to keep flotsam and jetsam from accumulating under the house. When Art tried to remove the fence-like structure to gain access to the stringers, he discovered he was trying to saw through metal bars protecting wood storage bins under the floor. "Not exactly where you would store firewood," he comments. "Ahemmm..."

In another house, he found he couldn't budge a refrigerator that he needed to move. He tilted the refrigerator and discovered a metal bin directly under it that blocked all attempts to slide the heavy appliance. The bin was exactly the depth needed to hold eight-inch high Mason jars just below floor level. No doubt it had served as an ideal hiding place for home brew during Prohibition.

Art often commutes to work in the boat he uses to haul materials to a job site. His partner Helen literally runs to a more conventional job as a nurse at a medical clinic on Seattle's "Pill Hill" near Swedish Hospital. For years, Helen and Art participated in a Scottish dancing group which led Helen to a deep interest in Scottish music. "Through several twists and turns, I became the West Coast manager of Chris Norman, a world class wooden flutist. I also play Scottish music on a wooden flute for a dance performance group and as part of a quartet. Art and I remodeled the front room and now instead of a weaving studio for my previous creative outlet, we've turned it into a music studio."

Helen also manages to find some time for maintaining an upstairs container garden on the deck outside their bedroom. She grows vegetables in containers on their lower deck as well as directly in the dirt of the adjacent land. "I had to replant my green beans four times this year, the geese were really hungry. But, my tomatoes are coming along fine," she reports.

Art tells the story of a neighbor who carefully planted two different colors of tulips with great attention to which color would blossom where. Since her tulips had been raided by raccoons the previous year, Helen carefully covered each newly planted bulb with an inverted clay pot. Not to be put off, the wily raccoons carefully lifted each pot, ate the one color they preferred, then dug up the less tasty bulbs to replace the ones they had eaten. Next the raccoons carefully patted the dirt over the bulbs they had just planted and replaced the clay pots. While no one witnessed their nocturnal caper, it's the only explanation for what happened the following spring; all the yellow tulips bloomed exactly where red ones had been planted.

Helen adds, "I've put various water plants in between our house and the shore for a small water garden. One time an old muskrat swam by and sat in the middle of the plants growing inside a floating recycled tire. He was so oblivious as he munched away at my plants I could reach down and pet him; I finally had to push him back into the water to rescue my tire garden."

Because Art and Helen have hosted a setting goose on their deck more than one summer, Art found it rather ironic when he had a job site shut down and the probable explanation was a neighbor who thought Art was threatening his nesting goose.

"Replacing stringers is dirty work," says Art, "but I enjoy the different and varied challenges of it. The fewer engines and cables you use, the safer it will be. From an engineering standpoint, you use the assistance of the water as much as possible. That means both the city water, which I use for my hydraulic jacks, and the lake water. I use the lake to commute to work, to haul the stringers, and to take old stringers and logs back home. I've never had to buy firewood; we burn the wood I bring from my work."

Cozy and content in their Portage Bay houseboat, Art and Helen, with their varied talents, are an integral part of the houseboat community.

VINTAGE GEORGE

His card reads:

George Johnston
FLOATING HOME SERVICES
Flotation installation (foam and barrels)
Deck & dock repair
Plumbing repairs & sump pump service
Diving (recovery & survey)
High Pressure Exterior Washing
Exterior painting & re-roofing

On a typical Sunday morning we find George adding flotation to George Yeannakis' home on a Fairview Avenue dock. George has already connected with the diver he often uses, Chuck Murray. Chuck is placing fifty-five gallon plastic barrels under the float of the Yeannakis' house. Each of the polyethylene barrels adds about 450 pounds of buoyancy once it's filled with air.

George explains, "The ecologists don't want used barrels in the land fill; the end users would have to cut them up first. So everyone is delighted I recycle them for flotation." He's standing on Yeannakis' deck holding a yellow tape measure extended to the level of the water so he can measure the increasing height of the deck above it.

Jan, whose home is directly across the channel, spies

George and leans out her upstairs window. "George, have you got a diver down there?"

"Yeah, what do you need?" he answers with a hint of New Jersey twang.

"I've had a couple of workmen over here that lost a pry bar and a ratchet set. Could you have him take a look?"

"Sure. I'll tell Chuck when he comes up."

Later that day George will write out a check to Chuck, but you can bet one hundred to one that Jan will never receive a bill.

All this is communicated over the whirring of an air compressor George uses to blow the water out of the barrels once Chuck's positioned them. The water is necessary initially so the barrels can be maneuvered under the home, a feat Chuck accomplishes without benefit of artificial light but with a fair amount of spatial expertise in basic geometry.

Another neighbor from near the end of the dock comes up.

"George, my sewer connection hose is too short, can you add a couple of feet to it?"

"I'll take care of it next time I'm back here," answers George.

As soon as Chuck surfaces, George tells him about the pry bar and ratchet set.

George explains, "Chuck loves foraging along the bottom of this lake. It's his favorite thing; he actually calls his business *Bottom Obsession*."

Meanwhile George Yeannakis reports his house is still a little low on the east side. George maneuvers three more barrels, one smelling distinctly of vinegar, into the lake and begins filling them with water. While George is leaning over the water handling the barrels another dock resident comes by.

"George, I've put in a terrific corner toilet I found down at Seattle Salvage. Could you use my old one?"

"Sure," he answers. "I'll put it in one of my rental houses.

A Classic Sprung Roof

"It's the nature of the work," explains George. "You never know what will come up next. The other day I was working at Jeanette Day's dock and she asked me if I could help find her dog, Skipper. The little schnauzer was blind and had been incontinent for the past couple of years, but Jeanette was absolutely devoted to him. Somehow Skipper had wandered out of the little box she'd made for him. She couldn't find her dog anywhere in the house and was afraid he'd fallen into the lake. She asked me to check under her dock hoping he had managed to crawl up on some of the logs. Unfortunately, I found him floating dead in the water. She was devastated. I helped bury him in that patch of flowers up by the mail boxes."

At this point Chuck surfaces without a pry bar or ratchet set, but with four hammers in his hand. George tells him they have to add another inch or so of flotation on the east side of Yeannakis' house, and Chuck disappears with one of the barrels.

When asked how he got into the flotation business, George replies, "If anyone had told me forty years ago I'd be doing this, I would have never believed it, but life takes funny turns."

George arrived in Seattle the summer of 1958 after graduating from what was still Antioch College of Yellow Springs, Ohio. His minor in chemistry landed him a job at Boeing in the shipping and packaging section where chemistry know-how was applicable in working with adhesives.

When Congress voted not to fund the supersonic transport, the Boeing Company shrank by approximately 70,000 employees in the Seattle area over a two year period. Like thousands of others, George was laid off in 1972, free to explore other career options.

"When I first came to Seattle I had some friends from Antioch who lived on a houseboat in Portage Bay, so I bought one a couple of years later. I paid $800 for it with $100 down. Since it had three bedrooms, all the appliances, a Franklin stove, plus a decent kitchen and living area, I rented out the two extra bedrooms and my house mates covered the mortgage payments. I decided this was a slick scheme, so I bought a second houseboat, rented it out, and then a third. I did most of my own maintenance on them, so I worked with the steel barrels we used for flotation back then. I realized the Styrofoam we used at Boeing would be much easier to install than steel barrels, so I was one of the first to start installing it for flotation. I still work with Styrofoam occasionally, but these plastic barrels are even better."

Bill Velte, now of Puerto Vallarta, Mexico, once rented one of George's houseboats in the 1960s as a graduate student at the University of Washington. A perpetual handyman himself, Bill reports George willingly shared his talent for improvisation with humor and fervor, as if to spread the word and call his fellow country men to domestic self-sufficiency. A classic example occurred in a kitchen where George had used his electric chain saw to cut Styrofoam blocks into manageable pieces.

The problem: a leak in the water pipe below the sink.

The theory: dislodged rust and Styrofoam particles will drift into the leak area and plug it.

The tool: a hammer.

George asked Bill to open the sink faucet just enough to allow the slowest possible dribble. George grabbed his hammer, thoughtfully tilted his moustache, and banged on the pipe slightly upstream from the leak.

The result: the leak dwindled to a mere drop or two per minute and then stopped.

"Ha!" George exclaimed gleefully, "plumbing boils down to a well-controlled leak."

The still legendary George has finally leveled the Yeannakis' home, so he heads toward his trade-mark 1988 van that doubles as his traveling shop. First he checks with Chuck to tell him the address of their next job on Westlake. The diver has found two twenty-five pound lead trolling weights which George admires while poking through the dock (paper recycle) dumpsters. "I'm always looking for semi-current magazines," he explains. Instead of magazines George finds three decent square wooden planters which he pulls out and places on the ground for anyone who might want them.

Then George reaches into his pocket to pull out his car key. It's on a two-foot long chain along with about twenty other keys attached to his belt. "I've lost keys in the water one time too many. I'd rather look like a biker than go through that again. I haven't lost a wallet in years, it's on a chain too. People on the lake wouldn't recognize me unless I'm in my field jacket, my wharf rat costume," quips George.

However he's dressed, George is available twenty-four hours a day and considered a rare treasure by floating home owners where the answer to almost any houseboat problem is three simple words, "Better call George."

THE MOVING MAN

Word of the latest houseboat sale leapt from dock to dock.

"He paid what?"

"Almost two million dollars...in cash."

Granted, the rather massive house spreads across two end moorage sites, blocking any view of the lake from the dock; but almost two million dollars? As word spread, astonished neighbors, especially those who had bought their own homes and moorage space for as little as $55,000, pondered the ever-increasing value of their property.

The escalating gentrification of floating homes has led to a relatively new phenomenon. New-comers often buy a houseboat with plans to remodel and add a second story. They sometimes decide it's simply easier to start all over or discover the existing float and depth of the site won't support the added weight.

One typical alternative is to build a new house on a new float, often working with a Canadian company, outside Vancouver, British Columbia, where the exchange rate favors the U.S. dollar. When the new house is floated down to Seattle, Sid McFarland orchestrates the complex process of moving the old house out and the new one in.

Sid grew up on the corner of Shelby Street and Furhman Avenue above Portage Bay with houseboats right before him. Sid's father worked for Libby, McNeil and Libby and could walk from Portage Bay over the hill and down to work at their Salmon Division headquarters on Fairview Avenue near the foot of Hamlin Street.

"I remember playing on the some of the cannery boats when they were in Alaska. Some of them still moor down there in the winter. Every summer, after school was out, we flew up to Alaska where my father was superintendent of a cannery. My mother, we three kids, and our cat flew up in a DC 3. It was quite an experience. The airstrips were frequently fogged in and it could take two to four days before we actually arrived at our destination.

"When we were back in Seattle I delivered papers on Fairview Avenue between E. Louisa and Boston Streets. Back in those days, the houseboats and docks went every which way in the lake. Sometimes I'd come to collect for the paper and a whole dock would be gone; it just disappeared. The houseboats were much more mobile back then. They'd rig a hose for the water and God knows how they always seemed to have electricity. I used to treat myself to a twenty-five cent long dog at the forerunner of Daly's Drive-in on Eastlake."

Sid attended his neighborhood Seward, Hamilton, and Lincoln schools and then the University of Washington. He primarily took business courses along with a generous dose of engineering, education, and psychology classes. His next assignment was flying helicopters in Vietnam. After the conflict ended, he flew helicopters in Alaska during the summer to support himself and his wife while working to finish a Business Degree.

"I worked as Service Manager for Motorola Communications, covering Washington and Oregon, got a divorce, and then finally decided I wanted to go back to flying in Alaska. A group of my fellow ski instructors invited everyone they knew that knew me for a going away party before I headed north. Jann came along with one of my friends and the two of us connected. She and her friends thought it was worth hanging around until the party ended when there were thirteen ski instructors in the group. We discovered we'd graduated the same year from Lincoln and Roosevelt respectively; I'd even dated some of her girl friends.

"I went on up to Alaska and flew that summer, but that ended my flying career. I returned to Seattle and Jann. I had a friend who worked for an electronics firm on Mercer Street. They needed someone to come in and work with production and help create a conversion to computers. It was a really good fit for me; I worked for there for fifteen years. Then the firm was bought by an outfit back East and that was end of that. The job market was such you'd go on interviews and they'd want to pick your mind but then hire someone fresh out of college who was younger and cheaper. I didn't play that game for very long."

Jann owned a houseboat before Sid met her, so he moved in. Sid did a very extensive remodel job on what he describes as her "single-story shack." The house had probably been built around 1910 on Lake Washington. The summer floating cabin moved to Portage Bay when evicted in the late 1930s, and ended up at its current location on Fairview when displaced by the 520 link to the I-5 freeway.

"After my experience with Jann's house I decided to start a business working on houseboats. I'd built houses before, and with my upbringing and engineering courses, all that stuff was second nature. I was able to fill a void down here. I look at what I do as sort of one-stop shopping. If somebody needs something done on their houseboat I can either do it or I know where to direct them. There aren't many people left who know about the old houseboats. A lot of the new contractors just want to level them to the float and replace them. They don't know how to work on a house where nothing is level and there's no such thing as square corners.

"I remember in our house we had a sinking refrigerator that kept going further and further down in the floor. We didn't do much about it because we knew we were going to remodel. When I finally tore up the floor there was a trap door, with the logs missing underneath it. We figured it was left from bootlegging days. We saved the trap door and may try to incorporate it in a future remodel.

"Sometimes houseboats are cantilevered out so far they can't help but sag. It's a challenge to work with the logs and try to lift the area up a little bit."

One time the owner of a big two story house on a cement float called Sid because his roof ridge beams were slowly pulling apart.

"It can't be," he insisted. "It can't be happening because I've got a cement float."

"I had to explain to him that cement can also bend. His older float had cement lattice but little floatation on the ends and the unsupported weight on each end was literally pulling the houseboat apart."

Sid points out the original cement floats displaced water to keep them afloat; but they had little ballast and were very shallow. During a winter storm, a house with that type of float began to tilt backward under the weight of heavy snow. A neighbor wanted Sid to help get the furniture out. Sid felt the house was too unstable. He looked at the back end of the house and decided to step on the front deck to see if that would stabilize it. When he did so, the house actually tilted toward the dock just from his weight alone, a sure indicator of how unstable it was.

Now many of the more recent floats, like Heinz Strobl's, have ballast tanks built in all four corners and a pump system to keep the house level.

With Sid's expertise on all things related to houseboat construction, it was only natural the owner of the first new house-boat built to replace an older one called on Sid to orchestrate the trade-off. This first move in the late 1990s presented a challenge: the home owners that needed to be moved out to provide access to the moorage site refused to move. "It was a whole new concept for them," explains Sid. "They'd never heard of such a thing and were concerned about the effect on their homes. Fortunately, I was able to work with the home owners on the small dock next door. There were only four houses moored there and the owners agreed to have their dock, with the houseboats attached to it, moved out to the Bay. Since it was a floating dock, all we had to do was disconnect the dock from the pilings rather then moving each individual home. We traded the new for the old house while the dock was tied up to a boat in the bay, then towed it back to its site, anchored it to the pilings, and reconnected the utilities. All in one day."

Sid thinks his biggest challenge was moving in Heinz Strobl's new house. Since his house is at the land end of the dock, Sid and his crew had to move out all six neighbors in front of him, ship his old house to the Center for Wooden Boats, where he had donated it, move in the new one, then return and reconnect all six houseboats. Heinz accommodated his temporarily homeless neighbors by supplying lunch and dinner for everyone on the dock. Once again, the move was completed in just one day, but it was a logistical challenge to do all that in one day.

When planning such a move, Sid always informs the Seattle Harbor Patrol, arranges for electrical contractors to handle the electrical connections, and he and his crew spend at least a day or so adapting all utility connections for a quick disconnect on the actual moving day.

"I try to educate long-term dock residents who will be moved as to what to expect. They're often a tad bit set in their ways, have never experienced a move, and they're understandably very worried about their property and what's going to happen. I have to help them understand the process.

"There's lots of prep work to do, and the move is always very weather dependent. If it's too windy we have to cancel and go to the next day; you can't tell Mother Nature what you want; she doesn't care. Sometimes we have to involve City Light. There're always surprises, always somebody on the dock who had other plans for the day, or is expecting guests, or took the previous day off to be around for the move but the weather prevented it. It's also important to have all the tools I need; for instance, I use an electronic instrument to measure across the water, a standard measuring tape just wouldn't cut it."

Now that five houseboats have been replaced, the old houseboats can become a liability if the owner can't recycle them either in the community or elsewhere. It can cost up to $10,000 to have an old house demolished. Even the old cedar logs now go to a land fill. Sid explains that the old logs are full of pins and stuff that might break a saw blade, so no one wants them.

When a houseboat sells for almost two million dollars, more of the older houseboats, especially those with large footprints, will be replaced. While moving houseboats comprises only a small portion of his work, Sid doubts he'll ever again find himself unemployed.

THROUGH THE YEAR

While we can only speculate as to the future of Lake Union's water dwellers, certain constants will always be a part of their environment: the ever-present dance of the water, the ballet of wind, rain, sunlight and moonlight on its flat or white capped surface, and the plants' and animals' response to the soothing, predictable order of the seasons.

On the lake the noisy pre-dawn honking of geese in early March will always signal the beginning of a new year far more significantly than a typically gray, wet first day of January. The birds' cacophony of various pitched honks marks the beginning of another mating season, during which the abundant fowl fight interminable battles for nesting space.

Purple, white and yellow crocus, then daffodils, tulips and iris blossom in window boxes, hanging baskets, whiskey barrels, and garden floats. Occasional bursts of sunshine draw residents outside, poking around in container gardens to ready them for planting as they shield their eyes from the shock of the bright sunlight.

A week or more without rain tempts owners of small boats, canoes, or kayaks, left wintering upside down on decks or hanging under porch roofs, to right their craft and slip them into the water.

Come April neighbors debate the best way to protect their

newly planted annuals from clear-cutting by geese, exchange advice on how to handle the yellowing leaves of spent daffodils and tulips, and report seeing the first gaggle of goslings or sighting a raccoon, beaver or muskrat.

May will always bring Opening Day of boating season in Seattle, a traditional parade of boats from Lake Union into Portage Bay where both expert and novice boaters salute the current Commodore of the Seattle Yacht Club before passing through the Montlake Cut into Lake Washington. Portage Bay houseboaters have a grand stand seat for the parade that features everything from elegant yachts to kayakers, canoes and homemade rafts. Bill's Espresso barge does a "water office" business among frequently cold and damp boaters. In the morning college rowing teams compete for the Windermere Cup in the quiet waters of the Montlake Cut as hundreds of spectators along the park-like border of the waterway cheer their favorite crew.

Opening day also heralds the return of the Duck Dodge to Lake Union. The Tuesday night sailboat race began years ago when a houseboater bought a new sail boat and challenged his neighbor to a race. The two had such fun they invited other salts to join them, and now up to a hundred boats join in the soft core competition. They compete not only among themselves for the winning trophy, a genuine yellow rubber duck; but also for space among the pleasure boats, tour boats, sail-boards, kayaks and seaplanes.

As the weather warms, friendly competition, not to mention peer pressure, begins on the various docks to see who will be the first to go swimming. Typically it's a youngster who takes the first plunge. Early swimmers recommend jumping into the chilly water, sometimes with a long preliminary run, and never, but never, stick your toe in the water first.

By June it is still daylight at 9:30 in the evening, families of now adolescent goslings can be seen sleeping on the grass at the edge of the shore, and hopefully the steam whistle of the Virginia V will be heard well into the next century. Designated a National Historical Landmark, the Virginia V is the last of the mosquito fleet, wooden boats that once serviced the many small towns on the shores of Lake Washington and Puget Sound.

June can also bring sun and hot temperatures that mean it's a "two-watering day." Container flowers begin wilting by mid-afternoon, and it's obvious they need another dose of lake water, typically dispensed by a teapot, bucket or sprinkling can tied with a string for lowering it into the water, or an old coffee can or cooking pan mounted on a wooden pole.

On July 3rd houseboaters with a view of the next day's fireworks make sure that everything they'll need for the Fourth is on board; driving anywhere on the Big Day risks having your parking space pre-empted. Guests are advised to carpool and plan to park at least three to four blocks away. Dock owners frequently require guest lists to make sure the hired security guard knows who belongs on the dock. The annual Wooden Boat Festival offers views of some spectacular classic boats sailing by while waiting for nightfall and the fireworks.

In August small craft skim the flat early morning water to pick breakfast blackberries from the steep banks accessible only by boat. Tomatoes, beans, basil, peppers, zucchini, chives, thyme, mint, oregano, sage, lavender and even corn and Brussels sprouts are harvested from containers. Returning salmon headed for their spawning grounds flash against the light blue sky and deep blue water. Warm summer evenings, especially when accompanied by a full moon, witness skinny dippers frolicking in the moonlight.

As the days noticeably begin to shorten in September, plants show signs of mildew and mold, giant V's of geese head southward, and piles of firewood for the next heating season arrive by truck or boat.

October witnesses dock pumpkin-carving parties, Dutch doors (useful for keeping out wandering wildlife) no longer open at the top, and a wind-down of outdoor remodeling. Before standard time returns the pre-dawn rowing shells on the lake sport flashlights mounted on their bow with duct tape as they glide through the darkness.

By Thanksgiving most small boats are hauled back up on decks; winter cabbage, chrysanthemums, and violas replace geraniums, cosmos, and mildewing impatiens. Smoke curls from houseboat chimneys heated by wood-burning stoves.

December brings the bright lights of decorated tour boats, the parade of various yacht club craft, and festive bonfires at Gasworks Parks. Squiggling lines of color shimmer across the dark water. The intrepid Kayak Carolers, flashlights in hand, offer Christmas carols in return for a hot drink and warm cookies.

New Year's Eve is often spent at home, especially along Fairview where small groups gather at the end of the long docks to watch the Space Needle announce the New Year. The following day non-football fans traditionally walk around the lake by way of the University and Fremont bridges.

January may bring the first snowfall, and the one or two snow shovels on each dock are shared among neighbors. Occasional electrical outages draw chilly houseboaters to the warm homes of neighbors with wood-burning stoves. New-comers are reminded to keep their cold water running if freezing temperatures are predicted; it's the only way to keep water from freezing in the above ground hoses and pipes.

Like their land-locked counterparts, by February many houseboaters desert their homes for a shot of sunshine, an ideal vacation time for those whose own homes offer superb summer vacation amenities. A week or so of warmth and sunshine, and we're once again ready for the squawking geese to announce the beginning of another year on the lake.

May it ever be thus.

Dock Mail Boxes

GLOSSARY

Aquatic lands typically refers to land owned by the state.

Abutting underwater shore lands the underwater property from the shoreline to the navigable water line.

Dead storage houseboats temporarily moored without utilities.

Duck Dodge a playful sailboat race on Lake Union every Tuesday night during boating season.

Dutch door a door cut in half horizontally so the top half may be opened independently.

End houseboat home at the end of a dock, usually the most valuable on a moorage.

Equity Ordinance Drafted to protect houseboat owners from arbitrary evictions and rental increases and to assure moorage owners of a fair and reasonable return on their investment. Necessitated by the artificial market created by the city's limitations on future houseboat moorages.

FHA	abbreviation for Floating Homes Association.
Flotation	whatever keeps a barge or houseboat floating, such as cedar logs, empty barrels, old barges, concrete and Styrofoam singularly or in combination.
Footprint	architectural term that refers to the dimensions of a float or deck.
Gentrification	the process in which a deteriorating neighborhood reverses that trend.
Grandfathered	Situations which are no longer permitted but allowed to remain because they predate existing regulations or codes.
Hooverville	designation for shanty-towns that sprung up during the Great Depression named after President Hoover.
Log-boom	a large quantity of logs held in place inside a rectangle of logs chained together.
Mill-pond	water or pond in which logs were floated to season or store them.
Navigable water line	a fixed line beyond which no permanent structures are allowed.
NOAA	National Oceanographic and Atmospheric Administration, a federal agency which bases some of its white research ships on the east side of Lake Union.